GOOD
is the FLESH

GOOD
is the FLESH

Body, Soul, and Christian Faith

EDITED AND COMPILED BY
JEAN DENTON

FOREWORD BY
JAMES C. FENHAGEN II

morehouse

Morehouse Publishing, P.O. Box 1321, Harrisburg, PA 17105

Morehouse Publishing, The Tower Building, 11 York Road, London SE1 7NX

Morehouse Publishing is a Continuum imprint.

Cover art: Robert Llewellyn/Superstock

Cover design: Thomas Castanzo

Library of Congress Cataloging-in-Publication Data

Good is the flesh: body, soul, and Christian faith / edited and compiled by Jean Denton; foreword by James C. Fenhagen II.
    p. cm.
Includes bibliographical references.
ISBN 0-8192-2131-7 (pbk.)
1. Health—Religious aspects—Christianity. I. Denton, Jean (Jean Margaret)
BT732.G66 2005
261.8'321—dc22

                         2004013749

Printed in the United States of America
05 06 07 08 09 10   6 5 4 3 2 1

Contents

Acknowledgments

How does one say thank you when the gift is so great? So many gifted people have gifted me. It is apparent that this book would not have come to be except for the willingness of authors to share their work. In unique ways, each of these inquisitive minds has probed the relationship between Christian faith and health. I am deeply grateful to them for sharing their gifts as writers and thinkers.

My heartfelt thanks go to the people of St. Paul's Episcopal Church in Indianapolis, who have, sometimes inadvertently, taught me what health ministry is. The Reverend Tom Stoll, rector when this ministry began, shared my vision and was a co-conspirator in establishing a health ministry. The Reverend Richard Winters, the current rector, guided me to shape each writing day with prayer. Melba Hopper, Paula Franck, John Hoard, Rita Goldenberg, Marge Olsen, Betsy Whaley, Nancy Campbell, and Raima Larter have never failed to remind me of the value of sharing what I have been given.

The people of National Episcopal Health Ministries carry the dream that every faithful congregation will engage in health ministry. Along with the members of the Health Ministries Association, they are making this dream a reality. Their work feeds my soul, and I thank them, each and every one.

Many of the contributors to this volume are women, and more than one is a self-described feminist theologian. I thank all my sisters who have brought the body back from the dead. Women have long known the value of the body.

And where would we be without editors? My sincere appreciation goes to Nancy Fitzgerald, who gently guided me through this process, and to Debra Farrington, who initially saw the possibilities of this compilation. Thanks also to Daniel J. Vice, who, as a young English major, offered great practical assistance from computer skills to writing skills.

I will never be able to properly thank my husband, Tom, and my children, Nathan and Annemarie, for believing in me, more than I deserve.

Foreword

In all the great religions of the world, and particularly in the Christian faith, contemplative prayer is related to the rhythm of breathing. To pay attention to our breathing in and breathing out is, in itself, a form of prayer. Simply by paying attention to the movement of our breath, we are open to a silence within us that is responsive to the presence of God.

When we speak of the soul, we are speaking of that part of our awareness that is responsive to the work of the spirit. The soul, as we understand it, is that part of our consciousness that is tuned to God's presence, both in us and around us. When our spiritual life and our physical life are in tune, wholeness emerges. Healing, therefore, in any form, is as much the work of our spirits as it is the work of our physical bodies. Paying attention to our bodies is a response to God's spirit, simply because our bodies and our souls (our inner lives) are one. To abuse our bodies or to ignore the disciplines that lead to health is to deny God's presence within us. The soul is the spirit within us that responds to the Spirit of God.

After many years of seeking a discipline of prayer that would open me to the movement of God's spirit, I finally discovered that the awareness of God's presence does not come by effort and stringent discipline, but by an awareness of God's address to us. God takes the initiative. This awareness began for me when I was told by my physician after an annual checkup that my blood pressure had risen and that I needed to do something about it. His cure was not medicine but the charge to lose weight. "Your body is out of balance," he said, "and needs attention." At first, I resisted, denying that the habits that I had developed needed to be changed. It was as though I was running away from what I most needed, until I gradually came to realize that denial was my response to a fear that I could not face.

And thanks be to God, I began to change, as I began to slow down in the quietness that only stillness can create. After several years, the pattern of exercise and early-morning walks I had adopted began to take on strength, and for the past several years, I've developed a habit of exercise that I look forward to with positive expectation. My exercise time is also a time of prayer, as I listen to my breathing and take notice of all that's around me.

I first met Jean Denton when we both served as faculty for a conference for Episcopal clergy inaugurated by the Church Pension Group of the Episcopal Church. The conference, and the many conferences that were to follow, was named CREDO, an acronym for Clergy Reflection, Education, Discernment Opportunity. The elements of the CREDO conference were quite practical yet remarkably deep. Each conference was built around personal vocation, spiritual awareness and practice, finances, and health. The aim was "to provide opportunities for clergy to examine significant areas of their lives and to discern prayerfully the future direction of their vocation and their response to God's call in a lifelong practice and transformation." I'd been invited to serve this conference as the chaplain paying attention to the needs of the spiritual life; Jean Denton was there as a nurse whose vocation had been in the areas of health and well-being.

I'd heard about Jean as one of the founders of the parish nurse ministry that had already begun to spread across the country. It was because of Jean's help that my wife had been able to establish a health ministry in our parish. As the CREDO conferences began to multiply, Jean and I had more opportunities to work together and we became friends. What makes this remarkable collection of life-affirming reflections that Jean has pulled together so important is her concern for the relationship of wholeness and health in the larger context of the many ways in which the ministries of healing take place. The very term "health ministry" isn't one you hear every day, and yet in the way Jean puts together the many different ways that health ministry takes place, she offers us a vision of wholeness where the spirit and the body are one.

I give thanks every day for the gift of health and for the strength to live with a body that needs continual care, especially as I grow older. As a Christian, I have come to appreciate the wonder of silence in which I meet the resurrected Jesus so that I might live in him and he in me. Jean's book draws together the wisdom of many people. In its totality, however, it is the story and the wonder of body and soul.

The Reverend James C. Fenhagen II
President and Warden
College of Preachers
Washington National Cathedral

Introduction

As a nurse, I've been invited into the most intimate places in people's lives. I've witnessed the miracle of a baby's first breath and a family being born. I've sat with people in stunned silence after a physician told of a devastating diagnosis. I've witnessed death, weeping while I served as a midwife to people who were passing from this life to be born into the next.

Visiting these holy places has taught me a simple and amazing truth: Body and soul are one. We can define "body" and "soul" and know them to be discrete concepts, but the division seems artificial in real life. Were you to meet my body without my soul, you wouldn't know me. Neither would you know my soul apart from my body, which mediates my soul to the created world.

The ancients believed they would eventually find the soul in the body—maybe in the pineal gland, or in the diaphragm. But one medieval Christian writer, Meister Eckert, suggested the opposite. He wrote, "The soul loves the body. Consider too how it is that the body is more in the soul than the soul is in the body."[1]

The dichotomy between body and soul, initiated by Hellenistic thought and reinforced by early Christian heresies, became a firm reality for the Western world with the thinking of René Descartes. If there is any doubt about this dualism today, a stay in a modern hospital will verify its existence. The health care system knows much about cure of the body, though precious little about care of the soul. The church, conversely, cares so much for the soul that it fails to take the body seriously. The church rarely speaks of stewardship of the body; it forgets to remind us that our physical selves are treasures from God loaned to us for tending. It seems that the body, failing the test of immortality, can be used and abused, without deserving any particular attention. Christians have become so inured to this dualism that little effort is expended on plumbing the issues or engaging the superb possibilities inherent in the potential demise of this heresy.

Unfortunately, some of the terms used in Christian dialogue have reinforced this dualism. The term "body" (*soma* in Greek) has become synonymous with "flesh" (*sarx*), which St. Paul uses to refer to a person's urge to sin. The flesh is weak and superficial. This interchanging of words has given the body bad press that continues to this day. "Soul," the ethereal and imperishable, has come to be contrasted with body. Yet soul is such a full-bodied word. Soul music is deeply personal and very much in the body. To be soulless is to be heartless, to lack sensibility—and sensibility comes through the body's senses. We have come full circle.

Why I Am Writing

As a registered nurse and an ordained minister, I've been exploring the body-soul connection and, by extension, the health-spirituality connection, for many years. I am one of many in mainline Christian congregations who are approaching this connection with new eyes and new hope for the mission of the church.

As I've delved into the literature, my own library has grown enormously. From my books, I've selected articles and essays for this volume, seeking to make these ideas available for a wider audience. I make no pretense of being comprehensive. I simply seek to engage more voices—including yours—in the dialogue.

To Whom I Am Writing

This book is addressed to people who want to explore the contemporary connection between mainline Christianity and health, from either a personal perspective or from the perspective of a local Christian community. It is for those who are curious about what modern Christian writers have to say about the body and about health. It is for those who are exploring the possibilities of a health ministry in their congregations and who seek a deeper look at the implications of being Christian in a society that divorces body from soul. And it is also written for those currently committed to health ministry, as support and further grounding for their vocation.

What to Expect in These Chapters

Chapter 1, Theological Roots of Health Ministry, offers the reader an opportunity to explore the foundations of a Christian theology of health and the body. With vivid imagery, "We Awaken in Christ's Body," written in the eleventh century by Symeon the New Theologian, opens our eyes to an ancient understanding of how our bodies are the body of Christ. James B. Nelson, who has been engaged in exploring body theology for decades, helps us reflect on body experience as a means of God's revelation in "Doing Body Theology," excerpted from his book, *Body Theology*. Elisabeth Moltmann-Wendel writes about the body from the perspective of a feminist theologian. In "The Crucified Jesus—The Bodily Jesus," excerpted from *I Am My Body*, she asks us to consider two Christs, one in a tortured body and one in a very ordinary human body. Then Linda L. Smith, a nurse and former nun, explores the biblical roots of healing and health in "Searching for the Roots of Healing" from her book, *Called into Healing*.

Chapter 2, Our Relationship with Our Bodies, addresses the relationships Christians have or might have with the body. The poem "Pax" by D. H. Lawrence can be read as addressing this topic. He speaks of what it means to be truly dependent on God and comfortable in the great household of creation, knowing ourselves in our bodies to be both loved and perfectly ourselves. Flora Slossum Wuellner shares insights into how it is that we have come to hate our flesh and been taught to deny it in "Reconciling and Celebrating with Our Bodies" from her book, *Prayer and Our Bodies*. Elisabeth Moltmann-Wendel invites us to consider what joy there is in the body's ability to feel in "Touching and Being Touched," also from *I Am My Body*. Margaret Mohrmann, who is both a medical doctor and a doctor of philosophy in ethics, reminds us that health and life are gifts from God; they are not gods to be worshiped, but secondary "goods"—gifts from the one true God. "The Idolatry of Health and the Idolatry of Life" comes from her book, *Medicine as Ministry*.

Health is a long continuum. On the one extreme is perfect well-being, and on the other is premature dying. Chapter 3, Christian Spirituality and Well-Being, explores a Christian view and experience of good health. Susan McCaslin's poem "Feet Addressing Head" humorously reminds us that we are not simply talking heads, but bodies grounded in the earth. Marilyn Chandler McEntyre shares her experience of well-being in her Saturday morning movement class in "The Presence of God and the Life of the Body," originally published in the spirituality journal *Weavings*. Cheryl A. Kirk-Duggan speaks of "Sacred flesh and blood/ walking and talking/ moving and grooving/ . . . temples embodying/ the pulse of life itself," in "Physical Health: Our Bodies, Our Temple," a chapter from her book *The Undivided Soul: Helping Congregations Connect Body and Spirit*. Eating well is certainly part of well-being, and Bruce G. Epperly takes on the challenge of exploring eating from a Christian perspective in "Soul Food and Spiritual Formation" from *Spirituality & Health, Health & Spirituality*.

None of us really lives on the "perfect well-being" end of the health continuum. Chapter 4 looks at Christian spirituality and illness. In her poem, "To the Wife of a Sick Friend," Edna St. Vincent Millay dares to describe the "unmitigated dark" that often accompanies serious illness. Flora Slossum Wuellner offers a possible way to experience our selves fully by "Relating to Our Bodies in Illness and Disability," excerpted from her book, *Prayer and Our Bodies*. Mary C. Earle takes it a step further, encouraging us to dare to read our wounds and scars in "Lectio," from her book, *Broken Body, Healing Spirit*. Closing this section is "Suffering, Spirituality, and Health Care" by Daniel P. Sulmasy, from his book, *The Healer's Calling*. As a physician, a monastic, and an ethicist, he poses this question, and then offers an answer: "In the face of [the fact that relief from suffering is not always possible], is mute silence all there is to consolation?"

Health is not a private affair; it is communal. At least, that is the truth of the Christian community that understands the interconnection of all of God's creation. Chapter 5 addresses health and justice. Patricia Benner's "A Litany of Penitence for Health Care" laments the failures of the current health care delivery system in the United States. Then, from the Universal Health Care Access Network, we have a set of facts and fictions to test our knowledge of health care in the United States today. Abigail Rian Evans, in "Health Care in Crisis" from her book *Redeeming Marketplace Medicine: A Theology of Health Ministry*, offers reasons for the failure of the current system. Churches have not been silent about this issue, and statements from several Christian denominations are included in

"Denominations Speak Out about Appropriate Health Care."

Where does this leave us? Chapter 6 describes "Health Ministry and the Parish," a way for local congregations to begin to address health issues. The popular hymn text "Where Cross the Crowded Ways of Life" by Frank Mason North starts the section, inviting Christians to put their spirituality into ministry. I write, in very practical terms, "Answers to Some Basic Questions about Health Ministry." Tom A. Droege's "Dialogue with Your Body about Illness and Health" is one of many exercises from his book, *The Healing Presence*. It offers a way to begin to introduce parishioners to getting in touch with their personal body stories and to their own body theology. In "A Day in the Life of a Parish Nurse," I invite you to enter the practice of parish nursing for a day. In "Congregational Practices Heal Us from Dis-ease," Brita L. Gill-Austern calls upon congregations to see themselves differently—as places of health and healing for body and soul.

By offering questions for your consideration following each section, I hope you will engage the material, both privately and with others. It is my hope that this reading will be both informative and provocative. It is my prayer that you will choose to take action based on what you learn here, and in so doing join with the faith-health movement in bringing the reign of God just a little closer.

Notes

1. Matthew Fox, *Meditations with Meister Eckert* (Santa Fe, NM: Bear & Co., 1983), 103.

1.

Theological Roots of Health Ministry

We Awaken In Christ's Body
–Symeon the New Theologian

We awaken in Christ's body
as Christ awakens our bodies,
and my poor hand is Christ, He enters
my foot, and is infinitely me.

I move my hand, and wonderfully
my hand becomes Christ, becomes all of Him
(for God is indivisibly
whole, seamless in His Godhood).

I move my foot, and at once
He appears like a flash of lightning.
Do my words seem blasphemous?—Then
open your heart to Him

and let yourself receive the one
who is opening to you so deeply.
For if we genuinely love Him,
we wake up inside Christ's body

where all our body, all over,
every most hidden part of it,
is realized in joy as Him,
and He makes us, utterly, real,

and everything that is hurt, everything
that seemed to us dark, harsh, shameful,
maimed, ugly, irreparably damaged,
is in Him transformed

and recognized as whole, as lovely,
and radiant in His light
we awaken as the Beloved
in every last part of our body.

The news media offer a cacophony of voices about health. Studies that show a vitamin will prevent an illness are discredited within a week. Health care policies are rolled out in an election year, and then wrapped safely and put on the shelf to protect them from the wear and tear of politics. The promises of health from good, clean living are broken as a strong and beautiful twenty-five-year-old is diagnosed with malignancy. There are so many voices, and they deliver such conflicting messages.

There are other voices, too—voices of researchers advising us that attending church is good for our longevity, and that meditation reduces our stress. These seductive voices tempt us to consider taking a Christian path to achieve personal, self-serving ends. This flies in the face of a Christianity that calls us to love God and to serve our neighbor, not ourselves.

There are yet other voices, voices from within our bodies that are muffled and censored. The aching back is ignored in favor of carrying the load just a little bit longer. The tightness in the throat is disregarded as less-than-lovely feelings are stuffed and silenced. The inflammation in the joints is disregarded as resentment builds about meeting an arbitrary deadline. To what voices are we to listen?

I believe it is important to take time out from listening to the chatter of the world and put ourselves in a position to hear God's voice. God's voice will not compete with the shouts of popular fads or be heard amidst the frenzied clamor of too-busy minds. God's voice will be heard in the quiet.

This section bids you to settle yourself into a place for silent reflection on some theological roots for health. First, you are invited to consider "body theology" as a way of hearing God speak. Second, you are urged to consider unusual thoughts about the bodily Jesus. Last, you are encouraged to review the way God has worked in health and healing throughout the Judeo-Christian tradition.

Reflect on these ideas, and see if God might be speaking a new word to you.

DOING BODY THEOLOGY
–James B. Nelson

James B. Nelson, Ph.D., is professor emeritus of Christian Ethics at United Theological Seminary of the Twin Cities, New Brighton, Minnesota. He has worked with SIECUS (Sexuality, Information and Education Council of the United States) and has served on the board of the Society of Christian Ethics. He has written thirteen books, and in each takes body experiences seriously and as central to the mystery of human experience and to the human relationship with God.

Until recently, most of the Christian and Jewish writings about the body and sexuality were one-directional. They began with religion and moved to the body, not the other way around. They began with such questions as these: What do the scriptures say about our bodily life and how we ought to live it? What does the Vatican say about this or that sexual expression? What does the church teach? The assumption was that religion had its truth, received or arrived at quite independently of our bodily-sexual experience, a truth that then needed only to be applied. Religion provided the instruction book that came with the body appliance, an instruction that often seemed to say "CAUTION: READ CAREFULLY BEFORE OPERATING!"

Remember Søren Kierkegaard's biting comment about his nineteenth-century contemporary, the German philosopher Hegel. In his monumental, abstract philosophy of religion, Hegel had rationally systematized the human experience of God. Kierkegaard's response was simple and to the point: the philosopher had forgotten only one thing—concrete, particular, existing individuals.

In an analogous manner, our religious tradition has too often forgotten the embodied self. Through the centuries, most theologizing, unfortunately, has not taken seriously the fact that when we reflect theologically we inevitably do so as embodied selves. Male theologians, in particular, have long assumed that the arena of theology is that of spirit and mind, far removed from the inferior, suspect body. Consequently, we have begun more deductively than inductively. We have begun with propositions and attempted to move from the abstract to the concrete. The feminist and the lesbian/gay liberation movements have now reminded us to take body experience as important theological data.

For centuries, however, it was not generally recognized that human bodies are active sources of meaning. Rather, it was believed that bodies were like cameras in a photographic process, simply recording external things mechanistically, things that were passed through the nervous system to form images in the brain according to physical laws. Now, however, there is reason to understand differently.[1] The body has its own ways of knowing. The body often speaks its mind.

Thus, our concern here is not primarily with the "body-object" as studied by the anatomist or physiologist, but rather the "body-subject," the embodiment of our consciousness, our bodily sense of how we are in the world. Our concern is the interaction of the "givenness" of our fleshly realities and the ways in which we interpret them. It is our bodily sense of connections to the world, our bodily sense of the space and time we are in, our bodily knowing of the meanings of our relationships.[2]

Body theology begins with the concrete. It does not begin with certain doctrinal formulations, nor with certain portions of a creed, nor with a "problem" in the tradition (though all of these sources may well contribute insight later). Rather, body theology starts with the fleshly experience of life—with our hungers and our passions, our bodily aliveness and deadness, with the smell of coffee, with the homeless and the hungry we see on our streets, with the warm touch of a friend, with bodies violated and torn apart in war, with the scent of a honeysuckle or the soft sting of autumn air on the cheek, with bodies tortured and raped, with the bodyself making love with the beloved and lovemaking with the earth.

The task of body theology is critical reflection on our bodily experience as a fundamental realm of the experience of God. It is not, in the first instance, a theological description of bodily life from a supra-bodily vantage point (as if that were possible, which in actuality it is not). Nor is it primarily concerned with articulating norms for the proper "use" of the body. Body theology necessarily begins with the concreteness of our bodily experience, even while it recognizes that this very concreteness is filtered through the interpretive web of meanings that we have come to attach to our bodily life.

After all, we know the world and respond to it through our embodiedness. That is how as little children we learned to differentiate ourselves from other persons: we touched them, heard their voices, saw their movements as other than our own. As children we learned to make sense of language through body motions and images. If as adults we have been taught to abstract much of our knowledge from the body, that only makes both our knowledge and our bodies less real. Moral knowledge, for example, is bodily: if we cannot somehow feel in the gut the meanings of justice and injustice, of hope and hopelessness, those terms remain abstract and unreal.

The way we feel about our embodiedness significantly conditions the way we feel about the world. Studies in body psychology, for example, disclose strong correlations between self-body connectedness and the capacity for ambiguity tolerance. The more connected and comfortable I am with my bodily reality, the more I am able to accept the confusing mix of things in the world I experience. Contrarily, there are also strong correlations between body alienation and the propensity toward dichotomous reality perceptions: the more I feel distant from my body, the greater my tendency to populate my perceived world with sharply etched "either-ors" (either me or not-me, we or they, good or bad, right or wrong, black or white, sick or well, true or false, heterosexual or homosexual).[3] Our body realities do shape our moral perceptions in ways we have seldom realized.

"We do not just *have* bodies, we *are* bodies." This sentence is both a hopeful statement of faith and a lived experience. It is part of our faith heritage. Hebraic anthropology was remarkably unitary about the bodyself, and when the Christian tradition is purged of its dualistic accretions, it too incarnationally proclaims the unitary human being. But let us be clear about the difference between a *dualism* and a *duality*. A dualism (like a dichotomy) is the experience of two utterly different elements at war with each other. At times they may exist in uneasy truce, but always there is hostility. A duality (or polarity) is the perception of two elements, which, while distinguishable from each other, truly belong together. Sometimes the two elements may be experienced in creative tension, but always they belong together. Thus, the alienation of body from spirit is dualism, or polarization. The sense that there are different dimensions of myself but that I am essentially one is the perception of duality, or polarity, within my essential unity.

While our self-experience is too frequently dualistic and divisive, we also know the reality of our bodyself unity. That, too, is our lived experience. We feel "most ourselves" when we experience such bodyself integration. When, in illness, the body feels alien to us, we say, "I'm not myself today." And we feel most fully ourselves when bodily connected with each other and the earth. The unitary bodyself, then, is not simply an abstract hope, a revelation "from outside" imposed on a very different reality. We are able to articulate this faith claim and we are moved to do so precisely because this too is part of our body experience.

On the other hand, we do live between the times, knowing well the ravages of our body dualisms very personally, but also socially and planetarily. We have been taught that not only is the body different from the real core of selfhood, it is also lower and must be controlled by that which is higher. Our language itself is often strongly dualistic: to say, "I *have* a body" seems much more "natural" than "I *am* a body." Certain experiences—notably illness, aging, and death—seem to confirm the otherness of my body. In those situations, my body seems radically different from me. Though the body is "me," the body is also "it," a thing, a burden to be borne, to be put up with, to be tolerated, sometimes an enemy lived with in warfare or uneasy truce. Then, though the body is "mine," I am also "its."

Thus, for good and for ill, the body has theological and ethical relevance in a host of ways. And our bodily experience is always sexual. Such experience, obviously, is not always genital—actually, only infrequently so. Sexuality is far more than what we do with our genitals. It is our way of being in the world as bodyselves who are gendered biologically and socially, who have varying sexual orientations, who have the capacity for sensuousness, who have the need for intimacy, who have varied and often conflicting feelings about what it means to be bodied. It is all of this body experience that is foundational to our moral agency: our capacities for action and power, our abilities to tolerate ambiguity, our capacities for moral feeling. Our bodily experience significantly colors our interpretations of social relations, communities, and institutions—which are the stuff of ethics.

Similarly, our body experience lends considerable shape to our basic theological perspectives. These days we have been frequently and rightly reminded that the images and metaphors we find most meaningful to our experience of God are inevitably connected to our lifelong body experience. In contrast to the anti-body images of experiencing God, listen to the positive body revelation in Brian Wren's hymn "Good Is the Flesh" (based on Gen 1:31, John 1:14, and John 14:23):

Good is the flesh that the Word has become,
good is the birthing, the milk in the breast,
good is the feeding, caressing and rest,
good is the body for knowing the world,
Good is the flesh that the Word has become.

Good is the body for knowing the world,
sensing the sunlight, the tug of the ground,
feeling, perceiving, within and around,
good is the body, from cradle to grave,
Good is the flesh that the Word has become.

Good is the body, from cradle to grave,
growing and ageing, arousing, impaired,
happy in clothing, or lovingly bared,
good is the pleasure of God in our flesh,
Good is the flesh that the Word has become.

Good is the pleasure of God in our flesh,
longing in all, as in Jesus, to dwell,
glad of embracing, and tasting, and smell,
good is the body, for good and for God,
Good is the flesh that the Word has become. . . .[4]

What, then, is body theology? It is nothing more, nothing less than our attempts to reflect on body experience as revelatory of God. How can we understand both the givenness of our body realities and the meanings that we ascribe to them, and how can we interpret these in ways that nurture the greater wholeness of our lives in relation to God, each other, and the earth? Obviously, there is no single path. But one approach of crucial importance to Christians is in exploring the meanings of "incarnation."

Webster's primary definition for incarnation is simply *embodiment*—being made flesh. Theologically, it means *God's* embodiment. Christianly, it means *Christ*. In particular, it means Jesus as the Christ, the expected and anointed one. Through the lens of this paradigmatic embodiment of God, however, Christians can see other incarnations: the *christic* reality expressed in other human beings in their God-bearing relatedness. Indeed, the central purpose of Christology, I take it, is not affirmations about Jesus as the Christ. Rather, affirmations about Jesus are in the service of revealing God's christic presence and activity in the world now.

While this understanding of the main purpose of Christology may seem at odds with much in the tradition, I believe it faithful to tradition's intent.

Christologies, our reflections about the meanings of Christ, serve best when they clarify the present activity and embodiment of God, not when they keep our vision fixed on a past epiphany. Indeed, traditional Christologies frequently have raised difficult problems. The formula of a hypostatic union of two natures was largely based on a dualistic metaphysic and has perpetuated it. Beginning with the assumption that divine nature and human nature were essentially foreign to each other, the question then became, how can these two utterly different natures be united in one being?

Confining the divine incarnation exclusively to Jesus has tended to make him a docetic exception to our humanity and has disconnected the christic reality from our experience. Docetism—the early heresy that believed God took on only the *appearance* of human flesh in Jesus, but did not really enter a fully human being—is, unfortunately, still alive and well. Further, focusing on who Jesus was (the divine and human natures) has relegated his actions and relationships to secondary importance. By suggesting to many Christians that belief in a certain Christological formula is necessary for their salvation, such theologies have encouraged Christian triumphalism and have been oppressive to many persons. . . .[5]

What is at stake for body theology is not the paradigmatic importance of God's revelation in Jesus. In our faith community's history, it is this figure and not another who has been and who is central for us. It is through him that we measure the ways we are grasped by the christic presence. But the marvelous paradox is that Jesus empties himself of claims to be the exclusive embodiment of God, and in that self-emptying opens the continuing possibility for all other persons.

The union of God and humanity in Jesus was a moral and personal union— a continuing possibility for all persons. Incarnation is always a miracle of grace, but the essence of miracle is not "interference" in the "natural" world by the "supernatural." It is the gracious (hence miraculous) discovery of who we really are, the communion of divine and human life in flesh. One essential criterion of Christological adequacy must be the moral test. Does this interpretation of Christ result in our bodying forth more of God's reality now? Does it create more justice and peace and joyous fulfillment of creaturely bodily life? Do we experience more of "the resurrection of the body" now—the gracious gift of a fundamental trust in the present bodily reality of God, the Word made flesh?

All this suggests that the human body is language and a fundamental means of communication. We do not just use words. We *are* words. This conviction underlies Christian incarnationalism. In Jesus Christ, God was present in a human being not for the first and only time, but in a radical way that has created a new definition of who we are. In Christ we are redefined as body words of love, and such body life in us is the radical sign of God's love for the world and of the divine immediacy in the world.[6]

This incarnational perspective, only briefly sketched here, is one critical way of beginning to move into the deeper meanings of our body and sexual experience. There are other ways. Yet this path is an important part of the Christian tradition, even if it has often been muted.

It was present, for example, in the later period of the Byzantine Empire, a time in which Christ's transfiguration was seen to be at the very center of our understanding God, ourselves, and the world. It was a time that affirmed that while the final mystery of God will always remain beyond the reach of our faculties, nevertheless, in the energies of the divine action and presence, God is revealed to our bodily senses. This vision of a transfigured world, a vision at the heart of Eastern Orthodoxy, was also present in the Anglican vision of the seventeenth century. In Thomas Traherne's work, for example, it finds remarkable expression: "By the very right of your senses, you enjoy the world. . . . You never enjoy the world aright, till the sea itself floweth in your veins, till you are clothed with the heavens and crowned with the stars, and perceive yourself to be the sole heir of the whole world, and more than so, because others are in it who are everyone sole heirs as well as you."[7]

True, the developments in science and philosophy in the latter days of the seventeenth century muted that theme in the West, and ever since then it has been more difficult to see the bodily consequences of an incarnational faith. The time is upon us for recapturing the feeling for the bodily apprehension of God. When we do so, we will find ourselves not simply making religious pronouncements about the bodily life; we will enter theologically more deeply into this experience, letting it speak of God to us, and of us to God.

The significance of all this has not escaped Toni Morrison in her Pulitzer prize-winning novel, *Beloved*. A central character is Baby Suggs, grandmother and holy woman of the African American extended family who had escaped from slavery in the South only to find continued oppression by the Northern whites. Speaking to her people, Baby Suggs "told them that the only grace they could have was the grace they could imagine. That if they could not see it, they would not have it. 'Here,' she said, 'in this place, we flesh; flesh that weeps, laughs; flesh that dances on bare feet in grass. Love it. Love it hard. Yonder they do not love your flesh. They despise it. . . . You got to love it. You.'"[8] Note carefully Baby Suggs's counsel. The only grace we can have is the grace we can imagine. If we cannot see it, we will not have it.

Notes

1. See Don Johnson, *Body* (Boston: Beacon Press, 1983), especially ch. 3.

2. See Kenneth J. Shapiro, *Bodily Reflective Modes: A Phenomenological Method for Psychology* (Durham, NC: Duke University Press, 1985).

3. See Seymour Fisher, *Body Experience in Fantasy and Behavior* (New York: Appleton-Century-Crofts, 1970); *Body Consciousness* (Englewood Cliffs, NJ: Prentice-Hall, 1973); *Development and Structure of the Body Image*, vol. 2 (Hillsdale, NJ: Lawrence Erlbaum

Assocs., 1986). Fisher says, "Although we are still in the early stages of understanding body image phenomena, we have discovered that body attitudes are woven into practically every aspect of behavior. The full range of their involvement cannot be overstated" (*Development and Structure*, 625). There is reason to assume that our bodyself experiences as females and as males are more similar than dissimilar. Here I am dealing in the basic human commonalities of body experience. Nevertheless, there are also certain important differences of world perception related to our different sexual biologies as well as to our sex-role conditioning. I have described some of these with their possible theological-ethical implications in *The Intimate Connection: Male Sexuality, Masculine Spirituality* (Philadelphia: Westminster Press, 1988).

4. Brian Wren, *Bring Many Names* (Carol Stream, IL: Hope Publishing Co., 1989). I wish to record my genuine gratitude to Brian Wren for dedicating this hymn to me.

5. For a helpful and extended discussion of these problems, see Tom F. Driver, *Christ in a Changing World* (New York: Crossroad, 1982).

6. Two writers who have grasped this insight well are Charles Davis, *Body as Spirit: The Nature of Religious Feeling* (New York: Seabury, 1976), and Arthur A. Vogel, *Body Theology* (New York: Harper & Row, 1973).

7. Thomas Traherne, *Poems, Centuries and Three Thanksgivings*, ed. Anne Ridler, 174, 177, quoted in A. M. Alchin, *The World is a Wedding: Explorations in Christian Spirituality* (New York: Crossroad, 1982), 41.

8. Toni Morrison, *Beloved* (New York: New American Library, 1987), 88

THE CRUCIFIED JESUS—THE BODILY JESUS
–Elisabeth Moltmann-Wendel

Elisabeth Moltmann-Wendel is a German theologian and prolific writer. Among her books are *Women around Jesus* and *A Land Flowing with Milk and Honey: Perspectives on Feminist Theology*. Her latest book, *Passion for God: Theology in Two Voices* is written with her theologian husband, Jürgen Moltmann.

What about the body of the central figure of Christianity? What symbolism is associated with Jesus?

A crucifix hangs in almost all churches and in the studies of many ministers as a symbol of Christianity. For many, it is a symbol of the hostility to the body which led Christian men and women to flee from and despise the body. How could a tortured, dying, dead body arouse pleasure and love in one's own body? In fact in Christianity the expression "body of Christ" refers only to the body on the cross and the risen body. In the Eucharist this body given in death, "Take, eat, this is my body which is given for you," is identified with the bread which is offered. And finally there is the body of Christ in the sense of the church, but this is again grounded in the body of Christ on the cross, which comprises all people of this faith. But is that the whole body of Christ of which the New Testament tells?

We must attack this dense tradition if we want to see the human body once again as God's creation and as a field of energy of unsuspected dimensions opened up to us. We must do this both with our experiences of our own bodies and with a critical approach to, a re-vision of, our tradition. And that also means a re-vision of the life and body of Jesus. Christian theology does not offer a good tradition for this, since it follows the apostle Paul, who did not want to know Christ "after the flesh" but was interested only in the crucified and risen Christ. But this view was and is one-sided. We have four Gospels—accounts of the life of Jesus—which were extremely interested in his flesh, in his life, and which we could ask about his body and life. They report his birth, his youth, his public career and his death. What is new about our question is that we do not want to ask about his human life generally but to start from the question of his body, which shaped his life like anyone else's: his body—the seat of feelings, the sphere of thought and relationship. Do these old accounts still have something to say for our questions today? Do they fall silent here, or do they give us new insights into the person of Jesus and a forgotten Christian message?

At first it was difficult for the early Christians—as it still is for Christians today—to understand Jesus' birth. Only the first evangelist, Mark, assumes a normal human birth and sees a kind of adoption by God first taking place through Jesus' baptism. The evangelists Matthew and Luke imagine that Mary became pregnant through the Holy Spirit, that her fiancé Joseph was frightened to death at this and on divine instructions was obliged to marry the mother of a child which was not really his. For them, a Son of God could not be conceived in the normal way. This view later began to become more and more established, and today is even to be found in the new Catechism of the Catholic Church, in which Jesus also may have no physical brothers and sisters, thus distorting some of the incarnation of God. The Gospel of Mark, which does not yet know such constructions, is also more human in its depiction of the humanity of Jesus than the later writers.

But Luke also relates human features: that after his birth Jesus was wrapped in swaddling clothes, in other words, he evacuated himself like other human beings; and that he was laid in a manger, the image of poverty and for later interpreters a prelude to the cross: the wood of the manger is also the wood of the cross. The later popular notions, which also appear in the mediaeval visions of Brigitta of Sweden, that Jesus lay naked on the naked earth, are much more earthy and emphasize Jesus' humanity more: here is a reminiscence of the powers of earth and the old earth mother, which communicate a physical life-force. Or there is the notion that he was born in a cave, i.e., in the depths of the earth. The picture of the savior who "springs from the earth," as in the Advent hymn "O savior, rend the heavens," recalls his earthliness and bodiliness.

The human Jesus of the Gospel of Mark also shows very marked human reactions that the later gospels have skillfully retouched. He is annoyed at the disciples (9:19; 8:17f.) and the Pharisees (3:5) and has outbursts of anger. He groans and sighs (8:12). He welcomes children and does not just use them as teaching illustrations (9:36; 10:16). He is full of compassion (1:41) and loves the rich young man with a love that does not come from above but is mutual, agape (10:21). It can also be said of him that he needs a cushion in the boat to sleep on (4:38) and that his family thinks him crazy, a ne'er-do-well (3:21). Mark also reports his desperate feeling of godforsakenness on the cross (15:34). These are images which show Jesus as vital person, needing company and tenderness, but also capable of passionate outbursts. Here is a Jesus who has a body, and the author of the Gospel of Mark has no problems about that. It is from this body—and not from his will, his head or his spirit—that the energies which heal the woman with the issue of blood emanate (5:30). Though a generation of theologians whose perception was reduced by the Enlightenment may have eliminated such details, we are again discovering them as central christological statements. Jesus is no Gnostic hero who brings us a change of consciousness. He brings liberation from social compulsions and healing for destroyed bodies. With his body Jesus is also drawn into the cosmos: in his anxiety in Gethsemane he falls on the comforting mother earth, which at the same time swallows people up (14:35). This earth quakes at his death and gives up its dead (Matt 27:52ff.). He came into this cosmos—according to the Gospel of John—to heal the divisions of the world (John 11:27).

With a balanced Jesus who could no longer be passionate, angry and tender, it was also forgotten that Jesus lived in and by relationships. Because he was always put on a higher level than other human beings, there was a failure to see that he needed other people for his development, and that the relationships necessary for a person of flesh and blood were also necessary for his spirit and its energies. In relationships we experience acceptance and gain detachment. Relationships are shaped by conflicts and their resolutions. And we experience these with our whole persons.

Jesus' conflict with his family also extends unmistakably into the stories that have been handed down to us. They wanted to see Jesus as a normal "citizen" and family man instead of as a revolutionary and a single person. And the group of disciples that he then joined did not give the resonance that he needed. These men in love with success disappointed him time and again. He found acceptance, stimulation and new lifestyles later with the women who stayed with him to his death, one of whom showed him his way to the Gentiles (Matt 15:21ff.) and another his way to death as the anointed king of Israel (Mark 14:3ff.). He did not understand his life as that of a husband and father, obedient to the family tradition and bringing up children, but as that of a man who devotes body and life to other values.

To this degree his notions of sexuality differed fundamentally from those of his environment, in particular from those of Judaism, as Elaine Pagels[1] has shown, though he did not make his lifestyle a law. But the later Gnostic Gospels relate that he had erotic needs. According to these, Mary Magdalene was his friend, with whom he passionately exchanged kisses. So for him love was not reduced socially to love of the neighbor. He reproaches the Pharisee who had invited him to his house for a cold and loveless meal. By contrast, the prostitute who suddenly burst into this male circle deeply moved him physically with her anointing. For him, her tears, her hair, her kisses were physical love that gave his body pleasure (Luke 7).

It is also striking what value the story of Jesus attaches to eating. The New Testament meals are too often immediately associated with Jesus' last meal, the Last Supper. But all the meals in his life must have been eaten with enjoyment: fish, lamb, bread, wine, herbs do not indicate asceticism. And the fact that his opponents spoke of him as a "glutton and winebibber" only confirms that he did not live his life grimly, but in a relaxed way, as a celebration. How parallel his own suffering, life and death were seen as being to human suffering and recuperation in the early period of the church is evident from many terms which can be found in the healing stories and in the passion narrative. In particular, the story of the woman with an issue of blood seems to have been understood as an exemplary passion story. The word "suffer" is used both of the woman who suffered under the physicians and of the suffering of Jesus (Mark 5:26; 8:31; 9:12). In Mark, the blood is both her and his blood; similarly, in Mark "body" occurs only in this story and in the passion narrative. The word "scourge," used to describe the woman's affliction, is also used in connection with the torturing of Jesus.

In these stories, Jesus' death is still seen in parallel to other human suffering and dying, in which at the same time the power and healing force of God are visible. His dying is still not sacrificial dying for human sin. Here with his uncompromising life he still fought for the life of others.

Later this suffering was no longer seen in the context of human suffering. The idea of representation was replaced by the notion of the atoning sacrifice that had to be offered for the sins of humankind. In this way his death came into a religious dimension which no longer allowed any comparisons with human suffering. Thus his body was distinguished from other human bodies and became the body of crucifixion and resurrection, which had virtually no relationship to his earthly life. His body was seen as a sacrifice which now had to draw other sacrifices after it: male sacrifices in war and female self-sacrifices.

For many people the question will remain whether as God's Son Jesus did not follow other laws, and his divinity is not to be compared with our humanity. I think that his deepest humanity makes up his divinity. As God became human—"clad himself in our poor flesh and blood" as Luther said—we can all freely seek Jesus' forgotten body. God and humankind encounter each other in the body. God encounters us in the human body. Those who fail to see their bodies fail to see God. The crucifix, which confronts us only with the tortured and dead body, misses the whole message of the Gospel.

Notes

1. Elaine Pagels, *Adam, Eve and the Serpent* (Harmondsworth, UK: Penguin, 1990), 9ff.

SEARCHING FOR THE ROOTS OF HEALING
–Linda L. Smith

Linda L. Smith, RN, MS, has spent most of her life in church work as a nurse and teacher. Her health care background includes critical care nursing, nursing education, home health, and hospice care. Linda is founder and director of the Healing Touch Spiritual Ministry Program. Energized by her passion to bring healing back into our Christian churches and ministries, she has taught hundreds of workshops on healing.

Looking for Healing in the Hebrew Bible

The role of healing in the Hebrew Bible is quite profound but not always obvious. Aside from a few direct references to healing, the larger concepts of sin, salvation, and ultimate destiny also relate to healing. Tom Harpur, an Anglican priest and writer, calls attention to the common thread of human brokenness and how we can be restored to health.[1] Our relationship with God was broken in the garden of Eden, he says, and everything since has been affected by our turning away from the face of God. The story points to our need to be restored to wholeness—to health—to be healed and restored to oneness with God.

The stories of the early Hebrews existed for thousands of years as an oral tradition. These stories addressed the meaning of life, including how people were to behave. Gradually, this oral tradition was written down as sacred law and gradually developed into what we now know as the Torah. It contains the five books of Moses and the books of the Prophets and the Holy Writings. All of these make up the Hebrew Scriptures or the Hebrew Bible. The Torah was written in Hebrew, typically without vowels. Understanding the meaning could be quite challenging, particularly since everything was viewed as a metaphor for hidden wisdom teachings. Unlocking the meaning of a passage was truly an accomplishment that was met with great rejoicing. The role of the sages was to memorize vast amounts of the law and the sacred teachings, a skill greatly relied upon by the people. In this way, they were able to live fairly ordered lives, knowing who they were as a people in relationship with God.

In the Old Testament we can trace beliefs about the people's relationship with God and how healing figured in their lives. The God of Abraham and Moses led the people through the wilderness and protected them by day and night. Yahweh was the giver of all good things and the dispenser of sicknesses of all kinds. The prophets warned the people to follow the law or grave things would befall them. Clearly, Yahweh was the bringer of both life and death and there was no escaping God's judgment. We find throughout the scriptures a compassionate God who could also be a harsh God. Illnesses and even natural catastrophes such as earthquakes and floods were viewed as God's wrathful visitation upon his people; healing was God's relenting compassion and caring for his people.

The ancient Hebrews struck a bargain with God in the form of the covenant. This bond tied them to Yahweh, the Source of all that is. Yahweh, in turn, agreed to care for the "chosen" ones. Obedience of the nation and physical health were linked, just as disobedience and disease were linked. The covenant was made with the whole people, not just individuals. When King David sinned, his punishment was visited upon the whole people.

There are details in the scriptures of all kinds of diseases that God would send his people when they did not live up to the covenant. These include consumption, fever, pestilence, boils, scurvy, itch for which there is no cure, madness, blindness, distraction of mind, burning fever, and inflammation. Every sickness not specifically mentioned was promised in payment for disobeying the law.

Nowhere do the scriptures describe attempts to influence God's hand in matters of life and death. If one "sinned," whatever punishment was meted out was deserved. "Sin" meant "missing the mark," being "off the path." A sinful life was punished with disease and misfortune. A righteous life, on the other hand, would be blessed by God with riches. This interpretation of the events of life was very straightforward as long as the "sin" could be identified. It faltered, however (as do all theologies), in explaining why bad things happened to apparently good people. The ancient Hebrews believed that surely some sin, perhaps even by one's parents, accounted for God's punishment.

The book of Job addressed this issue with an allegorical story about a righteous man who by all appearances seemed to be in disfavor with God. Even his family and friends tried to convince him to see where he had "missed the mark." But Job was steadfast. He knew that he was God's faithful servant. In the end, he was justified by God. The story questions the assumption that goodness always wins God's blessing and punishment always is meted out for evil. This story had to be a comfort to those ancient Hebrews as they searched for the meaning of suffering in their lives, just as it is a comfort for all those reading it today.

THE PSALMS—POETRY OF HEALING

The theme of healing in the Old Testament becomes quite personal in the Psalms. Tom Harpur calls the Psalms the "window through which we view the inner wrestling of the human soul." All struggles, hopes, fears, and longings of humanity are exposed to the presence of God in these prayers flowing from the heart of Jewish spiritual life. Tradition has it that the Psalms, seen as divinely inspired, are the most effective means in mirroring back the direct light of God. Since they believed that sickness was God's way of dealing with the individual, many of the psalms call us to trust in the Holy One as a healer of mind, body, soul, and spirit. There seems to be a deep conviction on the part of the psalmists that God's natural inclination is towards healing of all creation. However, there are other psalms that appear to contradict this thought. These psalms call upon God to reign down terror on one's enemies, including diseases and other ills.

Rabbi Simkha Weintraub[2] tells us about the Hasidic master Rabbi Nachman of Breslov who lived in the eighteenth century. This revered master identified ten psalms as having special power to bring a true and complete healing of body and spirit. He called them the *Tikkun HaKlali* or "Complete Remedy," and said they embody the concentrated power of the entire book of Psalms. Viewed together, the ten psalms reflect an unfolding of many emotions and reactions common to those dealing with illness. Mere recitation will have little value. Instead, you must identify with their contents in a deep and meaningful way, and seek to find yourself in every psalm. According to Rabbi Nachman, prayer is a dialogue between humans and their Creator and is absolutely key in the repair of the world. The ultimate goal in Jewish teaching is to bring the world to a state of *tikkun*. Rabbi Weintraub explains that this word implies repair, correction, wholeness, and perfection. *Tikkun* repairs the covenant relationship and bridges the separation between the people and God.

Another book available to the ancient Hebrews was the book of Proverbs, which is counted among the Holy Writings. It continues the theme found in the Psalms, the Torah, and the writings of the prophets. Here there are warnings that illness and misfortune are the results of sin. Over and over, we find this same theme: if we follow wisdom and the Law, we will be blessed with health and long life. These maxims were often committed to memory as words to live by.

For the Hebrews, life was seen metaphorically as a path to be walked. If they stepped off the path, they fell into sin. But what "influenced" them to step off the path in the first place? Were there greater forces out there working against God and ultimately against his people? Was there "evil" loose in the world? These were questions that their cosmology attempted to answer.

THE ROLE OF SATAN AND EVIL SPIRITS

For the Hebrews, Satan originally was not evil or opposed to God. On the contrary, he was one of God's angels (messengers) of light sent to stand in one's path much like an adversary, until you saw your sinful ways and turned back to the righteous path. The Greek term *diabolos*, later translated as "devil," literally means "one who throws something across one's path." The Hebrew storytellers would often attribute misfortune to human sin. At other times, Satan, by God's order or permission, would block human plans and desires. Elaine Pagels,[3] a respected scripture scholar, describes the Hebrew term, *satan*, as an adversarial role. If the path was wrong, then having Satan "throw a monkey wrench in the works" was not a bad thing. In this sense, God might be sending the messenger Satan to protect a person from worse harm. The story of Job is a classic example of this adversarial role of Satan. In the tale, Satan challenges God to put his favorite servant, Job, to the test of loyalty. God authorized Satan to afflict Job, but to spare his life. Job passes the test, and in the end, Satan remains an angel, God's obedient servant.

Demons had no place in the Old Testament, but it is interesting to see that the Hebrew Scriptures are filled with angels. They are often referred to as the "shining ones" who serve as God's messengers. They brought good news as well as bad. For the Egyptians and Babylonians, the power of darkness was at the root of all misfortune. This was not so, however, for the Hebrews. Not until the time of the exile, when the Jewish people were forced into captivity in Babylon, do we see spiritual powers being attributed to anything other than Yahweh. Until then, the only source of illness was believed to be Yahweh. During the exile, contact with Babylonians, Egyptians, and Persians began to affect Hebrew thought. They too began to accept that the powers of darkness somehow played a part in misfortunes and illnesses.

Satan became "The Satan" and took on a personality antagonistic to God. Stories began to give him various names such as Beelzebuh, Semihazah, Azazel, Belial, and Prince of Darkness. There are many stories about the fall of this great angel, who took a horde of angels with him down to *sheol*. The Satan took on sinister qualities. No longer one of God's faithful servants, he was depicted as swollen with lust and arrogance and blamed for humans' fall into sin. According to Hebrew cosmology, the forces of evil under the Prince of Darkness have continued to influence the people of the earth ever since. There is a great cosmic battle going on between the forces of good and the forces of evil. Even today, we use the expression "the devil made me do it!"

WHERE WERE THE TRADITIONAL HEALERS IN JUDAISM?

Among other ancient societies, there were diviners, soothsayers, sorcerers, and those who believed in demons and other spiritual forces. Often these individuals tended the sick and assisted in childbirth. We read in Leviticus that the witches, augurs, mediums, and wizards were to be stoned, presumably because they called upon other forces besides Yahweh. Furthermore, those who practiced medical healing were thought to be trained in divination and magic, which were strictly forbidden. Even the skills of physicians were not held in high esteem. However, in the book of Jeremiah, we hear the prophet lamenting the absence of physicians in Gilead. His cry was for his poor people, sinners that they were, whose health was in jeopardy. Zach Thomas, a Presbyterian minister, observes, "Judaism grew to be remarkably devoid of anyone designated as a healer."[4]

Since the scriptures are quite clear that Yahweh is the only source of blessing and curse, there are few references in the Old Testament to the use of medicine or to the role of the physician. People thought it was better to pray for deliverance from their pain than to suffer at the hands of physicians. There is the story in 2 Chronicles about a King Asa who suffered from a debilitating disease. He sought the help of physicians and died, proof of the importance of putting faith in God, not in earthly healers. His turning to physicians was interpreted as a "betrayal" and most likely involved pagan physicians.

The most positive reference to roles of the physician and medicine is in the apocryphal book of Ecclesiasticus (Sirach 38:9–12). The passage describes the conditions under which God will heal. Notice in this passage that in order to be made well or "whole," there are four things required:

1. Pray first to the Lord for deliverance.

2. Look within and see where you have missed the mark, then repent.

3. Make an offering, the best you have.

4. Finally, submit to the physician.

The passage was probably written in the century after the Chronicles (about 190 BC), and represents a much later development in Judaic thought. Here the writer is saying that the person in need of healing is fulfilling the law by placing all of his or her faith in God, who is the ultimate healer. Then, the person looks within his or her heart, repenting of any wrongdoing that may have brought on this curse or punishment. Important to all Hebrew ritual was making an offering or appeasement to God. This offering was supposed to be the very best of what the person had to offer and would show his or her sincerity in repentance. Finally, the sick person is advised to trust in the care and knowledge of the physician. The passage ends with words of wisdom that offer a "cheerful" thought: "If a man sins in the eyes of his Maker, may he fall under the care of the doctor."

This is the only passage in the Holy Writings that extols not only the role of the physician but also that of the pharmacist. Morton Kelsey, Episcopal priest and respected author, states that physicians and healers did attend the sick but were looked upon with great suspicion by the rabbis.[5] The main rabbinical schools forbade the practice of medicine and healing since they were viewed as akin to sorcery and magic. In the Talmud, there are references that say those who participate in these roles will have no share in the world to come. The Talmud is like an encyclopedia of the meanings and intentions of the law. It assisted the rabbis in interpreting the Holy Scriptures. Kelsey also points to a statement in the Talmud that Jesus was hanged on a tree on Passover eve because he practiced sorcery, which is a reference to Jesus healing the sick.

YAHWEH'S COMPASSION

There are some healing stories in the Old Testament that show God's mercy and compassion on individuals. In the book of Kings, both Elijah and Elisha heal a child and Elisha cleanses Namaan of leprosy. None of these incidents, however, include the idea that the presence of "sin" provoked illness. No reason is given for the illnesses; neither is there any judgment. There are other stories of healing after the proper sacrifices were made for sin, as well as stories of how plagues were stopped when Moses and Aaron prayed and made atonement for the people. At one point, Moses is told to fashion a bronze serpent so that anyone bitten by the vipers in the desert would be healed. In a story in the book of Samuel, King David builds an altar to the Lord and offers burnt offerings to appease God. The Lord answers his prayers by lifting a plague from the land.

In 2 Kings 20, King Hezekiah becomes ill and is told by the prophet Isaiah that he will die. The king prays for his own recovery. Isaiah then gets a message from God that fifteen years will be added to the king's life. Almost as an afterthought, Isaiah makes a poultice of figs to apply to the king's boils. Medicine and prayer work together for the king's recovery in this story.

In yet another story, Tobias heals his father, Tobit, of his blindness through the help of the angel Raphael. Raphael, whom Tobit does not recognize as an angel of God, tells Tobit to "take courage, the time is near for God to heal you." As the story continues, Raphael journeys with Tobit's son, Tobias, and teaches him about many things, including the healing properties of fish heart, liver, and gall. Burning incense made of the fish heart and liver will drive away demons and evil spirits that afflict people. Apparently, the smell can drive them all the way to Egypt! The fish's gall can be used to anoint a person's eyes where white films have appeared on them. Tobias, following the angel's guidance, peels away the white film that covers his father's eyes, and he is able to see his son once again.

These are representative of the healing stories in the Hebrew Bible. On the whole, the healing stories were intended to show the supernatural powers of God. The theme of healing is relatively minor in comparison to themes like sin and salvation. Yet, the Psalms, which were the prayers of the people, are filled with mention of the healing power of Yahweh. Although the healing stories may be few, belief in Yahweh's compassion and power to heal was strong.

The prophet Isaiah refers to the theme of healing in his references to the coming of the messiah—the one who will save the people. His writing encouraged many to hope for the day of Yahweh when all illness would be healed. "Be strong, do not fear," Isaiah tells us, "He will come with vengeance, with terrible recompense. He will come and save you!" And how shall we recognize the messiah? The dead will rise, the deaf will hear, and the blind will see. God will come not only as a savior but as *a healer of God's people.*

Healing in the New Testament

JESUS AS HEALER

Jesus entered his ministry after his empowerment through baptism into the Spirit. He was totally submerged in the Spirit and afterwards began his preaching and teaching with what the gospel writers described as "a new authority in his voice." The people were astonished because his teaching was not like that of the scribes. Jesus' authority was based on direct experience, on intuitive knowing, instead of on an intellectual conceptualization. He was so powerful that his very presence was enough to stir the hearts of many. His words compelled his listeners to change their lives. Some left everything behind to follow him. He did more than teach—he healed physical and mental ills. This was the mark of a true prophet. Wherever he went, he was besieged by those who wanted to be healed. For Jesus, healing was a manifestation of God's great love and compassion for all of us. Had Jesus believed that illness and suffering were sent from God for our good, he would never have intervened in God's process. Thus, it is obvious that he did not subscribe to this belief—even if we are tempted to do so at times.

By the time the stories about Jesus were actually written down (by most accounts at least forty years after the crucifixion), they had been told countless times, probably with some embellishment and changing of facts. This point is accepted by the majority of New Testament scholars. According to Tom Harpur, however, the accounts in the Gospel of Mark of Jesus healing the sick and driving out the demonic forces are too primitive and too pervasive not to have their roots in actuality. In addition, we know from John that many other stories could have been told as well, but were not written down.

Early in Jesus' ministry, John's disciples came to him with the question, "Are you the one?" When Jesus answered, he did not say, "Yes, I'm the one you have set your hopes on." Rather, he pointed to the prophesy of Isaiah. All those listening recognized the importance of his words and their hearts burned within them. They were an oppressed people, subject to the Romans. By walking from town to town and healing, Jesus gave messages of hope to all who heard him. He was letting them know that these were the signs that the reign of God had begun. God's people were being healed.

One-fifth of the content of the Gospels is about Jesus' healing ministry. There are forty-one distinct instances of physical and mental healings recorded in the four gospels. Some of these are retold in several gospels, so there are seventy-two accounts in all. Some of the accounts are about healing large numbers of people at one time; others describe individual healing or healing at a distance. Jesus taught his disciples to heal and empowered them to go out and carry out his ministry. Even from a brief look at the scriptures, it is obvious that Jesus expected his disciples to continue his work.

It is striking to see that in all three of the Synoptic Gospels, the "call" to ministry for the apostles and the disciples included healing. It was the mark whereby Jesus' followers would be known. Spiritual writers through the centuries have also connected the work of healing to a call from God. Many, however, defined that call so narrowly that few qualified in their eyes as "called by God." However, we now realize that we are all called into healing ourselves and, in various degrees, into healing our neighbor.

HOW DID JESUS HEAL?

Jesus healed by the power of God. Connecting with God, he was able to release the fire and energy of God in the form of healing. He employed various healing methods, selecting whatever was most effective for the individual or the situation before him. He did not always heal the same way and therefore did not leave us a formula of how to go about it. He healed through his very presence, through love, word, touch, faith, and what Dr. Dale Matthews calls the ancient medicine of "saliva."[6] There are healing properties in one's spit, he tells us, which was probably a well-known fact to the people of that day. But Jesus' most common means of healing was by speaking words and touching the person with his hand. When he saw a need, he healed from a compassionate heart.

Compassion means to know suffering together with another. Jesus so loved that he healed. When confronted with individuals who had been caught in "sin," his attitude was one of compassion as he healed and restored them to the community. Jesus looked into the person's very soul, into his or her heart, and brought wholeness and healing.

Nowhere in the Gospels do we find Jesus asking anyone what they had done wrong before healing them. Instead, he responded with compassion and met their need. Rev. Lawrence Althouse observed that we do not see Jesus judging whether someone was worthy of healing.[7] Personal worth was never a factor in Jesus' ministry. Jesus did not believe that God intended a person to be ill in order to grow in faith, patience, or any other virtue. He did not subscribe to the belief that suffering is good for you. If he had, he wouldn't have healed people.

THE HEALING TOUCH OF JESUS

Jesus often touched others, and people likewise liked to touch Jesus. Ron Roth, a modern-day mystic and healer, explains that Jesus had reached such a state of perfect communion with God that merely being in his presence and being open to God's grace could heal a person.

Nearly one-half of all the recorded healings in the Gospels involve touching. Jesus held children, washed feet, touched blind eyes and deaf ears, crippled limbs, dead bodies. He touched men and he touched women. Most shocking of all, he touched the untouchables, the lepers. He even allowed notorious women to touch him and to anoint him.

He was known for breaking all the rules and for putting human need above the law. As one might imagine, this angered the ones who upheld the rules. They accused him of healing by the power of Beelzebul, the Prince of Darkness. Obviously, this was as absurd to Jesus as it was to his followers. As we know, Jesus worked in God's light, so how could he heal from darkness?

The Gospels tell us that Jesus' opponents were most angered at his repeated healings on the Sabbath. He probably could have waited until the next day, but being totally present to the need before him, it mattered little to him what day it was.

CHRISTIAN COMMUNITY HEALING

Prior to Pentecost, the disciples performed healing miracles even though they did not understand Jesus' words about his coming death and resurrection.

Once they came to know and believe in Jesus, they were able to access the power and love of God. They were changed personally. When the pouring out of the Spirit came at Pentecost, it was an event of great power and fire. All four gospels relate that the coming of the Spirit was like the sound of wind—actually, the sound of an immense amount of energy. The Spirit descended in the form of flames (powerful energy) and then it transformed all those present. Immediately, they went out to preach to those they had been afraid of just the day before. We are told that "awe came upon every one"—they were powerfully transformed by this experience and strengthened to carry out Jesus' mission.

As the little community of followers increased, the Christian leaders in turn empowered others to act with compassion toward those who were suffering in any way. They had learned that the source of all healing is God, and they were to be instruments through which God would then manifest wholeness and healing.

In his letter to the early church, James stated that Christian healing is not a special gift only for a few. Rather, it is a gift freely given to the whole community, which means it is entirely within our capabilities. For centuries the church interpreted the meaning of James's writing as "the act of saving a person from spiritual death." Kelsey, however, states that modern studies on the original Greek text reveal that the words in Greek mean healed, cured, and saved from illness or death.

Jesus' words and ministry were about healing bodies and spirits, about wholeness, forgiveness, new life, and touching others from a compassionate heart. Jesus healed with compassion, as did the early Christians. As healers, they were the conduits of healing for the Spirit of God. They served as deacons and deaconesses in committed service. We do not see these healers stopping to question whether or not to relieve someone's illness when that action would restore the individual to God's love. Their occasional failure to heal did not stop their reaching out, nor did it stop their faith in healing. They visited and nursed the sick just as the Master had modeled for them.

Thich Nhat Hanh, a Buddhist priest writing about Buddhism and Christianity, observes that whenever we see someone who is loving, compassionate, mindful, caring, and understanding, we know that the Holy Spirit is there.[8] Those first Christians were intoxicated with the fire of the Spirit. They were "Christed" individuals for others, and that Spirit of God has continued to dwell in the hearts of men and women through the darkest of nights down through the ages.

Notes

1. Tom Harpur, *The Uncommon Touch: An Investigation of Spiritual Healing* (Toronto: McClelland & Stewart, 1994).

2. Simkha Weintraub, *Healing of Soul, Healing of Body, Spiritual Leaders Unfold the Strength and Solace in Psalms* (Woodstock, VT: Jewish Lights, 1994).

3. Elaine Pagels, *The Origin of Satan* (New York: Vintage, 1995).

4. Zach Thomas, *Healing Touch: The Church's Forgotten Language* (Louisville, KY: Westminster/John Knox, 1994).

5. Morton Kelsey, *Healing and Christianity* (Minneapolis: Augsburg, 1995).

6. Dale Matthews, *The Faith Factor, Proof of the Healing Power of Prayer* (New York: Penguin, 1998).

7. Lawrence W. Althouse, *Rediscovering the Gift of Healing* (Nashville: Abingdon, 1977).

8. Thich Nhat Hanh, *Living Buddha, Living Christ* (New York: Riverhead, 1995).

FOR PERSONAL REFLECTION

1. Dualism and duality are different—the first is "the experience of two utterly different elements at war with each other"; the second is "the perception of two elements which, while distinguishable from each other, truly belong together." What life experiences have caused you to experience the dualism of body and soul? When have you experienced a healthy duality?

2. Nelson says that we humans participate in the miracle of the incarnation, as incarnation is being "the gracious (hence miraculous) discovery of who we really are, the communion of divine and human life in flesh." So often, Christians understand incarnation as referring only to the experience of Jesus. How do you respond (both in your "gut" and in your heart) to Nelson's assertion?

3. Moltmann-Wendel offers a clear description of the bodily Jesus. In what ways can you imagine this description influencing your own relationship with Jesus? How does that influence your own theology?

FOR GROUP DISCUSSION

1. Both Nelson and Moltmann-Wendel speak of Jesus' sexuality, something that very rarely occurs in Christian circles. Yet sexuality is very significant in our bodies. What has been the result of this silence on Christian attitudes toward sexuality? On a comprehensive Christian theology of the body?

2. Smith writes of the ancient religious understanding that illness is caused by sin. What remnants of that understanding still exist in our culture today? How is the concept of Satan related to your religious tradition's view of illness?

3. In what ways did Jesus' ministry expand his culture's understanding of healing? If we adopted Jesus' attitude about healing in our own culture, what would the impact be? Would it change our theology?

2.
Our Relationship with Our Bodies

Pax
–D. H. Lawrence

All that matters is to be at one with the living God
to be a creature in the house of the God of Life.

Like a cat asleep on a chair
at peace, in peace
and at one with the master of the house, with the mistress,
at home, at home in the house of the living,
sleeping on the hearth, and yawning before the fire.

Sleeping on the hearth of the living world
yawning at home before the fire of life
feeling the presence of the living God
like a great reassurance
a deep calm in the heart
a presence
as of the master sitting at the board
in his own and greater being,
     in the house of life.

Having considered—and probably reconsidered—theology of the body, informed by contemporary Christian writers, we now move a little closer to home. From the realm of the conceptual, we move to the personal. How do we make our theology of the body "real"? How do we make it a truly practical theology?

For me, D. H. Lawrence's poem draws a picture of what it means to be in a truly right relationship not just with God, but also with myself. In accepting, embracing, and fully living my life, and in confidence that God is the Source of All Being, I can relax and enjoy my little place in the universe story. I, though made of mortal flesh, can feel at one with the living God.

Sometimes that's not the way I feel. I need to be constantly converted from the error of alienation from my body. I need to continue to face into the questions raised by Wuellner: "Why are we so often at war with our bodies? . . . What have our bodies done to us that we ignore, dislike, and punish them so?" Whenever I confess this sin, I am again graced that both God and my body forgive me and welcome me into a yet deeper relationship. I find that my body tells me truth, and I can trust it. I celebrate the reconciliation and the joy of being in relationship with my body. No longer is my body a tool, a machine to keep functioning smoothly 'til I die, but a means of relating to God and creation.

Lest I come across as a dualist, suggesting that I and my body are not one and the same, I offer you an analogy. When I say to you the word "ocean," an image leaps to mind—one of a great, wet, watery expanse. Were I to say the word "wave," another image would be evoked, probably of a swelling ridge of water, maybe lapping a shoreline. But where does the ocean end and the wave begin? Ocean and wave are inextricably part of each other. My body and I are inextricably part of each other. This intrapersonal relationship is complicated. It is also worthy of reflection and exploration.

The following essays address the matter of our relationship (or should that be *relationships?*) with our bodies. Moltmann-Wendel describes the influence of touch in how we know our bodies and thus relate to them. Mohrmann describes our relationship with the body in terms of ethics. Hers is a theological view, not a secular one. Her words are addressed to physicians, but the rest of us may listen in too and be edified.

RECONCILING AND CELEBRATING WITH OUR BODIES
—Flora Slosson Wuellner

Flora Slosson Wuellner is an ordained minister in the United Church of Christ. After several years in parish ministry, she entered a specialized ministry of spiritual renewal. She has led ecumenical retreats and workshops in the United States and Europe, authored ten books, and taught as an adjunct faculty member at the Pacific School of Religion, Berkeley, in the area of spirituality.

We pray constantly for peace in our homes, our communities, and our world. Why are we so often at war with our bodies?

"I hate my body!" I recently heard a friend say. "It's no better than second-hand goods. I'd like to trade it in for a new model!"

I recently read an informal survey reporting almost 80 percent of women dislike their bodies or at least many parts of their bodies. How often do we look in the mirror and think: *I wish I had a different face, I wish my eyes were a different color, I hate the shape of my legs,* or, *I'm too big . . . I'm too thin . . . too fat . . . too short?*

Some of us jog or exercise to the point of punishment. Some of us take diet pills or go on crash diets to "get rid of that ugly fat." We blame our stomachs for our eating problems, and we blame our sexual systems for our sexual behavior. When our bodies get ill or tired, we blame them for letting us down. When they are well, we take them for granted.

Many of us carry around unhealed inner hurts about our bodily, and therefore our emotional, selves. Perhaps our families and school friends teased or rejected us because we were hyperactive, slow in sports, clumsy with our hands, too tall, too short, too plump, or too skinny.

We spend a lifetime centered around the necessities of feeding, clothing, and sheltering our bodies, and we anxiously or impatiently take them to doctors when we are sick. But we almost never think about them in depth or listen thoughtfully to their signals of stress and distress.

Our Western culture almost brainwashes us into helplessness, anger, anxiety at the great physical transitions of life: adolescence, middle life, menopause, aging, and death. At these times, for many of us, our bodies are at best puzzling, scary machines, out of control or, at worst, malevolent, treacherous enemies.

What have our bodies done to us that we ignore, dislike, and punish them so? Do we merely aim for self-improvement, better health, and beauty? If so, these qualities (as we know with our children and even with our pets and plants) flourish best in an atmosphere of warm friendliness, encouragement, respect, communication, and sensitivity to ability and timing. It is far more likely that much unhealed anger, fear, and hurt underlie our dislike and suspicion of our bodily selves. For many of us, our bodies are the victims of our loneliness, our anxiety, and our need to control our environment.

Is this not the same underlying fear and hurt that exists among our families, communities, and warring nations? Is it possible that God is able to begin the reconciling, transforming work here in our own bodily selves?

There are many hopeful and joyful signs that the reconciling work has begun. There are new, more holistic ways of eating and drinking; there are new, helpful ways of taking charge of our bodies in illness and medical treatment; alternatives are now offered for childbirth, the middle years, and the challenges of aging. But these changes are still very much on the frontiers of our thinking and living. They have not yet taken deep root in our culture.

This is not only a cultural concern, but also a spiritual concern. The way we relate to our bodily selves profoundly influences the way we relate to God, to one another, to prayer, to all of life.

Unfortunately, there is still a widespread mindset in many churches and Christian communities that our bodies are *hindrances* to our spiritual lives. It is still too often implied, if not actually taught, that the body is, by its very nature, lower, inferior, separating us from God. Some of our most loved hymns reinforce this concept, such as the beautiful hymn by Whittier, "Dear Lord and Father of Mankind," in which the last verse urges: "Let sense be dumb, let flesh retire." This seems to confirm the ancient heresy that the flesh is a prison in which the spirit is trapped and tempted. But this concept is not the incarnational, biblical witness.

A careful reading of Paul's epistles clears up many misunderstandings. For example, in his letter to the church in Galatia, in which he contrasts the works of the flesh and the works of the Spirit, we see that the problems he lists as belonging to the flesh include many things that are not especially related to the body at all: "idolatry, sorcery, enmity, strife, jealousy, anger, selfishness, party spirit, envy" (5:20–21). It is obvious that Paul means by flesh not the body itself, but the fragmented, sinful condition of the *whole* person who is not yet healed and transformed by Christ.

Paul's basic teaching about the body is clearly stated in his letter to the church in Corinth: "Do you not know that your bodies are members of Christ? . . . Do you not know that your body is a temple of the Holy Spirit within you which you have from God? . . . Glorify God in your body" (1 Cor 6:15, 19–20).

With equal power, he wrote to the church at Philippi: "It is my eager expectation and hope that I shall not be at all ashamed, but that with full courage . . . Christ will be honored in my body whether by life or by death" (1:20).

The witness of Jesus is stated simply and completely in John's gospel: "Jesus answered them, 'Destroy this temple, and in three days I will raise it up.' . . . He spoke of the temple of his body" (2:19, 21).

Throughout the Bible, we see many perplexities of the body, many sufferings in the body, but always the triumphant affirmation that "God saw everything that [God] had made, and behold, it was very good" (Gen 1:31).

If God created, loved, and honored our bodies and so blessed them by the incarnation, then our bodily selves were meant to be to us priceless, incomparable gifts.

This does not mean that we are to idolize our bodies or obey every physical impulse or abandon attempts to improve health and appearance. Nor does it mean that we may never have to compel or even sacrifice our bodies for love of others. Rather, it means that we are to be healed of our dislike for our bodies. We are to learn to listen to the signals of our bodies, honoring them as one of the main ways God speaks to us and by which we can learn much unencountered truth about ourselves and our communities.

Who is this "I" or "we" that listens to and dialogues with our bodies? Certainly it is not some "ghost in the machine" or some spiritual entity hovering above the ground. The "I" is our *conscious* self, the perceiver, the interpreter. It is not detached from the body or the deep self; it is like an island that is the only visible part of an underwater mountain range or a ray of light from a lighthouse that focuses on specific parts of the surrounding mystery of darkness.

When I speak of relationship with the body, I do not deny the oneness and unity of our whole selves, for that would be unholistic fragmentation and compartmentalization. But a healing process can result from the focus on our various physical and emotional aspects as if they were beings in themselves. By thus visualizing and communicating in prayer with these "identities" of our bodies and feelings, we often experience deepening healing and unity. Fragmentation results when we are *out* of touch with our emotions and bodies. Through encountering these two aspects of ourselves with awareness and love, they become increasingly unified, vital parts of our whole selves. This relationship between our conscious selves and our bodily selves was meant to be exciting, enjoyable, trustful, alert, and nurturing, with each part sharing its own special gifts and powers.

The first step in this new marriage of our powers is often the healing and forgiveness for the wounds of contempt and compulsion. If for years we have disliked, ignored, or repudiated parts of our bodies, quite possibly the level of consciousness in every cell and organ has picked up these thoughts and feelings. We know that even very young children pick up our attitudes, and there is much evidence that this is also true of our pets and plants; so shouldn't this also be true of the living cells of our bodies? And what has this done to us over the years?

We should not pretend or try to force ourselves to love what we do not love. That can do even more harm. But we can face our true feelings and pray that the anxiety or anger that underlies the feelings may be healed. We can pray for awareness that our disliked bodily parts are part of us and have served us faithfully. We can stop blaming our bodies for our own decisions. For example, it is I, not my stomach, who decides what I will eat and drink. My stomach sends out signals of distress at my decision and is the victim, not the perpetrator. We can pray for awareness of the deep mystery of our bodily selves. It is helpful to think of our bodies as microcosms of our whole earth, even of our universe. I recently came across a glorious little poem by Madeleine L'Engle:

> I am fashioned as a galaxy,
> Not as a solid substance but a mesh
> Of atoms in their far complexity
> Forming the pattern of my bone and flesh.
>
> Small solar systems are my eyes.
> Muscle and sinew are composed of air.
> Like comets flashing through the evening skies
> My blood runs, ordered, arrogant, and fair.
>
> Ten lifetimes distant is the nearest star,
> And yet within my body, firm as wood,
> Proton and electron separate are.
> Bone is more fluid than my coursing blood.
> What plan had God, so strict and so empassioned
> When He an island universe my body fashioned?[1]

Such awareness of the awesome mystery of our bodily selves is one of the first ways to encounter the vaster mystery of God.

We can learn from a loving family or any other group bonded in tenderness how to respond to the signals of distress or hurt from our bodies. We all know how one crying, distressed child involves the whole family in concern—in a healthy family. It is the same with our bodies: contempt of even one small part is deeply damaging to the whole. Celebration of even one small part is deeply healing to the whole. In his comparison of the human body to the human community, Paul writes:

> The body does not consist of one member but of many. . . . If all were a single organ, would the body be? The eye cannot say to the hand, "I have no need of you." . . . On the contrary, the parts of the body which seem to be weaker are indispensable, and those parts of the body which we think less honorable we invest with the greater honor. . . . If one member suffers, all suffer together; if one member is honored, all rejoice together. (1 Cor 12:14, 19, 21–23, 26)

How can we begin our own reconciliation with our bodies? Try a deliberate encounter with some bodily part you have ignored or disliked. Maybe you have always been somewhat ashamed of your hands, their size or shape. Look at your hands and inwardly speak to them, somewhat in this manner: "Dear friends, you have served me faithfully every day of my life. I do my work and I touch other people and the world around me through you. Forgive me that I've been ashamed of you. I'd like to learn to *rejoice* in you!"

If you have taken the service of your eyes for granted recently, try to take a moment occasionally to lean back, place your palms gently and warmly over your eyes, praise them for their service, and encourage them in their work.

If this inner communicating seems uncomfortable and embarrassing at first, it is enough just to glance at your hands in a friendly way and thank God for them or think of your eyes occasionally and praise God for the gift they are.

Notes

1. Madeleine L'Engle, *A Winter's Love* (New York: Ballantine, 1984), 152–53.

TOUCHING AND BEING TOUCHED
–Elisabeth Moltmann-Wendel

Elisabeth Moltmann-Wendel is a German theologian and a prolific writer. Among her books are *Women Around Jesus* and *A Land Flowing with Milk and Honey: Perspectives on Feminist Theology.* Her latest book, *Passion for God: Theology in Two Voices,* is written with her theologian husband, Jürgen Moltmann.

We get a bit closer to the healing stories if we do not remain fixated on Jesus the miracle-worker but look more closely at the processes of becoming whole. Accustomed to start from the almighty word and its sole power, we have overlooked how important the touching of the sick is. Our senses, above all our tactile senses, have long been stifled in a verbal culture. We are reading the stories with new senses today and are touched by the skin contact that is reported in them. We can very rapidly translate the apparently magical element in these stories into our own present, if we are open to what touching means for our own modern existence. Touching grasps, stimulates, changes our bodies. Words, too, can have something of the same effect. But they can also resound ineffectively. One cannot miss a touch. The body notices being touched.

The medium of touching is the skin. Let's first turn to its significance and function, which is being rediscovered today, but which for more than two millennia was the same.

The skin is our largest but also our least known organ. It is one of the organs of the senses like the eyes, the ears and the nose. It thus belongs with the group of sense organs that develop smell, taste and feel; the other sense organs, eyes and ears, are more familiar to us, conveying experiences like seeing and hearing.

What makes the skin unique as compared with all other organs is that it is turned both outwards and inwards, so that it can communicate what is happening within us outwards and outside experiences inwards.

The skin covers the body, is about 1.6 square meters in area, makes up a sixth of our body weight and is divided into an epidermis (upper skin), dermis and subcutaneous tissue. It protects the body against external stimuli, stores fluids, regulates warmth and exudes sweat and poisons. As it is the largest organ, its nerve center is also represented most strongly in the brain. It has a great variety of functions, transmitting cold, warmth; stimuli causing pain, itching and tension; and general feelings of pressure and contact. No one can survive without it, whereas people can live without eyes and ears. Its psychological function is as comprehensive as its physiological significance, as we shall soon see.

However, the skin is mostly an unknown organ to us, the importance of which we overlook. It does not seem to be an active organ like the eye, the loss of which we immediately detect. We usually notice the reactions of the skin when they are unpleasant, when it gets red, goes pale, exudes sweat, produces goose pimples, is diseased or broken. If we don't feel anything, it seems to us to be normal. However, to "feel" this normality could help us to greater sensitivity to our body and our environment. The skin is also the organ that visibly gives away youth and age and—as youth has become a cult—can set off alarm signals in people. The first wrinkle can then be the way out! Its functions as a surface usually make the skin seem very superficial to us. But those who suffer from skin diseases, of the kind that the author John Updike keeps describing, have difficulties with their self-esteem. The color of a person's skin is still taken as a signal for what is within. To be tanned seems to white people to be healthy and dynamic. Black and yellow skin has long discriminated against those who have it, and rethinking in this area is still far from complete.

Unlike ourselves, our language still contains deep-rooted experiences of what our skin means for us. "Thin-skinned" indicates great sensitivity. "Thick-skinned" points to the capacity to allow unpleasant things to bounce off. What gets "under our skin" is something that obsesses us, and so on. So the skin comprises our own most personal realm, and is a protective covering for our intimate sphere.

The special thing about skin is its capacity for perception. Its sense of touch enables it to communicate with the world and again to feel the world. The significance of perception by touch is becoming increasingly clear today. Helen Keller, who was born blind and deaf, touched the world and in this way learned to communicate. What people normally communicate to the brain by eyes and ears can also be communicated to it by the skin's sense of touch. What we may not "touch" we may later find difficult to "understand."

This capacity already begins in the embryo—long before ears and eyes form. The embryo communicates through the skin with its environment, the mother's body. At birth this primal state ends, and a far-reaching change takes place: the contractions of the womb stimulate the child's skin and prepare it for the new state of independence. In animals, the mother licks the newborn offspring to make this process possible. In human beings, the process of change, without which a child would be incapable of life, takes place through suckling, stroking, lying on a parent's lap. For the unborn child, the skin was the organ of experience and learning, and this continues with the baby. What it learns through its skin— tenderness, indifference—shapes it. By contrast, what it sees and hears is almost secondary. At least, seeing and hearing are shaped by touching: "The skin is the mother of senses and all the other senses derive from it."[1]

So the skin is the greatest organ of learning, even in a spiritual sense. Our language still betrays these connections. We are "grasped"—we "grasp." We cannot grasp what does not grasp us. Or we "grasp" only in a grasping, violent sense. Those who keep alive their bodies, their feelings, their skin as levels of communication will find it difficult to fall victim to an abstract "grasping," but will constantly retain bodily thought.

In touching we experience the world and one another. In today's ecological

ethics the skin and the sense of touch associated with it become unusually important. "As I touch, so I am touched."[2] Experience of self and experience of nature
coincide. The Western self bids farewell to manipulation and exposes itself to new
experiences.

The most intense form of touch takes place in love. Unadorned skin also
allows love to be experienced again. A French feminist has said: "We have so often
used cosmetics to please him that we have forgotten our skin. Outside our skins
we remain far from ourselves. You and I, far from one another."

From the first to the last day, touching is experienced as assurance, confirmation of the self and healing. Physical healing can also take place in touching; for
example, it can lower high blood pressure. An incubator can be dispensed with
for babies if they are stroked and massaged several times a day.

However, there are also rituals of touching. The inferior in the hierarchy does
not touch those above him. An American president cannot allow himself a familiar gesture to a queen. But it often happens that a boss puts a friendly hand on the
shoulder of his employees.

In addition, different cultures have different types of touching: shaking
hands, rubbing noses, kissing the hand in certain European circles, the socialist
fraternal kiss, the "'holy kiss" in Paul that still existed in earliest Christianity.

However, many rituals involving the skin involve only males. Women are
often excluded from them; as the lowly ones who are to be honored, they
are made contact with (kissing of the hand) or are helplessly at the mercy of
excessive skin contacts. They seldom initiate touching in public life.

Shaking hands with one of the "great" people of the world gives many people
a sense of deep confirmation. Something magic has gone from the great person
to them. A small existence is confirmed and transformed by a great existence.

In the healing stories of the New Testament to which we now return, there
are different kinds of touching. There is the energetic *kratein*, grasping, rescuing
from the anguish of death—an expression that is also used for saving an animal
from a well. So Jesus grasps the hands of Peter's mother-in-law (Mark 1:31) and
Jairus's daughter (Mark 5:41) and snatches them back from death. The same
expression is also used for the dramatic rescue of the epileptic boy (Mark 9:27).
Women grasp the feet of the risen Jesus just as energetically, rescuing themselves,
reassuring themselves; this gives them the assurance that he is alive and their
existence is confirmed (Matt 28:9).

There is also the more official laying on of hands (*epitithenai*) by Jesus, with
which the bent woman can set herself upright (Luke 13:13) and the blind man see
again (Mark 8:23ff.). Here the power of the healer goes over to the sick person in
a special ritual. The power goes from the stronger to the weaker. Jesus himself is
clearly seen as the source of power.

Another term for touching is *epilambanein*, seizing a person.

But the most interesting expression for touching is *haptein*, which simply
means "touch" and which occurs in several passages. It seems to be the democratic

kind of skin contact, for Jesus touches lepers (Mark 1:41), children (Mark 10:3), and disciples (Matt 17:7). And again—as was hardly the case with the other kinds of bodily contact—people touch him or his garment, which according to the traditional understanding is synonymous with his person (Matt 14:36; Mark 3:10; 6:56; Luke 6:19). Anyone who touches his garment is made whole. So the woman with an issue of blood also touches his garment and thus himself. The woman who was a sinner touches his feet (Luke 7:38). The risen Jesus says to Mary Magdalene that she should not touch him. So she probably ventured to touch him previously (John 20:17).

This *haptein* thus does not stand for any official rites, but for contact between people between whom energies can flow. These are loving, confirming contacts, which raise people from the shadows in which they are. The lepers, the children, the women, the typically underprivileged get self-confirmation and experience acceptance in the loving consensus of humankind.

And Jesus in turn experiences love and recognition, confirmation of his way, when his head is anointed by the unknown woman in Bethany, when his feet are anointed by the prostitute. In his defense of the sinner he chides the Pharisee who is his host for the disembodied lovelessness of his hospitality. The Pharisee did not kiss Jesus on the mouth, anoint his head, wash his feet and dry him with his hair. The love of the great sinner lies in her body language.

The touching by Jesus and in earliest Christianity, in its manifold forms, later became consolidated in the tradition of the laying on of hands, in the gesture of blessing, in the anointing of the last rites. Here an element of skin contact remained in the church, but no life-giving mutual contact.

The apostolic succession, which is communicated by the laying on of hands in an uninterrupted chain, still contains the idea that body and skin contact are important confirmations of existence. But since they are communicated above all by a male elite to a male elite, they have already lost their earliest Christian charisma.

I touch and am touched. This knowledge creates a new community of those who had no confirmation for their existence, who, as a result of sickness, their gender, or social contempt, had found no acceptance and now themselves become those who give, challenge and confirm. In the church of the word, in a society full of phobias about touching, in which the deep significance of touching has been forgotten, we should look for forms of touching both old and new. To touch means to stimulate people in their whole existence, with their senses and their spirits, heal their brokenness and make them once again capable of contact, thought and experience: "You will stretch out your hands and touch, and it will go well with you."[3]

Notes

1. Ashley Montagu, "Die Haut," in Dietmar Kamper and Christoph Wulf, eds., *Das Schwinden der Sinne* (Frankfurt am Main: Suhrkamp, 1984), 211.
2. Klaus Meyer-Abich, *Wege zum Frieden mit der Natur* (Munich: C. Hanser, 1984), 252.

3. Carter Heyward, *Our Passion for Justice: Images of Power, Sexuality and Liberation* (New York: Pilgrim Press, 1984), 185.

THE IDOLATRY OF HEALTH AND THE IDOLATRY OF LIFE
–Margaret E. Mohrmann

Margaret E. Mohrmann, MD, is a practicing physician and associate professor of pediatrics at the University of Virginia School of Medicine. She also holds a Ph.D. in religious ethics.

In 1979, the philosopher Alasdair MacIntyre wrote a provocative article in the *Journal of Medicine and Philosophy* titled "Theology, Ethics, and the Ethics of Medicine and Health Care." He began his essay with the following question and answer:

> What ought we to expect from contemporary theologians in the area of medical ethics? First—and without this everything else is uninteresting—we ought to expect a clear statement of what difference it makes to be a Jew or a Christian or a Moslem, rather than a secular thinker, in morality generally. Second . . . we need to hear a theological critique of secular morality and culture. Third, we want to be told what bearing what has been said under the first two headings has on the specific problems which arise for modern medicine.[1]

I shall not pretend that I am going to give a complete response to all that MacIntyre asks for in this passage. I do agree, however, with his insistence that any offering from theological ethics to the practice of medicine include statements of the unique theological bases of our ethical thought, criticisms of conventional culture, and the implications of theological beliefs and critiques for the sorts of issues that must be dealt with as we minister to those who suffer.

Let us start, then, with the premises that differentiate theological reflection from secular reflection—the premises that God exists, that God loves us, and that God is the Creator. One immediate corollary of the last statement is the understanding that, because God has created everything else, everything else is not God. We are, after all, monotheists, the coinheritors of the ancient Jewish revelation of the oneness of God. We are addressed in the Shema: "Hear, O Israel, the Lord our God, the Lord is One"; and we are disciplined by the commandment given at Sinai: "You shall have no other gods before me."

It is perhaps by now a cliché to say that, in our care for the suffering, we are assaulted, much like the Jews in the land of Canaan, by many temptations, many opportunities to put other, lesser, false gods before the one God. For example, it would be easy at this point to hold forth on the temptations of wealth for the physician. However, I shall not focus on this issue, because I think it is self-evident. No matter how bad physicians may be at acknowledging and combating the temptation of wealth, most of us are aware of it, at least at some level, and many of us even worry about it regularly. I doubt that I need to create discomfort about the queasy relationship between medicine and money.

It is another facile commonplace to bemoan our idolatry of medical technology and of those who know how to use it. Mother Teresa, for one, has called the neonatal intensive care units that populate American hospitals "obscene"; she could as easily have called them "blasphemous." But our adoration of machines and high-tech procedures is a superficial issue, and its elimination—even if that were possible—would still leave intact the deeper idolatry that supports it. The history of Israel shows us quite clearly that the destruction of the golden calf did not abolish idolatry from the hearts of the people of the covenant. Likewise, a wholesale attack on the worship of the icons of medicine will not eliminate the idolatry in our hearts that too often corrupts our use of those undeniably good inventions.

That idolatry within our hearts is more insidious and, I believe, far more worrisome than any enchantment by money or machinery. It takes two forms: the idolatry of health and the idolatry of life. The two are opposite faces of the same coin, both exhibiting the paradoxical mixture of pride and despair that characterizes the worship of false gods. David Barnard, in an essay on the relation of religion and medicine, has defined idolatry as "the denial of that wider context of meaning that endows the forms of worship with their sanctity."[2] I believe that both our idolatry of health and our idolatry of life manifest precisely such a denial of the wider context of meaning—the theological meaning—that alone gives health, and even life itself, whatever suggestion of sanctity either one may bear.

The Idolatry of Health

Reinhold Niebuhr has said that evil in its most developed form is always a good pretending or imagining itself to be better than it is.[3] The idolatry of health is a good example of this process, of pretending or imagining that the relative, subordinate good of health is better than God intends it to be. Evidence of the idolatry of health in our society is clear, manifesting itself in our fickle, shifting obsessions with diets and exercise machines and with jogging down every primrose path to perfect health, whether it is the path of vitamin C or brewer's yeast or no yeast at all or oat bran or whatever the latest "cure du jour." We have all been treated to, and have perhaps participated in, the spectacle of reasonable, pragmatic citizens of the last half of the twentieth century fearing and finding carcinogens everywhere, in much the same way our ancestors feared and found demons and witches everywhere.

It is also apparent that our idolatry of health goes hand in glove with an idolatry of the body, a presumption that health is entirely comprehended in physical health and, more particularly, in the physical health of a youthful body. Our single-minded focus on the health of the body is evident in the observation that even our interest in being mentally healthy—in handling stress, in expressing our feelings, in learning to be open and vulnerable—is often aimed at keeping us physically healthy. We try to be calm so we can avoid ulcers and heart attacks. We try to learn to laugh more so our arthritis will go away. We try to think positive thoughts so our immune systems will be stimulated to do their jobs more enthusiastically.

A true and complete understanding of health includes mental and spiritual health as important ingredients in their own right, not just as promoters of physical health. The biblical perspective on human life does not allow us to be dualists of the sort that denigrate the body as the prison of the spirit, but neither does it allow us to be dualists in the opposite sense, giving pride of place to the body and reducing our mental and spiritual faculties to mere maintainers and enhancers of our physical well-being.

What, then, are the implications of this situation for us who practice the ministry of medicine? What theological understanding of health can we bring to our ministry that can counteract and even redeem the idolatry that we find in our own hearts as well as in the hearts of those we serve?

First, we can bring to our work a balance and a perspective that come only from knowing that health can never be anything other than a secondary good. God is our absolute good; health is an instrumental, subordinate good, important only insofar as it enables us to be the joyful, whole persons God has created us to be and to perform the service to our neighbors that God calls us to perform. Any pursuit of personal health that subverts either of these obligations of joy and loving service is the pursuit of a false god. Health is to be sought in and for God, not instead of God.

Second, we must be aware of the extent to which the idolatry of health represents a failure of trust: trust, for example, in our own bodies to get us through life given a reasonable amount of care, trust in the food God provides and in those who supply it to us. It is certainly true that part of being good stewards of the bodies we have been given is to be careful. We need to recognize, for example, that there are practices in the food production system that can potentially endanger health, that there are some significant toxins floating around us, that there are ways in which our bodies break down despite reasonable care. However, such appropriate caution should be exercised in the context of a fundamental attitude of confidence that we have been created as far less fragile creatures than we fear we are.

A corollary to the belief that the God who loves us is the Creator is the belief that everything God has created is good. This does not mean that we cannot or do not contaminate what God has created. It means that we must not lose our basic theological assumption that our bodies and our food supply are to be trusted as good things, not feared as disasters waiting to happen. It is our task, as theologically formed ministers of health and healing, to witness to the goodness and the stability of God's creation, to be an antidote to the mistrust of creation manifested in obsessive searches for safe food and invulnerable bodies.

Even if we are not successful in transmitting our own faithful trust to those whom we serve, at least we can refuse to participate in that ignorance of God's creating goodness. For example, we can reject the assumption that normal children routinely need additional manufactured vitamins in order to be healthy, and the assumption that normal menopause is a "disorder" that routinely requires medical therapy, and even the assumption that a common symptom like the cough, God's brilliant mechanism for clearing the airways, routinely requires suppression whenever it occurs. Sometimes we are ridiculous.

Third, we must recognize the extent to which the idolatry of health represents a fear of death and often a denial of death's inevitability, both of which indicate a failure of hope. Several years ago, while browsing through a medical school library, I came upon a book titled *The Conquest of Death*, written in the mid-1960s. I examined it out of curiosity and found it to be a lengthy defense of the thesis that, given the pace of advances in medical knowledge and techniques, by the year 2000 no one will die except from catastrophic events like auto accidents and tornadoes. No one will die from disease or aging. There will be no "natural" death anymore.

The author was not very clear on whether our twenty-first-century immortality would also be accompanied by an arrest of the aging process. When I read the book, I found myself remembering the myth of Tithonus, the handsome hero loved by Eos, goddess of the dawn. She asked Zeus to grant him immortality, and Zeus did, but she had forgotten to ask also that he be given eternal youth. Poor Tithonus got older and older but could not die. Eos eventually had pity on him, after he had become so wizened that he had to be carried around in a basket, and turned him into a cicada. I thought the book was a pretty good joke—medicine as a producer of immortal crickets—until I started mentioning the book and its claim to groups of medical students. I found that at least half of them saw nothing odd in it at all and could not understand my reaction of amused disbelief. They really thought—and, I suspect, many of them still think—that eventually, by the grace of medicine, death will no longer be anything but an accident that befalls some but not most of us, and that we shall all coincidentally remain eternally twenty-five years old.

Odd books are not the only evidence of our fears and denials. The carelessness of the language we use in speaking of death reveals an underlying, and unexamined, assumption that at least some of us may be able to escape death. We speak of "preventing deaths" from cigarette smoking when we can only mean that people will then die, presumably at a more advanced age, for some reason unrelated to tobacco. We claim that people who fail to engage in certain health-promoting activities are generally "more likely to die," as though the general risk of dying could be anything less than 100 percent. These may not be intentional denials of the reality of death, but such linguistic slips betray a belief that drives the health-seeking behavior of many of us. It is the unspoken, but strong and pervasive, belief that if we just learn enough, do enough, prevent enough, exercise enough, eat the right stuff, purify our air and water and food, none of us will have to die.

We know better. We know that we are going to die. We know that death is the natural end to our earthly stories and even that it is to be welcomed as the mercy that it can be.

Some of us in the ministry of medicine do have the task of preventing untimely death, death that comes before the story has spun itself out; we rightly do this with all the medical know-how at our disposal. Others of us in the ministry of medicine have the task of preventing meaningless death, death that comes before the story has started to make sense; we do this by helping those we serve find some sense in the story. But none of us has the impossible task of preventing death. And all of us have the theological task of imparting hope—sometimes hope for an extension of earthly life, but always hope for life beyond death, in God.

We may not always be able to transmit our hope to those to whom we minister, but at least we can refuse to be part of the lie, part of the denial of the fact of death. That denial is an illusion that theology and theological ethics simply do not allow to enter into the ministry of medicine.

In Georges Bernanos's thoughtful and moving novel *The Diary of a Country Priest*, the priest's spiritual mentor tells him, "Our Heavenly Father said mankind was the salt of the world, son, not the honey. And our poor world's rather like old man Job, stretched out in all his filth, covered with ulcers and sores. Salt stings in an open wound, but saves you from gangrene."[4]

Whether or not the salutary effects of salt on gangrene would bear scientific scrutiny, it is true that we are called to be salt and not honey. Moreover, we are all rather like Job, bearers of open wounds, one of which is often a dread of death that leads us to suppress our knowledge that it will happen. Part of our task as salt for the world is to sting that wound, to remind each other of something we would choose to forget, that Lazarus died again.

Many philosophers have said in various ways that it is the certainty of death that gives life its meaning. Flannery O'Connor expressed this idea in her own inimitable way in her short story "A Good Man Is Hard to Find." An escaped convict kills a foolish, garrulous, terrorized grandmother, just after she has granted him the touch of grace that is the hallmark of O'Connor's stories. He then says, "She would of been a good woman, if it had been somebody there to shoot her every minute of her life."[5] So would we all.

I do not suggest that we continually hold a gun to the heads of our patients, our parishioners, or our friends to remind them that they are going to die. We are talking about ministry, not about haranguing or terrorizing. But remembering that death will happen, that there is a limit to this life, changes the questions we ask of ourselves and of those to whom we minister. The question is not, "What can I do to live longer?" The question is, "How shall I live the life I have?" Health-seeking behavior is not death prevention; it is life enhancement. This change in attitude restores perspective and balance to our lives. It returns health to its proper, subordinate place as a means to living a joyful life of service, not as the goal in a death-denying search for immortal youth.

The Idolatry of Life

Along with the denial of death that drives the idolatry of health comes the other form of idolatry, the one to which I fear we of theological bent are particularly inclined. It is the idolatry of life, marked most distinctively by the all-too-frequent use of "sanctity of life" arguments in ethical discussions. Theologically speaking, there can be no argument based on a purported "sanctity of life," both because there is no "life" as such and because we are on very shaky ground when we speak of anything or anyone but God as unqualifiedly sacred. Let me explain what I mean.

When I was a youngster, my pastor once asked my church school class to find in the Bible the book of Hezekiah. It took all of us a few minutes of flipping through our bibles to realize that there is no such book in the Bible; it simply *sounds* as though it should be there. I suspect you could play the same sort of trick on any number of people by asking them to find in the Bible the place where God says, "Let there be life." It sounds as though it should be there, but there is no such statement. God did not and does not create anything called "life." God created and creates living beings.

> Then God said, "Let the earth put forth vegetation: plants yielding seed, and fruit trees." . . . And God said, "Let the waters bring forth swarms of living creatures and let birds fly above the earth." . . . And God said, "Let the earth bring forth living creatures of every kind." . . . Then God said, "Let us make humankind in our image." (Gen 1:11, 20, 24, 26)

There is no life except as embodied in living beings, a truth we seem often to forget. Common enough to have become a standard caricature is the person who claims to love humankind but cannot stand people. Frighteningly common is the person who argues for sanctity of life while remaining oblivious to the plights of individual beloved beings who are the only forms in which that life exists.

When we, as persons who wish to live by a morality that is wholly theologi-cally determined, are asked what we think about such issues as abortion, euthana-sia, withholding hydration and nutrition from persons in the persistent vegetative state, or taking organs for transplant from anencephalic infants, the theologically appropriate response, the response of Christian ethics, is to ask in return, "To whom are you referring?" How can such issues even be addressed if we do not know whom they are about, or why they are being raised, or how the conclusions may be used?

Who is considering abortion and why? What is this person's story? Who is in a persistent vegetative state and what are the family members saying and doing? The policies and laws we help create must leave room for these queries. They must also ensure that the responses can be brought to bear on the decision in thoughtful, compassionate, and nondiscriminatory ways that consider the particulars of the situation without lapsing into reliance on the fraudulence of relative desert and worthiness.

The reply to the impersonal and empty claim of the sanctity of life, then, is always first the question, "Whose life?" Christian ethics is personal. As Dietrich Bonhoeffer wrote, "Christ teaches no abstract ethics. . . . Christ did not, like a moralist, love a theory of good, but he loved the real man. He was not, like a philosopher, interested in the 'universally valid,' but rather in that which is of help to the real, concrete human being. . . ."[6]

Christian ethics has always required attention to the details of the situation. Despite Jesus' explicit acknowledgment of the importance of the law, he did not take up a rule, such as "Thou shalt not steal," and apply it as though it were a blind bludgeon, heedless of the circumstances. Consider his treatment of the thief Zacchaeus, whom he loved into restitution; or of the thief Judas, whose theft from the common purse Jesus seems to have ignored in his persistent attempts to have his love penetrate Judas's misconceptions; or of the thieves who were money changers in the temple, whom he scourged; or of the thief who hung beside him on the cross, whom he forgave. These are all very different reactions to what some would call basically the same crime. They are all manifestations of divine love acting in the situation.

We always act within specific situations, and we must always be aware of and responsive to the details of those situations; the circumstances must be a vital part of what forms our moral decisions. In that sense, Christian ethics is very much situation ethics; it is not, however, the sort of rootless, painless, unrealistic situation ethics that Fletcher[7] preached.

> Now there was a woman who had been suffering from a hemorrhage for twelve years; and though she had spent all she had on physicians, no one could cure her. She came up behind him and touched the fringe of his clothes; and immediately her hemorrhage stopped. Then Jesus asked, "Who touched me?" . . . When the woman saw that she could not remain hidden, she came trembling; and falling down before him, she declared in the presence of all the people why she had touched him, and how she

had been immediately healed. He said to her, "Daughter, your
faith has made you well; go in peace." (Luke 8:43–45, 47–48)

Jesus surely had the power to heal anonymously, but he chose not to. He
insisted upon making that magical healing his own, accomplished on his own
terms. He insisted also upon making the healing her very own, the healing of his
particular daughter whose particular faith, and not some undirected magical
power located in the fringe of his robe, had brought her into contact with divine
healing love. We have no evidence that Jesus ever healed in any other way. When
he fed the five thousand with loaves and fishes, he also had the power to award
them a sort of blanket healing for whatever physical ailments they happened
to bring with them that day, but he did not do so. To argue that he should
have would be to misread both the nature of his power and the meaning of the
incarnation.

The woman with the hemorrhage was healed before Jesus knew who she was,
but he would not have it remain so. He would not be a party to magical, faceless
healing. So it must be with us. "Who is this?" is always the question that must be
asked by us if we are to evoke and enable the sort of healing love that God has
manifested to us in Jesus. When the questions arise that attempt to put the biggest
dilemmas of living and dying in terms of populations or generic categories or
abstract descriptors—such as persistent vegetative state or unwanted pregnancy
or Alzheimer's disease—the Christian is obligated to speak Jesus' words, and
thereby to do what Karl Barth insists all Christian ethics does: to repeat the good
that has been said.[8] We are to say, "Who touched me?"

In the earliest days of Christianity, a common pagan objection to the idea of
Jesus as the Christ was what is termed the "scandal of particularity." The "scandal" is the outrageous idea that God would become incarnate in one particular
human being, subject to all the vicissitudes of a truly human, individual life.
Although we know that our faith and our redemption are founded on the truth
of that very particular incarnation, we keep repeating the pagans' mistake by
refusing to accept the fact that the scandal of particularity continues, that such
outrageous behavior is part of the essence of the nature of God. Christians do not
believe that God is somehow generically present in something called "life." We
believe that God is present in individual human persons. It is those persons
whom we are called upon to love and serve, to respect and even revere in all their
difficult and scandalous particularity.

Jesus does not call me to love the Ground of Being and to love life wherever
I find it as much as I love the life force within me. I am, rather, called to love the
very distinctive, singular, personal God of Abraham, Sarah, Deborah, and David,
and to love the unique, imperfect, redeemed person who is my neighbor—just as
I am to love the equally unique, sinful, and redeemed person who is myself. . . .

Scripture is clear and consistent: God alone is sacred. That we are created
bearing the image of God does not mean that we, too, are sacred beings. The sort

of reverence we owe to the lives of human beings—including our own lives—is never absolute. God alone is holy. The church's traditional esteem for martyrs and scriptural warrants for believing that there are things worth dying for make no sense if human life is to have absolute value. Christian teaching affirms respect for every human being but it does not assume an infinite value for human life.

We may refer to human life as "sacred" only if we also admit the qualifications that only God is holy and that any holiness that can be attributed to any human being is derived from God's holiness. Our derived and conditional "holiness" is a function of our having been created by God, of our having been marked with God's image, and of our being loved and redeemed by God. As Reinhold Niebuhr put it, the command to love our neighbor is not based on the fact that our neighbor is equally divine or even that our neighbor is a person, but simply on the fact that our neighbor is beloved by God.[9] This is the source of the respect, and even awe, that we owe to every human being, and God's love, the source of our worth, is not given to us as faceless outcroppings of some generic life force.

The "sanctity of life" claim is unacceptable because it is impersonal and empty. It is an impersonal claim because the word "life" has no meaning except in the context of its embodiment in a particular person. It is an empty claim because our relative "sanctity" does not automatically tell us anything about what is to be done. "Sanctity" can be neither a synonym for "keep alive at all costs" nor, on the other hand, a code word for the sort of misguided compassion that assumes that the proper way to eliminate suffering is to eliminate the sufferer. "Sanctity" can only mean "beloved by God," and the God who loves us calls us by name.

God loves us as individual persons with unique characteristics, with hairs that can be numbered. This is how we are called to love one another—never as "sacred life," but always as beloved and particular living beings, with different needs, different problems, different stories. Because our stories, like our names, are different, honoring my life may require something very different from honoring your life.

When the time comes that I am suffering, or dying, or in an irreversible coma, and there are difficult decisions to be made on my behalf, I do not want those who care for me to talk about the "sanctity of life" as though the phrase has meaning. I want them to say, instead, "Here is God's beloved, Margaret. How would God have us love her here and now?" I want them to look at me the way God looks at me. I want them to remember who I am, the themes of thought and action that have run through my life, and to make decisions for me that are congruent with the whole of my life as I have lived it. Christian ethics is personal; it is within that personal context that we must accomplish our tasks of ministry and healing.

Notes

1. Alasdair MacIntyre, "Theology, Ethics, and the Ethics of Medicine and Health Care," *Journal of Medicine and Philosophy* 4 (1979): 435.

2. David Barnard, "Religion and Medicine," *Soundings* 68 (1985): 455.

3. Reinhold Niebuhr, *An Interpretation of Christian Ethics* (San Francisco: Harper & Row, 1935), 53.

4. Georges Bernanos, *The Diary of a Country Priest* (New York: Macmillan, 1937; repr., New York: Carroll & Graf, 1983), 11.

5. Flannery O'Connor, "A Good Man Is Hard to Find," in *The Complete Stories* (New York: Farrar, Straus, & Giroux, 1971), 133.

6. Dietrich Bonhoeffer, *Ethics* (New York: Macmillan, 1965), 84–85.

7. Joseph Fletcher, *Situation Ethics: The New Morality* (Philadelphia: Westminster, 1966).

8. Karl Barth, *Church Dogmatics* (Edinburgh: T. & T. Clark, 1961), II.2.537.

9. Niebuhr, *An Interpretation of Christian Ethics*, 131.

FOR PERSONAL REFLECTION

1. "Old messages" tell us our bodies are not satisfactory, and many voices call us to change our bodies. Yet our theology tells us that we were made in the image of God. In whose image do you try to cast yourself?

2. "The way we relate to our bodily selves profoundly influences the way we relate to God," says Wuellner. What have you experienced in your own life that either reinforces or contradicts her statement?

3. Mohrmann boldly states, "Health is to be sought in and for God, not instead of God." Have there been times in your life when you have sought health as an end unto itself, or sought health for the wrong reasons? How has that influenced your spiritual life?

FOR GROUP DISCUSSION

1. If we as a society were indeed to be healed of our dislike of our bodies, what impact would that have on our communities of faith? On our health care delivery system?

2. A good case has been made by Elisabeth Moltmann-Wendel for the benefit of affirming touch within the Christian tradition. Yet due to misuse of trust and subsequent fears of the legal ramifications of inappropriate touch, our society now has rules that preclude touching. Touch that had been acceptable is no longer acceptable. What do you think the impact of this will be on our faith communities? On our society?

3. Mohrmann reminds us that the reverence we owe to our lives and the lives of others "is never absolute. God alone is holy." Do you agree? Do you think that our culture reveres "the sanctity of life" as an abstract absolute? In what situations have you seen this? What would be the consequences of valuing "life," not as an abstraction, but as embodied in living beings?

3.

Christian Spirituality and Well-Being

Feet Addressing Head
–Susan McCaslin

Hey, dude, give us some space and turf,
you, rumbling up there
in your bright, abstract buzz.
You could go flying off, incapacitated
without us down here to keep you real,
you in your bulbous, bloodless dome.

Remember, we are your contact with ground zero,
Bathe us with myrrh and balm,
massage us once in a while
and maybe we will remember you
when the two of us lie tip to toe
partnered for the long journey home.

In an earlier section, Margaret Mohrmann stated that health "is an instrumental, subordinate good, important only insofar as it enables us to be the joyful, whole persons God has created us to be and to perform the service to our neighbors that God calls us to perform. Any pursuit of personal health that subverts either of these obligations of joy and loving service is the pursuit of a false god."

I am struck by her idea "obligation of joy." Experiencing joy in my body is not something I was taught in Sunday school. Investment in so passing a thing as flesh was not encouraged. Not until my maturity did I find the visceral, bodily joy of swimming laps and lifting weights and mountain hiking. Only recently has the pleasure of conscious, mindful eating become part of my experience. It is still somewhat foreign for me to consider such joy an obligation, so deeply writ is the childhood message that caring for my body is essentially a waste of time.

Yet, if our bodies are indeed temples of God, how ought we to care for them? A friend suggested that though we are told to treat our bodies as "temples of the Holy Spirit," we often treat them as tenements. What would be involved in caring for a temple? Some thoughts that come to my mind are keeping it clean from pollutants, seeing that the air is fresh, assuring that it is appropriately attractive and pleasant, seeing to it that necessary preventive maintenance is done, caringly repairing any damage using the best contractors we can find, and enjoying both its beauty and function.

Stewardship is a term we need to apply to our bodies. We understand ourselves to be stewards of our "time, talent, and treasure," as we are reminded when it is time to build the church budget. But what about stewardship of the temple— or torso, if you prefer? What about the care we are obligated to give to the distinct piece of creation that we call ourselves? What about our "obligation of joy"?

THE PRESENCE OF GOD AND THE LIFE OF THE BODY
—Marilyn Chandler McEntyre

Marilyn Chandler McEntyre, Ph.D., is an associate professor of literature at Westmont College in Santa Barbara, California. She is the author of *In Quiet Light: Poems on Vermeer's Women* and *Drawn to the Light: Poems on Rembrandt's Religious Paintings*. She is a contributing editor to the journal *Literature and Medicine* (John Hopkins University Press), and serves on the board of the Center for Medicine, Humanities, and Law at the University of California, Berkeley.

Part of the basic training I remember as a child was being told to sit up straight, not to slump, slouch, slide down in the chair or let my shoulders sag. Good posture, it seemed, was part of good manners—right up there with offering our seats to elders and chewing with our mouths closed. Perhaps a sociologist would regard such training simply as acculturation to the middle class, but in our household, everything that mattered, even good posture, was part of living rightly with God. In retrospect, I can see some danger in pervasive "spiritualizing"; the weight such reasoning can put on the ordinary, especially for a child, can be daunting and inhibiting. Still, that God gave us bodies, that the Spirit of God dwells in us, and that care of the body is a dimension of Christian stewardship provided a helpful framework for me, growing up female in a culture that commodifies, commercializes, and otherwise exploits the body as a receptacle or agent of dubious pleasures.

As age progresses and the life of the body impinges upon consciousness in new ways—small aches, stiffness in the joints, fatigue—I find myself revisiting matters as basic as posture, exercise, and nutrition with a new appreciation of their relationship to the life of the Spirit. I have taken some measures in the past year that began as "purely practical" efforts to maintain health and physical well-being, only to confirm once again that nothing is "purely practical"—every incident in the life of the body is reflected in some movement of the Spirit. The long walk, the half-hour swim, the infrequent and oh-so-welcome massage invariably leave me in a more open-hearted state, readier to listen, to prepare food, to return calls, to pray. Attention to my body opens not only the clogged pathways of the digestive, circulatory, and nervous systems, but the channels through which the Spirit flows who is the very breath of life.

One of the forms of attention I have begun to give my body is a Saturday morning movement class. Based loosely on principles derived from yoga, from chiropractic, and from common sense and close observation, the class focuses on what I think of as "deep posture"—my term, not the instructor's. In deceptively simple and slow exercises, we focus on balance, breathing, noticing underutilized or overstressed muscle groups, and ordinary movements like walking. We learn to walk like animals and breathe like babies. This learning, I begin to see, can become a way of practicing the presence of God.

The instructions in class are given in a language that links body and spirit. Repeatedly the instructor tells us as we resume our basic stance, "Lift up your heart." This is a physical directive, followed by "Pull your lats back, relax your shoulders, let your head float, knees bent, butt slightly out." The liturgical echo in "Lift up your heart" always reminds me that we "lift them up to the Lord." Like plants that stretch toward the sunlight or children who reach upward to be held, we find our actual physical stability in reaching toward the source of life.

Part of the work in this class is what the instructor calls "cross training," a term he uses to mean coordinating the two sides of brain and body. We do work that alternates the use of opposite limbs, working right arm and left leg, left arm and right leg, or tapping right hand and right foot, then switching. All of us, he explains, develop one-sided habits of dominance. We work to reunite both sides. As I listen to the refrain, "Opposite arm, opposite leg," I think about how often truth is two-sided—how persistently Jesus taught in paradox. Lose your life and find it. Rejoice and know that those who mourn are blessed. The law abides and grace abounds. The wrath of God is great—and be not afraid (Matt 10:39; Matt 5:4; Deut 1:34; John 6:20 NRSV). Something of the truth that must be told from both sides abides in the very design of our bodies. As we walk, we constantly shift our weight from one side to the other, activating different sides of the brain, going again and again through the slightly precarious moment of letting go with one foot as we receive with the other.

An hour into our lesson we walk across the room, hearts lifted, slowly enough to notice the bad muscle habits we have fallen into protecting some at the expense of others. The instructor tells us, "Keep your eyes up. Don't look at your feet. Your body knows what to do. Be intentional. Walk as though you're walking toward a beloved person, perhaps a beloved Master who is waiting to receive you." Again what might be taken as a mere visualization device becomes an occasion for spiritual reflection: I become aware that in my whole daily journey I am walking toward a beloved Master who is waiting to receive me, and that the right thing to do in his presence is to be as fully who he made me to be as I can—to claim my whole body, open my whole heart, awaken my whole mind to awareness and deliberation, attentiveness and expectation.

The practice of heightened alertness to the subtle signals of body and environment is certainly, but not only, a spiritual practice. As our instructor keeps reminding us, the animal who is not alert or balanced, the animal who "walks funny," is "somebody else's lunch." Called into life, we are called to stay alive by the wily strategies generations have devised as they clambered out of caves and learned the skills of sword and ploughshare. "Therefore choose life" (Deut 30:19 RSV) has always seemed to me one of the most vigorous and challenging commandments in the Old Testament. To obey it involves us in learning and fine-tuning not only the spiritual attitudes but also the animal behaviors that are part of the design for survival. To choose life is not to be—or walk like—a victim. It is to receive the gifts of the body gladly and use them fully and freely. To use all the muscles we were given, to stretch to our full range of motion, to tune the taste buds, the fingertips, the listening ear, the kinesthetic antennae to finer discrimination—all the work we put into staying fully alive is a way of consent to that injunction, saying yes to the One who called us into life and who wishes us to have it more abundantly. The African proverb, "If you can talk, you can sing; if you can walk, you can dance," might be read as both invitation and admonishment: Why stop short of full use of the body's gifts?

We truncate those gifts by the way we live now, so many of us office-bound screen gazers. We sit long hours though we are designed more properly to stand, move, lie, or squat. We privilege vision and hearing and often ignore information we might be receiving from other quarters, the whole body being designed to receive and offer information to the brain. We eat in ways that obscure the real appetites, and medicate ourselves in ways that often interfere with the body's own gradual and gracious healing processes. As Gerard Manley Hopkins put it, well over a century ago, "The soil is bare now, nor can foot feel, being shod."[1] If we want our feet to feel, or any of the millions of sensors built into our fearful and wonderful systems, we have to be deeply intentional about reclaiming the body as an instrument of grace and a receptor of the Spirit.

Of course such a reclamation project, like any other human endeavor, can become an exercise in narcissism or worse. "Health" practices or exercise routines can become obsessively self-focused, as anyone knows who has watched muscle-ripplers communing with themselves in the mirrors that line the walls of "health" clubs. (Luther's definition of sin, *curvatus in se*, "being turned in on oneself," finds apt illustration in our temples of self-improvement.) When diet and exercise programs are not linked to the source of life and fueled and guided by the Spirit, they can defeat the deeper purposes they might serve. But those purposes depend upon our active consent to the terms of our incarnate life, which is why I am coming to believe that right attention to the body's needs and inbuilt desires is an integral part of practicing the presence of God.

God is present to us in our bodies not only because we are manifestations of divine creative imagination, not only because God's work is apparent in the intricacy of anatomical design and the radiance of human beauty points to God. God is dynamically present in every breath and heartbeat. In each breath we draw, the Spirit gives life. Who that is a parent has not wished at some point to give more to a child unwilling to receive the time, attention, advice, affection we have to give? I wonder whether we are like those petulant children when we take little shallow breaths, let whole areas of the body go unused, fall into habits of self-protection and cheap comfort, become couch potatoes or armchair athletes. If every breath is a gift, why not receive the whole gift, with hearts lifted up in thanksgiving?

Learning to reclaim the deep, nourishing breaths of infancy is a part of basic training not only in health and movement classes, but in prayer and meditation practices all over the world. The deep, full breathing that is required to sing well may have similar importance in praying well: Nothing reminds us more literally than inbreathing and outbreathing that we continually receive life and must continually release what we have received in order to receive again. What sustains us is not static, but is renewed in every moment, like manna. And the "breath prayer" that is practiced by so many contemplatives may be readily and importantly adaptable to lives lived on the go, in the car, multitasking as we move, too often breathlessly about our busyness.[2] What would it be in the midst of all that busyness to be about God's business?

When Jesus described his work in that way, he had stopped in the Temple to ponder the scriptures with rabbis rather than continue the journey back to Nazareth where he doubtless worked as Joseph's apprentice (Luke 2:41–47 NRSV). He was not just prolonging the vacation; he was stopping in the midst of things, slowing down, making a point about the call of the moment. In our culture, one of the most important disciplines of body, mind, and spirit is slowing down and stopping in the midst of things. Everything around us tells us to speed up. So we buy personal digital assistants and cell phones and press the gas pedal a little harder. But in my Saturday morning movement class we move slowly. The discipline of slowing and stopping yields amazing results almost immediately. We do not move less—just more deliberately. Indeed, slow movement is often more strenuous than fast movement, requiring more balance, attention, and care. Slowing down, we reconnect movement with intention. And full intention involves the mind, the heart, and even the belly, with its visceral responses to the signals always coming in from the immediate environment. Jesus' message to Martha, who was "busy about many things," is a timely one for us. Mary, who had stopped in the midst of things to listen—not passively, but actively, attentively, acutely, expectantly, and lovingly—had chosen the better way. She listened, I believe, with every fiber of her being (Luke 10:38–42 NRSV).

Again and again, Jesus called individuals to reclaim the life of the body. So they stood and walked; they stretched out their hands; they washed their own bodies in healing waters or each other's feet after a journey. The blind learned to see again, and differently. Lazarus came forth (Mark 2:9; Matt 12:13; Mark 3:5;

John 5:2ff.; John 13:14; Matt 9:28ff.; John 11:44 NRSV). My pilgrimage to reclaim a neglected body becomes more and more clearly a spiritual pilgrimage. These days I am hearing the Lord say to me as he did to so many others, "Stand up and walk" (Matt 9:5 NRSV). And as I lift up my heart, pull my lats back, relax my shoulders, let my head float, knees bent, butt slightly out, I feel myself making room for the breath that gives me life and the Spirit who abides in us and in whom we abide. Very specific gifts of the Spirit come in the stretching and adjusting and breathing: clarity, trust, open-heartedness, receptivity, hope, delight, and thanksgiving. I begin in a new way to understand incarnation—humility of dust lit by divine fire—and I want, like David, to dance before the altar.

Notes

1. Gerard Manley Hopkins, "God's Grandeur," in *Gerard Manley Hopkins, The Penguin Poets Series* (New York: Penguin, 1961).

2. See Ron DelBene, Mary Montgomery, and Herb Montgomery, *The Breath of Life: A Simple Way to Pray* (Nashville: Upper Room Books, 1996).

PHYSICAL HEALTH: OUR BODIES, OUR TEMPLES
–Cheryl A. Kirk-Duggan

Cheryl A. Kirk-Duggan, Ph.D., is director of the Center for Women and Religion and assistant professor of theology and womanist studies at the Graduate Theological Union in Berkeley, California. She is ordained in the Christian Methodist Episcopal Church. Her publications are many and include *Mary Had a Baby: An Advent Study Based on African American Spirituals*, *Soul Pearls: Worship Resources for the Black Church*, and *Refiner's Fire: A Religious Engagement with Violence*.

Made sacred; alive:
Divine Sculpting,
Divine Grace-filled Breath
Infusing cells, body and mind,
Soul identity,
Magnificence unbounded.

Births and deaths,
Love and laughter,
Family traits of height and girth,
Seriousness and mirth,

Eyes and hair and limbs,
Intellect and habits,

Legacies of DNA:
That signature won't betray.
Sacred flesh and blood,
Walking and talking,
Moving and grooving,
Singing and praying,
Temples embodying,
The pulse of life itself.

The human body is a living, vital vessel magnificently created by God. Our bodies contain over 600 named muscles and 206 bones. Our brain, spinal cord, millions of nerves, and over 50 billion other cells throughout our body make up our central nervous system, which controls our body. Our heart is a muscle that contracts and relaxes about seventy times a minute at rest, squeezing and pumping blood through its chambers to all parts of the body by way of an amazing series of blood vessels—a rubbery pipeline with many branches. Strung together end to end, these blood vessels could circle the globe two and a half times. Our lungs contain almost 1,500 miles of airways, over 300 million alveoli, which process about thirteen pints of air every minute. Plants are our partners in breathing. We inhale air, use the oxygen in it, release carbon dioxide; plants take in carbon dioxide and release oxygen.

Our physicality allows us to exist and be together in community, as opposed to being disembodied souls. The body is an extraordinary creation that serves us well when we take care of it. This divinely given instrument is a temple, a sacred house of worship, which we tend to take for granted and minimize its elegance, power, possibility and nobility. The symmetry, balance of components, and the beauty lines bespeak the body's elegance. The strength, agility, and ability to engage in artistic movements—skating, basketball, ballet, dance, lifting, writing, painting, and playing musical instruments—indicate the body's power. The variety of shapes, colors, and sizes of persons that make up the human race signify the possibilities and nobility of individual and global community. Because the body is sacred, we have the remarkable ability to know consciousness and to love ourselves and others. So wonderfully made, the many functions of our bodies are self-contained and efficient. This magnificence of God, made manifest in the beautiful architecture of the human body, is vast. The creative spirits that exist and have existed through time emerge from the totality of ourselves. Our grace-filled bodies bring life, and when done, these bodies die no less sacred. Our bodies make the music of laughter and experience the animation of God's angelic chorus, singing together.

Meditation 1
Seeing, touching,
Smelling, hearing, tasting,
Radiating energies of sacredness,
Speaking volumes
Of our souls.

These bodies of ours,
God's marvelous, majestic configurations.
Bombarding atoms,
Over the consciousness of time,
Grouped into families,
In love, in pain, in hope.

Moment by moment
Electric impulses
Feed the data of our hearts;
Stimulating our minds,
Nurturing our souls,

Caressing our bodies,
One sacred being, indivisible.

The two accounts of creation in the biblical text provide a poetic backdrop for heightening our consciousness about the blessed gift of our physical bodies and the marvelous, majestic design of these precious, sacred temples. Genesis 1 unfolds as God creates an orderly world from chaos and speaks everything into being within six days, then takes a rest on the seventh day, the Sabbath. On the sixth day, God creates male and female in God's image, blesses them, gives them dominion over the earth, and pronounces *everything* created as good, including the physical body. The second creation story account follows from a different tradition and offers a different order of events.

This second creation story opens as the Lord God, Yahweh Elohim, creates earth, heavens, and waters for the whole earth. God, like a potter, then shapes and forms the male person, "adam," the creature from the earth, "adamah," breathing into his nostrils, and the male person becomes a living being. Yahweh Elohim then creates a garden in Eden, with many trees, including the tree of life and the tree of the knowledge of good and evil. God gives the male creature free access to the garden with the exception of the tree of the knowledge of good and evil, and announces the creation of a helper as the male creature's partner. Yahweh Elohim creates every animal and every bird out of the ground and gives the male creature permission to name them and have dominion over them. Yahweh Elohim puts the male creature to sleep, takes one of his ribs, closes that place up, and fashions a woman from that rib. In both stories the creation of humanity by the Divine expresses a dynamic orchestration of life, a picture of blessed benevolence.

Because of skewed theology, many believe that the stuff of the body is evil because flesh is weak: this is a misinterpretation of the scripture, a denigration of a beautiful creation by God, and is problematic to any kind of redemption. To think that the flesh is inferior or the root of evil can induce a schizophrenic mindset and rejects our sacred selves. To say that the body is not good contradicts the reality that we are created in the image of God, by God, given the belief that the character of God is good. That goodness manifests in some beautiful, awesome ways. The beauty of sight provides a panoramic view of all the world. The colors of bougainvillea and orchids, of sunrises and sunsets, of newborn babes and nodding older folk in the evening of their lives, of birds and bees, and of night and day provide us with a palette of memories. The beauty of sightlessness for the blind may heighten other senses or may hamper fulfillment. The blessedness of touch provides connection, sensuality, and consciousness. When touched in healthy ways, we know love, nurture, and comfort. When touched in ways that violate our personhood, we know fear, pain, and hatred for the perpetrator and ourselves. Divine touch, directly from God or mediated through an individual, re-creates and heals us.

The beatitude of hearing makes us familiar with melodic offerings of music, languages, noises, conversations, plays, poems, and broadcasts—sometimes a cacophony, sometimes distinct harmony. The beatitude of being deaf is the grace of privacy or the curse of secrecy. The blissfulness of taste is the joy of Epicurean delight, the gratitude for the privilege of having more than enough food. The curse of taste occurs when deadened taste buds can no longer relish the characteristic qualities of foods and drink or are defeated by anorexia or gluttony. The bounty of smell is the ability to appreciate the various aromas of foods, perfumes, flowers, and tragically, the stench of pollution, toxic waste, and death. The benevolence of not being able to smell is the avoidance of foul scents, acrid or sour. The five senses are fine-tuned sensors that bring pleasure and completion to our lives and to the sacred moments of sensual experience.

Meditation 2
On wings of grace
We live and move,
Sing and laugh,
Dream dreams fantasizing,
Have visions mesmerizing,
Sharing bits of love.

We use our arms to hold and lift,
Bend and toss,

Swing across.
With hand and hand
We come to moments
of decision.

Our legs are gifts
That let us run
'Cross rolling plains,
God's great domains.
Wildflowers grow,
Birds soar above,
On wings of Grace.

The experience of flying is magical. A seemingly impossible possibility occurs when objects heavier than air are able to soar. The sons of a Methodist preacher had a vision that people could fly. Bicycle makers Orville and Wilbur Wright saw the splendid marvel of birds flying and dreamed they could invent a machine that would take human beings into the air. Today we fly daily with tons of cargo and people throughout the world; we send astronauts into space beyond the earth's atmosphere. As we soar physically, we are blessed to be able to soar mentally and emotionally within our imagination. We think and envision and remember through the marvels of our brain system, our intellect. This ingenious mechanism, our brain, designed by God, is the central repository of our own database; it controls the functions of our body. We think because of our sacred command center. Our brain allows for our consciousness and creativity, coordinates most voluntary movement, and controls and monitors our unconscious bodily functions like breathing and heart rate. In acknowledging the sacredness of the body, we are better able to love ourselves.

One reason to treat the body well is that the body works well for us. We can lift and hold and bend and toss, run in fields and up stairs, and kick and jump and dance. We can hold and be held. We can sing and laugh and be affectionate. When we experience physical challenges and our bodies refuse to function well, we often feel betrayed. Some challenges are congenital; some are the results of poor health care, accidents, or environmental elements. The frailty of our physical bodies reminds us to embrace an attitude of gratitude for the services our bodies provide, and encourages a sensitivity to those who cannot take such things for granted. Such mindfulness invites us to regard the care of our bodies as an issue of faith: the context for being sensitive to the needs of those experiencing challenges; being sensitive in a way that affirms their reality without being condescending or offering pity. With covenant faith we realize that every individual matters and that we are called to love and respect everyone. Such awareness shapes what and how we eat, our attentiveness to hygiene and exercise, our attitudes regarding proper clothing; it makes us concerned about the amount of sleep and rest we get, and shapes our concern for the safety of our environments. Making our surroundings safe ensures that we are conscious of our language and thought processes, and that our buildings need to be accessible for physically challenged individuals. In faith we must become so conscious that we omit those attitudes and behaviors that rob others of their dignity. Most important, we must understand that an individual's challenged physical state is not the result of punishment by God of them or their ancestors.

Much about God and life is mysterious. Despite our advanced technology and scientific discoveries in the twentieth century, we have yet to cure the common cold. Conversely, researchers are now working on using the cold virus as a carrier for a cure for AIDS. We have named many diseases for which we do not know the causes or the cures. We have learned the importance of washing hands, the use of antibiotics, and the importance of DNA in determining who and what a child will become in life. So much is unpredictable. Nevertheless, we can embrace the gift of our physicalness. We can take the very best care of ourselves as possible and make physical well-being an issue for our entire families. We can teach families and congregants to practice preventive health care, including the significance of eye and dental exams, physical checkups, healthy eating, exercise, and being aware of family health profiles as part of our faith practice.

Meditation 3
Open eyes,
Seeing mysteries;
The beauty, the sadness,
The puzzles of existence,
Trapped in the morrows.

Dear sacred ones:
Strong not invincible;
Muscles, tissues, cells,
Like a prayer,
Musical tapestries,
Ever sensual,
Move one to ecstasy.

Hallelujah Joy!
Feet of clay,
Withstanding tests of time.
Having borne thousands
From ship to shore
From east to west; Nine to five,
These weary travelers sustain.

Eyes, lenses that see and windows that afford insight into soul, are significant to our physical selves. When we use our eyes in meaningful, aesthetic ways, we experience profound insights and are privy to wisdom and knowledge. Often when we look, we do not see, or see fully. We see either the trees or the forest, but not the trees and the forest. Sacred seeing is a way to appreciate the magnificence of God and God's creation as we value the privilege of being able to see with the physical, spiritual, or mental eye. What we see depends on when, where, and how we look and our various motives and reasons for wanting to see. Sometimes we do not see because we are not prepared or we have not been forthright in our presentation, as Joseph warns his brothers in their sojourn to Egypt (Gen 43:1–8). The eye, like a camera, scans and takes in thousands of snapshots. Most camera eyes can discern the spectrum of colors. Persons who are color-blind may not be able to detect certain color distinctions, such as the distinction between red and green. Some of our camera eyes see colors but miss textures, distinctive dimensions, and shapes. Sometimes we look but have no desire to see. When we refuse to see the good, to see God, we begin to worship gods of stone and wood that have no redemptive power (Deut 4:25). Sometimes people only see our weaknesses before we acknowledge our strengths, the very strengths that when known to our enemies become our weaknesses (Judg 16).

The gift of sight opens up our world to know continuums—from beauty to ugliness, happiness to sadness, or existence to death. As we see, we gain knowledge and information (1 Sam 23:23). Those who see without their physical eyes have a wealthy experience of our blessed, awesome, mysterious, elegant creation given to us by God. The Hebrew Bible understanding of *ra'ah* refers to the experience *to see*, both direct and implied. *To see* means to have an experience, to gaze, to take heed, to behold, approve, appear, or view. Sometimes to see is to experience the affliction of others (Neh 9:9), to no longer see that which is good (Job 7:7), to see someone's destruction (Job 21:20), or to see one's corruption (Ps 16:10). Sometimes to see means to experience in grandeur and beauty the goodness of the Lord (Ps 27:13). To see, one can know the love in the light of the Lord (Ps 36:7–9), see the face of the voice of one's beloved (Song 2:14) and the blessedness to the glory of the Lord (Isa 39:2). To see is to encounter revelation, announcements, and disclosure.

The experience of seeing is a knowledge of reality, a perception of mundane and divine proportions. The Hebrew word *chazâh* means to gaze at, to perceive or contemplate mentally; to dream, to behold. This way of seeing is the act of beholding God while we are yet in our flesh (Job 19:26–27), an experience of a prophetic dream (Isa 13:1), of having false visions (Isa 21:29). When we look and desire to see, it is important to be prayerful and discerning.

In the New Testament, there are many terms—*optomai, diablepo, blepo,* and *eido*—that pertain to the act of seeing. *Optomai,* used in certain tenses, means to gaze with wide-open eyes at something remarkable: the blessed see God (Matt 5:8); one sees the heavens open (John 1:50); and when, through the power of the

Holy Spirit, those who have never heard of Christ Jesus will see him (Rom 15:21). *Diablepo* and its related *blepo* focus on the notion of to look at, behold, be aware, look (on, to), perceive, regard, see, take heed, to confirm through voluntary observation. When Jesus touched the eyes of two blind men, through their faith their eyes were opened. Sometimes those who have heard preaching and teaching see and hear, but do not perceive or understand (Mark 4:12). One can see through a mirror (1 Cor 13:12), though the reflection may not be a clear image. One can, however, see with recognition (Eph 5:15; Rev 1:12). *Eido*, used in the past tense as a more mechanical, passive seeing, means to know, behold, be aware, perceive, be sure, or tell. One can see the light of God, of witness in others (Matt 5:16), watch the process of events as they transpire (Luke 2:15; John 1:33), and observe, take note, or want to be in one's presence (Gal 6:11; Phil 2:28; 1 Thess 3:6). To see, then, is to observe, to expand one's horizons, to encounter, to witness, to consider, to experience, to receive, and to understand.

Meditation 4
Hearing music,
Viewing heaven;
Smelling rosebuds,
Ambrosia oozing forth,
Tasting sweet elixers,
Mercy, life is good.

Palpating rhythms of life,
Touching hands together,
Caressing, hugging, loving,
Moments of intimacy:
Signifying Grace.

The largest mountain,
The infinitesimal nutria,
The whale and the mustard seed,
An ocean, a continent,
The great, the small,
All signify God.

Awesome wonders,
Physical splendors,
Intricacies and details,
Unimaginable connectedness,
Safety and health,
Relies on the breathing of us all.

Sometimes we experience lack and hurt because we live on the street of desperation, at the intersections of limits and unconsciousness. With the emergence of a new day we often fail to look and grasp its newness, its uniqueness. Sometimes our pains and angst loom so large that we cannot see the splendor in the grass or the twinkling of the stars. Prayertime can provide room for the shift from pain to appreciation. Prayer, human petitions to God or the Divine, as *t*ᵉ*phillâh*, involves supposition, intercession, and is engaging (2 Sam 7:27), a certainty that God hears and will deliver (Neh 1:6; Isa 38:5). Prayer may involve an imperative tone amidst a pressing awareness of distress (Pss 4:1; 39:12), or a caution about who one prays for (Jer 7:16).

Prayer, *proseuche*, involves praying earnestly, implies oratory, with a belief that prayer requested in faith produces results (Matt 21:22), describes one of the functions of a temple (Luke 19:46), helps refocus a group toward unity (Acts 1:14), and is a means to overcome anxiety (Phil 4:6). Prayer, as *deesis*, is a petition and supplication, for awesome blessings (Luke 1:13), shaped by one's heart's desire (Rom 10:1), and is a vehicle of deliverance (Phil 1:19). Prayer can give us clarity, a sense of well-being, and a heart more in tune with God, in gratitude, intensifying our many senses. A stance of appreciation is an opportunity to see and hear and smell beauty; to know life as possibility, as good. Just as in seeing, hearing provides another modality for being with God. To hear, as *shâma*, engages the intellect toward obedience, discernment, and perception.

In the New Testament, *akono* denotes the ability to hear in various ways and to give or attend as an audience. When listening to parables as a keen observer of life, one who has ears ought to hear (Matt 13:8*b*). One can also choose to leave when others refuse to hear (Mark 6:11). Part of the life of the faithful is to be supportive, to preach and teach so that others might hear and believe (Rom 10:14). The epistles reinforce a cautionary tale: we listen quickly, fastidiously, but speak and move to anger slowly (Jas 1:19). The gift of smell heightens our ability to interact with ourselves and our communities.

The experience of smell is closely related to the sense of blowing. *Ruwach* means to blow, to smell, to perceive in anticipation, to enjoy. Sweet smells of spices and frankincense are holy to the Lord and appropriate for worship rituals (Exod 30:38). *Reyach*, related to *ruwach*, means savor, scent, smell. We can smell the smell of one's garments (Gen 27:27), and with lovers we can smell delicious, intoxicating fragrances of bodies, ointments, and gardens (Song 1:12, 4:10, 7:8). Sweet smells, such as freshly bathed and talcumed babies along with sweet smells exuding from kitchens, often provide comfort and signify an experience of nurture and love. Appreciating the sense of smell can serve as a warning or an invitation. Bad, virulent, gaseous, ammonia-like smells warn us of stress and unrest; good, sweet smells evoke pleasure and often relaxation. Relaxing is key to gaining pleasure from one's body and one's surroundings. Reckoning with or evaluating one's present reality from the context of sensitiveness and thankfulness opens up a new vista and a new way of seeing things that we often take for granted. Sensitivity to the inner connection of life helps us embrace the various rhythms that go on in our bodies and in nature. Awareness of these textures helps us celebrate our senses as we come alive, know intimacy, know God, and ultimately begin to know ourselves.

SOUL FOOD AND SPIRITUAL FORMATION
–Bruce G. Epperly

Bruce G. Epperly, Ph.D., is the director of the Alliance for the Renewal of Ministry and Continuing Education and associate professor of practical theology at Lancaster Theological Seminary in Lancaster, Pennsylvania. Ordained in the Christian Church (Disciples of Christ) and the United Church of Christ, Bruce has served as a university chaplain, congregational minister, medical school professor, spiritual director, and consultant in spirituality and healing.

As they journeyed toward the promised land, the Israelites were warned that two paths of life stood before them—the first path led to death and the second led to life. Without oversimplifying the nature of human and divine decision making, we too find ourselves facing two paths. Will we choose life and health or death and disease? Will we follow the divine bias toward health or turn toward habits and practices that injure both body and spirit? The counsel of God both then and now is to "choose life."

Diet figures prominently in the biblical story. The Israelites were called by God to be holy even as God is holy. Their holiness or "set apart-ness" was to be reflected in their ethical treatment of one another, in the observance of the Sabbath, in hospitality to the stranger, and in their dietary habits. For reasons known to God alone, certain meats and fish were appropriate for consumption while others were taboo. What persons ate and their attitudes toward eating reflected their relationship to God.

Diet is also a matter of importance in the New Testament, most specifically in the writings of the Apostle Paul. Paul's challenge to the strict adherence to Jewish dietary laws was grounded not in issues of health but in issues of ethics, equality, and theology. In Galatians, Paul asserts that Christian freedom may involve transcending a legalistic understanding of the Jewish dietary laws and the practice of circumcision. In Christ, there are neither unclean persons nor unclean foods. Our relationship to God is based on God's love for us, first of all, and not on any specific dietary prohibitions.

Nevertheless, Paul sees our eating habits as an issue of faith. To those Corinthians who saw issues of diet and lifestyle of little consequence, Paul asserts that our eating and drinking must be grounded in our participation in the "body of Christ" and our care for "the temple of God." "All things are lawful" to the Christian, "but not all things are helpful" (1 Cor 10:23).

What we eat, Paul counsels, may even have an impact on our neighbor. While we may "eat whatever is sold in the meat market without raising any question on the ground of conscience," even if this food is sacrificed to idols, we must take care that our eating and drinking is not a stumbling block to our "weaker" brother or sister (1 Cor 8:9–11).

Further, at the agape feasts of the Corinthian church, the rich came early, bringing the best food and wines, and then consumed their dinners before their more humble neighbors arrived. The agape feasts, Paul proclaims, are to mirror Christ's own eucharistic feast. While "food does not commend us to God" and "we are not worse off if we do not eat, and no better off if we eat" certain types of food, our eating must glorify God and bring us closer to our neighbor. The health of "the body of Christ" requires that our eating bring health to the souls of our neighbors and ourselves. Eating, as today's experts on world hunger suggest, has ethical consequences when it involves gluttony, on the one hand, and starvation, on the other. As Paul proclaims, "whether you eat or drink, or whatever you do, do all to the glory of God" (1 Cor 10:31).

While fasting has always been part of monastic spiritual formation and the practice of many devout laypersons, the nineteenth-century Seventh Day Adventist movement brought the issue of diet and abstinence once again to the forefront of Christian reflection. Although the Adventist movement was ridiculed for its obsession with health and its expectation of the imminent Second Coming of Jesus, the dietary practices of the Seventh Day Adventists have been vindicated as contributors to health and well-being. Many of today's healthy diets, such as cardiologist Dean Ornish's "heart attack-prevention diet" or the Pritikin diet, reflect the wisdom of Ellen B. White, the mother of the Adventist movement, and her disciples.

At the heart of Seventh Day Adventist thinking is the belief that what we eat has spiritual ramifications. Persons should live in accordance with the divine laws of health and embodiment. Ellen White asserted that the eating of meat, the use of tobacco, and the consumption of alcohol numb the mind and deaden the spirit. Many of us, sadly, can testify to this fact! The soul is most appropriately nourished by a diet consisting of grains, fruits, and vegetables—a far cry from the high fat and cholesterol diets of both the nineteenth century and today. The Adventists believe that we prepare ourselves for the Second Coming by presenting our bodies as "a living sacrifice" unto God and following God's laws of nutrition, rest, and exercise. The vegetarian orientation of the Seventh Day Adventists is reflected in longer lives and fewer cases of hypertension and heart disease, on average, than the fast-food, meat-eating culture of most Americans. The God who resurrects the flesh on the last day is concerned with how we treat our flesh today!

In the spirit of the Adventist movement, Christians are discovering that diet is a matter of stewardship both of our own bodies and the bodies of others. Paul's gospel of Christian freedom did not, as some suggest, give Christians the license to eat whatever they want. Freedom in Christ leads to a responsible and loving lifestyle. We take care of the temple because it is part of God's creation and we affirm the bodies of others because they, too, are members of the body of Christ. We also recognize that irresponsible eating and drinking may lead to illnesses that burden our families, friends, and the social structure, as well as tax the health resources available to our communities.

According to today's medical wisdom, what we eat and how we eat are matters of life and death. Dean Ornish and other physicians have noted that at least 50 percent of heart attacks and other forms of cardiovascular disease are related to lifestyle and eating habits. The traditional risk factors for heart disease and high blood pressure center around diet, lack of exercise, obesity, and smoking, as well as age, gender, and genetics. We are a society plagued by cardiovascular disease: physicians estimate that 60 million Americans have some form of high blood pressure, hardening of the arteries, or heart disease.

Dean Ornish has been a pioneer in responding to heart disease in America. Ornish believes that the occurrence of cardiovascular disease may be an invitation to personal transformation. Through a transformed and healthy lifestyle, we can both reverse and prevent heart disease. Ornish believes that the current medical focus on heart bypass operations simply bypasses the spiritual, emotional, and dietary issues that lead to cardiovascular disease. Prevention and recovery require a transformed mind and a commitment to life and health.

Ornish's program for healthy living involves a healthy diet, moderate exercise, quitting smoking, stress management, and spiritual formation. Ornish's diet follows closely the spirit of Adventist Ellen White. In contrast to the typical American diet, which is high in animal products, fat, cholesterol, salt, and sugar, Ornish advocates a diet emphasizing beans, legumes, fruits, grains, and vegetables, all of which are high in fiber and low in fat and cholesterol. If we are aware of what we eat, we can "eat more and weigh less" precisely because the foods we eat are low in fat and high in fiber. Further, as I will suggest later in this section, the Ornish and Adventist diets are also ecologically and morally sound, since the foods suggested are low on the food chain, require less processing, and, because of their vegetarian orientation, minimize the use of grain as animal feed. Many cookbooks today emphasize both a healthy diet and a healthy attitude toward the environment and the needs of persons in underdeveloped nations.

Heart disease can be a catalyst for transformation insofar as it challenges us to rethink our priorities and choose new behaviors. An essential aspect of the Ornish program is "eating with mindfulness." While the term "mindfulness" has its origins in Buddhism, Christian leaders have also spoken of the importance of awareness and observation of our eating and of habitual behavior patterns in the process of spiritual formation. When we eat, we are challenged to eat slowly, tasting the food, and noting its impact on our bodies and minds. Ornish believes that many of our problems with food arise from the use of food to respond to emotional needs and to our failure to listen to our bodies and their needs. The body has a wisdom that we disobey at our own peril. Andrew Weil, another physician concerned with health, asserts that what we eat and drink and our lifestyle can enhance or depress our body's natural healing processes.

Most of us are virtually unaware of what we eat. How often have you eaten a meal while watching television, reading the paper, or planning the day ahead, and then, afterwards, asked yourself, "What did I just eat?" Clinical psychologist Elizabeth Wheeler notes that people often eat quickly and are surprised at how good food tastes when they eat slowly and mindfully. When persons eat with awareness, "they're less likely to eat when they're not hungry, and less likely to eat beyond the point of fullness."

Eating with mindfulness challenges today's Christian to choose between "fast food" and "soul food." This is not a matter of otherworldly salvation but a response to God's call to abundant life right now. In the spirit of Ornish and others, Christians can begin their personal transformation by exploring a spirituality of eating and serving. Such joyful and prayerful eating was at the heart of Jesus' table fellowship. Eating was as important as preaching for Jesus. He fed the five thousand, he ate with sinners and the wealthy, he transformed water into wine at Cana. Eating was a theological and ethical act that embodied God's love for the outcast and the sinful.

If we are to claim the spirit of Jesus' table fellowship, we must, first of all, surround our food with prayer. Too often, we cook, serve, and eat in a hurry. We pay little attention to our companions at the table. We barely notice the taste and are oblivious to the impact of certain foods on our well-being. We eat merely to "fill the void" or replenish an "empty gas tank." Our eating habits often negatively reflect our spiritual and emotional needs and disregard our nutritional and relational needs. Such compartmentalized and mechanistic eating habits lead to illness of both body and spirit.

Many liberal and mainstream Christians have abandoned mealtime prayer as archaic and repetitious. No doubt, some persons associate mealtime prayer with parental supervision, ritualistic repetition, or fundamentalist piety. In contrast, Jesus saw eating as a way of encountering God and trusting in God's bounty. Surrounding our meals with prayer can transform our food so that it becomes food for the spirit. It is an invitation to eat with an awareness that our diet is a spiritual issue. Today's Christians are called to follow the Native American image of eating in a holy and thankful way.

In my own cooking and food preparation, I seek to maintain a prayerful attitude. I follow the example of the kitchen mystic Brother Lawrence, who compared his time in the kitchen or shopping for supplies to his time spent at the Eucharist. I take time out to be thankful as I chop the vegetables, cut the fruit, or slice the chicken. I remember those for whom I am cooking and take a moment to pray for each one of them. If I become bothered or frustrated, I take a few breaths to center myself and ask that God be in my heart and mind as I cook and eat. While we do not always have regular mealtime blessings in my family, we try to spend the meal with one another in conversation and silence. We have learned the significance of doing one thing at a time and have, for the most part, broken the habit of "time-sharing" our eating with the evening news and the sports page. Such times of family eating enable us to commune with one another in a more leisurely fashion and to discover what is important in each other's lives. As we surround our meals with blessing, our food becomes holy food, it becomes for us "the body and blood of Christ," and our spirits as well as our bodies are nurtured.

Eating is a form of celebrating the ordinariness of life. Surely this sort of celebration, which transforms the everyday into a celebration of God's presence, was at the heart of Jesus' own table fellowship. We can see this same celebration of the ordinary and the temporary in the Japanese tea ceremony, the celebration of the eucharistic elements of bread and wine, and the Navajo sand painting and hunting rituals. All these activities are transitory, but by our openness to the holy within these temporary events, we find personal balance and become part of the rhythms of nature and the divine.

Today, many Christians are reclaiming the ethical aspects of eating. In an era of widespread starvation, we must "live simply, so that others might simply live." Today, as we consume our processed foods and animal products (both of which contribute to cardiovascular illness), we must remember that other weight problem. As Ronald Sider states, "we are an affluent island in the midst of starving humanity." Over one billion persons suffer from malnutrition. Over two hundred million children will suffer brain damage from lack of protein in their diets. The Apostle Paul notes that one of the greatest, yet in our time forgotten sins, is gluttony. Today, as we heap our plates full at the bountiful buffet of fast foods and high-cholesterol meals, we must turn our attention to those who beg for a morsel at the gates of the city all across the globe.

The prophet Amos once suggested that the wealthy and well fed will experience a "famine" of the word of God because of their injustice to the poor (Amos 8:11–12). Are we on the verge of such a famine? When we learn about the relationship between cattle raising and the destruction of the rainforest and the threat to the planetary ecosystem, we are convicted by the possibility that our current eating habits may jeopardize the survival of our children's children. Ronald Sider's suggestions for a "lifestyle of justice" are surprisingly similar to Ornish's counsels for a healthy lifestyle: substitute vegetable protein for animal protein, fast regularly, oppose the misuse of grain for beer and alcohol.

Diet is both a personal and a social issue. An ethical and ecological diet is also a healthy diet. Since all of life is interdependent, what is good for the "body of Christ" as a totality is also good for each individual part! As we live more simply, we consciously share in the lives of others and experience our connectedness with the world beyond ourselves and our families. Isolationism in diet, lifestyle, and economics is unhealthy for ourselves and others. As we experience our connectedness with God and the body of Christ incarnate in our companions on the planet, we will begin to eat with a sense of holiness and care.

Many contemporary physicians suggest a completely vegetarian diet. I see nothing wrong with eating flesh sparingly and with mindfulness. But ask yourself how meat makes you feel. Which meat products add zest to your life and which depress your system? How do you feel about the killing of animals? We are not called to be dietary legalists, and there is no one norm to which we must conform. From time to time, I enjoy chicken and on occasion will order a steak. But, for reasons of ethics as well as health, these occasions are becoming more and more rare. We are called to be countercultural in our eating habits and to eat meaningfully and spiritually. Remember Paul's challenge to the Christians at Rome: "Be not conformed to the world, but be transformed by the renewing of your mind" (Rom 12:2). In addition to thanking God for the blessings of the hunt and the harvest, we are called to be grateful to the food itself as well as to those who have prepared it for us.

Many Christians have found both a spiritual and a physical benefit in fasting. Fasting must be done, however, with care and discipline. When fasting becomes obsessive or injures the body, it violates the temple of God. Fasting is best employed when our motivation is to deepen our spiritual lives or live in solidarity with the poor and malnourished persons of our planet. Some persons contribute the money saved on fast days to local soup kitchens or hunger relief programs.

Fasting and other dietary practices should be done with grace and gentleness. For some, a fast supplemented by water will suffice; for others, juice is a necessity. Other persons, who require three regular meals to maintain their health or energy, can take time out before and after their meals to thank God for the gift of life and food and commit themselves to using their energy for the well-being of the neighborhood and the planet. Perhaps the fast most appropriate for many of us who work long hours and lead busy lives is the abstinence from one meal, from time to time, or between meal or bedtime snacks. Such times, when devoted to God and our neighbor, are spiritual disciplines that focus the mind even as they relax the digestive system.

Diet is important in our spiritual and ethical formation. What we eat and how we eat can be a witness to our faith and a commitment to participating in God's healing work in our bodies and in the body of Christ. When we eat with mindfulness, ethical sensitivity, and gratitude, then every meal participates in Christ's own eucharistic feast.

FOR PERSONAL REFLECTION

1. Wuellner suggests that our bodies might flourish "in an atmosphere of warm friendliness, encouragement, respect, communication, and sensitivity to ability and timing." Kirk-Duggan paints word pictures of just such an atmosphere in her friendly and intimate description of the body. Use her meditations for your own meditations, and see if Wuellner's truth is your truth as well.

2. "Whether you eat or drink . . . do all to the glory of God," admonishes St. Paul. In what ways do your eating and drinking reflect your consciousness of God? Do you believe that changing your eating patterns would increase that consciousness? What would be involved in making those changes?

3. "Thankfulness opens up a new vista and a new way of seeing things that we often take for granted," says Kirk-Duggan. Meister Eckert said, "If thank you is the only prayer you utter, it is enough." What do you think the impact of thankfulness would be on your well-being?

FOR GROUP DISCUSSION

1. "Every incident in the life of the body is reflected in some movement of the Spirit," says McEntyre. Similarly, Kirk-Duggan says, "Muscles, tissues, cells, / Like prayer . . . / Move one to ecstasy." Has this connection between movement of the body and movement of the spirit been your experience? If so, in what ways, and under what conditions?

2. Epperly tells us that in the times of the Bible, "what persons ate and their attitudes toward eating reflected their relationship to God." Is this reflected in our modern society? How do you see that lived out? What are the spiritual ramifications to what we eat?

3. "Diet is both a personal and a social issue. An ethical and ecological diet is also a healthy diet," writes Epperly, reflecting the multidimensionality of food. Is it reasonable to think that Western eating habits can change? What would be needed to make this a reality? What would be the drawbacks, the obstacles, and the benefits to making this change?

4.

Christian Spirituality and Illness

To the Wife of a Sick Friend
—Edna St. Vincent Millay

Shelter this candle from the wind.
Hold it steady. In its light
The cave wherein we wander lost
Glitters with frosty stalactite,
Blossoms with mineral rose and lotus,
Sparkles with crystal moon and star,
Till a man would rather be lost than found:
We have forgotten where we are.

Shelter this candle. Shrewdly blowing
Down the cave from a secret door
Enters our only foe, the wind.
Hold it steady. Lest we stand,
Each in a sudden, separate dare,
The hot wax spattered upon your hand,
The smoking wick in my nostril stone.
The inner eyelid red and green
For a moment yet with moons and roses,—
Then the unmitigated dark.

Alone, alone in a terrible place.
With only the dripping of the water on the stone,
And the sound of your tears, and the taste of my own.

Edna St. Vincent Millay's poem speaks of the wind. Could that wind be *rhuach*, the uncontrolled and uncontrollable Spirit of God that blows where it will? Our God is not gentle or tame; our God is wholly other, and we experience God as a *mysterium tremendum et fascinosum*, both terrifying and irresistibly attractive.

With the candle lit and sheltered from the wind, the explorer experiences some control of the venture. She can see the landscape. She finds it intriguing, mysterious, new, even exciting. Is that not the first blush of our experience with powerful illness? We enter the experience with some light, and we know we are on holy ground.

But too soon the wind, "our only enemy," gusts. Our dependable candlelight is extinguished. We no longer know where we are, or why, save that we are alone and in a terrible place. Is that the way it is when our old understandings about suffering are blown away by intimate and weighty experience? Is that the result of platitudes failing to hold truth when new truth is unbearable?

Suffering teaches us what joy cannot. Yet who among us would ask for such teaching?

Wuellner invites us into dialogue with our ill or disabled bodies, to have the conscious-self talk with the body-self, and to keep an honest dialogue alive. Earle encourages us to encounter the many layers of meaning of our wounds, listening to them, letting them illumine one another, and avoiding slick answers that are not hard won.

Sulmasy sets a context for the experiences that Wuellner and Earle address. Sulmasy writes as a careful ethicist, and his original work, *A Healer's Calling*, is addressed to health care professionals. Yet he has words for us as well, and we would be wise to eavesdrop and put human suffering into the context of what it means to be human. He argues that "if one suffers and in that suffering experiences limitation and finitude but still manages to hold out hope for the infinite . . . one is on the road to salvation." See if you agree.

RELATING TO OUR BODIES IN ILLNESS AND DISABILITY
—Flora Slosson Wuellner

Flora Slosson Wuellner is an ordained minister in the United Church of Christ. After several years in parish ministry, she entered a specialized ministry of spiritual renewal. She has led ecumenical retreats and workshops in the United States and Europe, authored several books, and taught as an adjunct faculty member at Pacific School of Religion, Berkeley, in the area of spirituality.

It's all very well to write about the signals, powers, pleasures and participation of our bodies when all our bodily parts are able to move, respond, communicate, and cooperate. But what about our bodies when they are paralyzed, blind, deaf, lame? What about our bodies when they are in pain and weakness or trapped in progressive disease? Where is our communication and empowerment when our body feels quite literally like a prison or even a torture chamber?

During this past decade, special thought and help has been given to the special problems of disability. (Rather than speaking of "disabled," we prefer to say "other-abled" or "physically challenged.") Every day I see men and women going about their work in electrically operated wheelchairs, guided by specially trained dogs, or learning to move and communicate through other ways and abilities. I have often talked with these men and women in our professional schools and have learned many things. To be other-abled is not necessarily the same thing as illness. One can be lame, paralyzed, blind, deaf, or mute and still be in basic good health. But the relationship of an other-abled individual with the body is of a unique poignancy.

> For probably all of us, at least at times, being disabled hurts. Even if the larger community would adopt totally fair and appropriate attitudes toward people with disabilities, this would still not eliminate the sense of loss, the frustration, and indeed the anger we feel just because we are disabled. . . .
> Because we are disabled, many of us have pretty low self-esteem. Our physical appearance, for example, often does not fit any traditional standards . . . we cannot do one or more basic life function. This . . . can also be extremely demoralizing. . . .
> . . . Positive thinking can, of course, be quite useful. . . . But if a newly disabled woman is constantly surrounded by only those spouting worn-out "it could be worse" clichés, she is likely to develop a very strong urge to strangle them all. . . . nothing they can say or do can make that disability disappear. It's there, and it's real, and it must be coped with.[1]

So how does one relate to one's body? Is it really possible to *have* a vital, loving relationship with the bodily self at all under such circumstances?

"How do you manage? How do you feel about your body?" I recently asked a church leader who had permanently lost the use of both of her legs in a car accident. She was in an electrically operated chair. A rather plump woman, she was dressed in warm, attractive colors, and her eyes shone with enthusiasm for her work.

"My paralysis of my legs is a fact, a given," she answered bluntly. "It's a fact of my life now, just like the fact that I am short and have curly hair. Yes, I do some-times think of the way I used to be, and yes, I do sometimes grieve bitterly. I had to face that and work through it. You can't cut short the grieving and the anger. You have to stay with it and work it through.

"But I don't need to *stop* there. I have gone on. My body is my friend, more than ever. I can pray for it, relate to it. I communicate with it, and I feel a response. Maybe not in my legs any more, but they are still *my* legs, part of the family even if I can't feel them. There is still circulation going on there, cellular change. Yes, my legs, though paralyzed, are still working in many ways for the good of my whole body.

"I am relating to my body—just as much as you do, though I've had to learn new ways of relating. I thank my legs for the work they are still doing, and I ask the rest of my body to take over as much as possible their missing functions."

As I listened to her and to others with similar problems, I realized there *was* a real relationship with the body possible, a relationship in many ways much deeper than mine had ever been. I realized that though one bodily ability is cut off or limited, there are other powers, awarenesses, abilities that develop. This is why the word "other-abled" is a much more descriptive word than "disabled."

A blind man once said to me some years after losing his sight, "I can hear more deeply what others are saying and feeling. It's as if I had a way of sensing or discerning that I didn't have before. I don't quite know where to locate this ability, or where in my body it's focused, but it is certainly real and very present."

We must neither misunderstand nor dishonor this kind of witness by thinking that there is no sense of loss, anger, or grieving. It is unrealistic and dangerous to try to gloss over our woundedness. I have recently read in the newspapers of a twenty-one-year-old girl who is totally paralyzed for life by a random bullet from a sniper. In one minute, a beautiful young body was rendered unmoving, bedridden for life. We have all heard of similar tragedies, and as we pray for such people, we wonder how we would be feeling in their place: Longing for death? Grateful for life? Anger? Despairing loss? Grief beyond description? Acute awareness of the love of others? Determination? Anger at God? Closeness to God? Probably we would feel all of these at different times, or even simultaneously. These are fully human feelings, bodily, emotional, relational, honored and understood by God. This humanity of ours must be encountered and lived. One of the most powerful and comforting aspects of the Bible is that human feelings are never negated. Hatred, fear, loneliness, despair, and longing are fully expressed, with knowledge that God hears and understands. Just leaf through the book of Psalms. No one is playing games with God or trying to repress or hide feelings in the Psalms! Jesus never hesitated to weep, feel anger, or express grief, need, or loneliness. To feel our feeling is a necessary part of our wholeness.

We must not make the mistake of thinking that God has sent us tragedy to punish us or to improve us. As a child, I used to listen to the singing of a powerful old song about a blind farmer. The whole song was in praise to God, who took away his sight so that his soul might see. Though I loved the beautiful melody, I worried a lot about that song. It made God seem scary and cruel. I hoped God wouldn't take any special notice of me! But as I grew older and began to read the New Testament, I noted that Jesus never refused to heal the blind because it was better for their souls. He never told anyone that God had sent illness upon them for their own good.

There were apparently times when Jesus couldn't heal very extensively or effectively, such as in his own home town of Nazareth: "He could do no mighty work there, except that he laid his hands upon a few sick people and healed them" (Mark 6:5). There are often blocks to our healing, but that is not God's wish for us. The God we see through Jesus is always on the side of healing and grieves for us and with us in our suffering.

Illness or other physical disasters are not the same as the cross that Christians are called to carry. These crosses are tasks of loving, sacrificial involvement with others, bearing their burdens. These are offered to us freely, and we are free to accept or reject them.

Our personal disasters are more like Paul's thorn in the flesh (2 Cor 12:7–9) and may come for many different reasons in our lives, but never as God's will for us. There may be blocks to their removal, but God works with us for healing, even if they are, for some of us, lifelong problems. We do not know why healing is sometimes so delayed, why it may come only in part, or why it perhaps may never come fully to our bodies. Recently a friend suggested to me that there might be a difference between being cured and being healed. I found this to be a helpful distinction. Perhaps the new creativity that God's grace helps us bring from our "thorns" is a healing, though the cure may not be complete in this life. Thus, in the midst of the "thorn" experience, we are promised freedom from bondage. Bondage is the feeling that our lives are out of control; that we have no choices or alternatives; that there is no more "new creation"; that we are living in captive obedience rather than in relationship. God sets us free to discover that each moment, within grace, opens endless creative possibilities.

We discover, as did my friend whose legs are paralyzed, that our bodies are a precious part of us. Our bodies are to be loved, not because of the problem (which would be masochistic), in spite of the problem (which would be patronizing), or even through the problem (which could be too idealistic). Rather our bodies should be loved within the problem, as part of our whole life's experience. Such a concept is expressed with unsurpassed poignant power in *With the Power of Each Breath*:

> Our bodies are our most precious and often our only posses-
> sions. . . . Some of us live in chronic pain, some with chronic
> unpredictability, and others with chronic stares. . . . We need to
> see our bodies as worthy parts of ourselves in order to invest the
> time and energy it takes to care for ourselves. . . . We are regard-
> ed as "defects." . . . Value judgments are assigned to our "good"
> and "bad" parts. . . . Our integrity as persons has been under-
> mined. . . . We claim our bodies and our integrity as disabled
> women. We insist on our right to make informed decisions about
> our bodies. We do not have good parts, bad parts or inner
> beauty. We come in many sizes, shapes and colors. Our bodies
> deserve our love, tenderness and pleasure.[2]

Relating to the body while undergoing illness and pain often presents very different problems from those of disablement. (As indicated earlier, dis- or other-ablement may not necessarily involve pain or disease.) Illness and disease may be chronic or temporary, but there is always a sense of struggle and unease as the body works to cast off bacterial invasion or to regain its chemical balance and vitality. The very work the body is doing makes it hard for us to love and communicate with it. It is hard for us not to hate and repudiate our body when it signals extreme discomfort and pain. It is hard not to blame it, or at least to ignore and escape from it, by merely deadening the symptoms. When caught by the misery of even just a bad cold, I for one am all too apt to feel totally unspiritual, merely enduring with intense dislike the close presence of my struggling life partner, my body! I talked once with a woman who had several operations for recurring cancer, moving through them with unmatched courage and good cheer. But when she broke her little toe while vacationing on a beach, she reacted with complete outrage to the pain!

"I experienced more pain with that toe than I ever had in my cancer," she told me, both laughing and indignant. "My whole body hurt! I never realized how much weight we put on the foot and how much we take the foot for granted. I think I know now what Paul meant when he wrote that the head can't say to the feet 'I have no need of you.' But I still can't help being mad at my foot for hurting me so!"

How can we best relate to and communicate with our bodies at these times? Probably it is best not to try to engage in long, intense meditations, but it is essential to keep some form of repeated, encouraging thought going toward our bodies. Our bodies are working with full force to preserve and keep us well, like a brave friend carrying our burden and fighting our battles. It must be allowed to do its full work without distraction, but with awareness of our appreciative concern and with forms of encouragement and imagery that help along its brave struggle. This does not mean we do not face and express our feelings of anger and dismay. Open admission of feeling will not block the body in its work. Unadmitted feelings are far more unhealthy and damaging. But along with the admitted feeling, we can choose many ways of helping our bodies with our conscious focusing. Some suggest visualizing the immune system encountering and overcoming in various ways bacterial and viral invaders.

If the body is experiencing an organic imbalance or deficiency, it is helpful to speak lovingly and encouragingly to the main organic systems involved, thanking them for the work they do, envisioning the healing light or healing waters of God surrounding and permeating them. We do this in the same way we would pray for a friend carrying a hard burden or working through a problem. Ask your body what you, your conscious self, can do to help in the way of diet, rest, exercise, and daily life. Do not set timetables for healing, and do not push or force. We need to respect the body's own rhythm of timing and healing. Remind yourself that the body has not suddenly become your enemy. Your body has not attacked you. It, too, is undergoing attack. It is helping carry the burden of your spirit and the pain of your community.

Like a brave, wise friend who works closely with you, your body will give signals, make suggestions, share its wisdom. Dr. Bernie Siegel, a surgeon specializing in cases of cancer, quotes the witness of a young pregnant woman recovering from a mastectomy, but knowing that cancer had spread to her lymph glands:

> As soon as I left the hospital, I tried to listen to my insides. I wanted my body and mind to tell me how to help them survive. I got some answers, and I tried to follow them even when I was too depressed to move or care. My body said: "Drink orange juice," a curious craving I'd never experienced before. I drank and drank, and it felt right. . . . I told my food to make me strong. I told each vitamin . . . to go to the right places and do the right things. . . .
>
> My body said, "Move, Lois, and do it fast!" Thirty minutes after I came home from the hospital I went for a walk.
>
> I told my body through exercise that I loved it and wanted it to be healthy. . . .
>
> My mind and body said, "Make love," and they were right. . . .
>
> I told my body to be well. I told my immunological system to protect me. . . . I watched my blood flowing strongly. I told the wound to heal quickly and the area around it to be clean. . . .
>
> I think of cancer every day, but I also think of how strong my body is, how good it feels most of the time. I still talk to my insides. I have a feeling of integration of body, mind and, probably, spirit, which I have never before experienced.[3]

Norman Cousins, in his book *The Healing Heart*, shares his own experience after his recovery from a massive heart attack:

> The belief that illness is something that comes into us from the outside . . . is so firmly ingrained in us that we naturally look to available outside forces to do battle with it and evict it. Since we are attacked from without we tend to believe we can be rescued only from without. We have little knowledge of, and therefore little confidence in, the numberless ways the human body goes about righting itself. . . . What can the individual do? First of all, it is important to be aware of the body's natural drive to heal itself, once freed of the provocations that played a part in bringing on the illness. . . . Each individual presides over the totality of himself or herself.[4]

Above all, therefore, in times of illness, it is essential to be in close touch with the body's wisdom as it works for healing. And if we have entered into a warm, appreciative, listening relationship with our bodies before illness strikes, it is all that much easier to hear and cooperate.

In our close work with our bodily selves during illness, it is absolutely necessary not to fall into the trap of guilt, believing that we are personally, totally responsible for all of our illnesses. As I pointed out earlier, we *do* live in a world in which there are bacteria, viruses, pollution, and genetic problems, and we *do* live in human communities whose burdens and stresses we share. Up to a point, our unhealed stress and our unwise lifestyles can and do make us vulnerable to illness, but seldom does illness rise solely from our personal mistakes. In our excitement over the new options of claiming responsibility for our own bodies, sometimes we go too far and imply in our attitudes to others that they must have done something against the laws of God or nature, or they wouldn't be sick! This puts us right back into the errors of the "comforters" of Job. This is glib, simplistic, and ignorant of the mystery of interweaving, between ourselves and our communities, ourselves and the problems of this universe in which we are embodied.

Somehow we must maintain the miracle of wholeness and healing when the body and mind work together in loving unity within God's embrace and at the same time acknowledge the presence of mystery, knowing that we do not have all the answers, knowing that God works ceaselessly with our body and mind to bring light out of darkness. This is a difficult balance, and yet it is the biblical challenge to us. There is excitement in God's unfolding work, in the realism that we have just begun and that there is so much to learn and, above all, that we are all bound together—God, humanity, the world around us, and worlds to come— in such love that if one suffers all suffer together; if one is healed, all share the life and joy.

With this humility always with us, let us move boldly into the exploration and excitement of the possibilities that unfold when we enter the new relationship of tenderness and fellowship with our bodies.

A minister shared recently that he called on a woman in the hospital who had had surgery and was recovering successfully in all areas but one; her bladder was not yet functioning. The doctors refused to release her from the hospital until it did. Each day she was getting angrier at her bladder for its behavior. The minister listened lovingly to her anger, and all of a sudden heard himself saying, "I can understand how you feel, but don't you think it's time now that you became *friends* with your bladder? Why don't you speak to it with love and encouragement and picture Jesus touching it with healing hands? Your bladder is your friend and needs your help." This was a totally new idea for the woman. That night she prayed this way for her body, and the next morning the bladder began to function spontaneously.

We do not always experience such a swift, complete response. The timing of our bodies is not always the same as that of our conscious minds. The body has to get in touch with the depths of the subconscious mind and do quite a lot of other work before the outer symptoms begin to change. But this change is set in motion when our attitudes become friendly and encouraging. The body hears, and *something* always begins to happen, even if there is not always a complete cure.

Often one of the first changes we notice is in the pain level. When in pain, while sending loving messages to the bodily powers of healing, work also on the pain by visualizing the painful part of the body breathing in and out slowly, gently, as if it had its own mouth and nose. Try this with an arthritic finger. Either before or after doing your finger limbering exercises, let the finger lie relaxed and visualize your whole body breathing through that finger as if it had its own breathing organs and was inhaling the healing light of God through each breath. Let your finger breathe as long as feels comfortable and then return to your ordinary way of breathing. Next, flex the finger. It is an almost incredible pain relief. This localized "breathing" is effective for any part of the body. (Naturally, continue to take any needed medication. God also reaches us through dedicated doctors, and many of God's miracles reach us through medical help.)

Never try to carry the burden of pain and illness alone. Not only does God's help reach us through medical means but also in profound ways through friends or a trusted prayer group. Ask others to hold you through their thoughts and prayers in God's healing light. The combined prayer of even a small group is of inexpressible power. It is significant how often Jesus, in his works of healing, called together a little group of faith, sometimes only two or three people, to help channel his healing power.

. . . If healing is delayed or if it seems likely that it will not come fully in this life, never feel that you are disqualified from praying for others and helping to bring healing to others. This was again shown to me at a recent meeting I attended while in acute pain from lower back spasms. I sat next to a minister who, through neurological illness, had lost the use of his legs and was sitting in an electric wheelchair. He had a most observable loving radiance about him. In the midst of the meeting, my pain suddenly and dramatically left me.

"Did you pray for me?" I asked him afterwards.

"Yes," he answered quietly. "I observed that you were in discomfort, and I channeled God's healing light to you.

"Has this happened before?" I asked.

He hesitated, and then said, "Yes, I have noticed that sometimes God can use me to help others."

I think this was very much Paul's experience when the removal of his thorn in the flesh (whatever it was) was delayed, and he heard God saying to him, "My grace is sufficient for you" (2 Cor 12:9). This does not mean that God wants anyone to be hurt or in wheelchairs, but rather that God can and does bring our lives into creative power even when healing is delayed.

This was an especially significant realization for Paul. The orthodox of many cultures and faiths in his time believed that physical imperfection disqualified a person from the full sacramental service of God and channeling from God.

Unless you were a perfect physical specimen, you were considered neither to be in the true likeness of God nor worthy to be set apart sacrificially for sacramental service to God. Unfortunately, many today still believe or are told by others that if they are chronically ill or disabled, they cannot minister to others. It is not easy for the physically challenged to find churches willing to train and call them as pastors, though their experiences have enriched their powers of compassion and intuitive awareness.

Even in temporary illness, we often hesitate to work for the healing of others. It is true that, when ill, we must learn how to let ourselves receive and be nurtured, and we should not undertake strenuous forms of meditation or intercession. But a quiet visualization of others held in the healing light of God while we rest in bed, the quiet inner speaking of another's name along with the name of Jesus, is prayer of great power.

Notes

1. dia r. thompson, "Anger," in Susan E. Browne et al., eds., *With the Power of Each Breath* (Pittsburg: Cleis Press, 1985), 79–81.

2. Deborah Abbott, "This Body I Love," in Browne, et al., 246–47.

3. Bernie S. Siegel, *Love, Medicine, & Miracles* (New York: Harper & Row, 1986), 120–23.

4. Norman Cousins, *The Healing Heart* (New York: Norton, 1983; New York: Avon Books, 1984), 188–90.

LECTIO
—Mary C. Earle

Mary C. Earle, M.Div., is an Episcopal priest, writer, poet, and retreat director. Her ministry focuses on spiritual direction, contemplative prayer, and interfaith dialogue. She is adjunct professor of pastoral ministry at the Episcopal Theological Seminary of the Southwest in Austin, Texas, and assistant rector of St. Mark's Episcopal Church in San Antonio.

What Is This Text?

In the early years of the church, when texts were laboriously copied by hand and many people were illiterate, this phase of *lectio divina* was a process of recalling the scripture rather than reading it. Hearing was more important then, and so was learning from memory. As the scripture took up residence within the person, becoming one with the person through regular repetition, the phrase or line would come forth in prayer. The person praying began to have within himself or herself an inner text, ready for the direction of the Holy Spirit. The remembered scripture could come unbidden, a gracious bit of direction during a time of discernment. Or the scripture might be more consciously invited through linking it to a particular activity or time of day, as we do with the Episcopal practice of praying the Daily Office. The opening lines of Morning Prayer, taken from Psalm 51:15, "Lord, open our lips / And our mouth shall proclaim your praise," have become part of our remembered scriptural heritage, as well as the heritage of the early years of the devotional practice of the church. Our illness offers us another scripture to read and internalize, another scripture through which the Spirit speaks.

LITERAL INTERPRETATIONS OF ILLNESS

Just as in the early church *lectio* was accomplished through recalling and remembering scripture, so too with the experience of falling ill and living with illness. We are invited to recall and remember. The text in this case is the text of the body, particularly this afflicted body. The body—wedded to the soul and shaping us as unique persons—is itself a living word, spoken into being by the God in whom we live and move and have our being. This living text of the various microcosms of our organs and bodily systems is also a living metaphor, a figure of divine speech that invites our listening. Yet that meaning cannot and should not be assumed, prescribed, or dictated.

Like any rich and intricately detailed text, the body cannot and should not be reduced to one layer of meaning. Have you ever had a high school English teacher who proclaimed the one—and only—meaning of a poem or story? Alternative meanings were not acceptable. Have you ever experienced the literalism of some within the Christian community as they interpret scripture? Both cases are examples of reductionist thinking, where meaning has been reduced to a sound bite, hindering us from knowing the deeper, fuller meaning. When we read on only the simplest, most literal of levels, we often miss the point.

Sadly, this sort of interpretation has also invaded the realm of health and spirituality. Guides to interpreting illness are everywhere, leading those who are ill and vulnerable to simplistic and sometimes guilt-ridden ways of reading their experience. Some authors, for example, imply that emphysema results not so much from environmental toxins or cigarette smoking but from not breathing one's life. Breast cancer signals trouble with womanhood, and so on. While there may be clues about the text of an illness in the organ affected, it is harmful to reduce the experience to this level of direct cause and effect

From within Christian quarters, a different kind of fundamentalism can reign. This is the kind of belief and practice that subjects the sick person to continuous, smug evaluation. Comments such as "You know, if you just prayed harder, your bipolar disorder would be healed" or "God has given you the cancer so that you can learn a lesson" have behind them a theology that has little to do with the Trinity of Love. These comments are based, rather, on fear and uneasiness with mortality. It is fear and anxiety that tend to force us into simplistic interpretations, whether we are interpreting scripture, our lives, or our illnesses.

Again and again, I hear from those under my spiritual direction and from those who participate in my classes that these sorts of comments abound. Because a person who lives with physical or mental affliction is already experiencing a degree of distancing, these comments can be especially injurious. However, when two or three persons whose lives are marked by illness come together, they can support one another in Christ by peeling away interpretations that are false and misleading, if not downright punitive. They can hear what one another's bodies and illnesses are saying. They can offer one another a little community in which to practice *lectio* of the illness.

DISCOVERING THE TEXT

The body, which is a living word from the Word, is a text with many layers of meaning. These layers await our taking the time to encounter them, to listen to them, and to let them illumine one another. This discovery of the text of the body allows us to befriend the body, to perceive this flesh as a wonder, even when we are engaging in terribly difficult medical regimens. Illness, from this perspective, is part of a lifelong encounter with the divine mystery. The person who chooses to engage this reading of the text of illness will not so much be looking to a symbol dictionary or the latest version of "Your illness means . . ." from the best-seller list. The person who chooses this path of *lectio* will be entering a process of deeply listening to the experience, to the body, to the life that unfolds through physical diminishment. This can be daunting. It's like taking off from a well-known shore and setting sail for a new land. It's a little like going on a pilgrimage.

The Metaphor of Pilgrimage: Getting into the Coracle

From the early church in the Celtic lands (now Scotland, Wales, Ireland, Brittany, Cornwall, and the Isle of Man) we receive a version of pilgrimage that serves well as a metaphor for this *lectio* of the body. In Celtic tradition, rather than starting off with a destination in mind, such as Jerusalem or Rome, pilgrims got in a little boat known as a coracle, round in shape with no oars. Once on board, the pilgrim trusted the currents of the sea or the river to take the little boat to a destination hid with Christ. The current was the means by which the pilgrim was brought to the "place of resurrection," the geographical spot where the pilgrim would live out his remaining days and eventually die. But the "place of resurrection" is the place where we encounter the living Christ who has burst the tomb and whose radiant presence frees us from all imprisoning and demeaning interpretations of our lives.

I point to the Celtic pilgrims because the engagement with the text of illness may lead away from well-known shores and familiar interpretations, too. This engagement, without claiming to offer answers or solutions or definitive spiritual insight, calls us to muster the same sort of courage that a Celtic pilgrim needed to have. Setting off toward Jerusalem or Rome was a pilgrimage fraught with danger, but at least the destination was a given. Getting into the coracle involved a degree of trust that most of our religious training has succeeded in extinguishing. When I offer this metaphor for the life of faith in classes, inevitably there is a sharp intake of breath and a chorus of "OH!" We are startled that living faithfully might look like this kind of trust. We have tended to think of faith as a set of propositions about doctrinal truth that we need to affirm intellectually. The metaphor of the pilgrimage in the coracle reminds us that faith and trust are two faces of the same reality, and that faith involves our selves, our souls, and our bodies.

This sort of trust is precisely what we need to honestly engage the experience of illness and to forsake the ready answers that our health-conscious culture provides. This sort of trust invites us out of tombs of literalistic attitudes toward living with illness, into the freedom of the place of our resurrection. We are invited, through this sort of reflection, to befriend the fact of our mortality and creatureliness. We are led to remember, as the Benedictine Rule counsels, to keep death at our shoulder daily. This is not a morbid practice. It is simply an honest one.

For many persons who have been living not only with the stress of illness but also with the stress of others' anxiety for a cure, this trusting may come slowly. But it may also feel dizzily freeing. In my classes, even among those living with a so-called terminal diagnosis, some experience a real quickening of spirit when their own deep intuitions are called forth. When the truth begins to be spoken in love, they may experience "bright sadness," a term used by the early church to encompass joy and pain simultaneously, without negating either. It's ultimately an embrace of the Christian proclamation that even at the grave we make our song: "Alleluia, alleluia, alleluia!" Getting into the coracle, entrusting ourselves to the currents of divine love, and seeking the place of our resurrection implies that we are embracing the truth of our mortality—we wouldn't need a place of resurrection if we weren't mortal. As we learn to number our days, and to remember that each person's days are numbered, living, even living with an illness, becomes a process of moving toward the infinite love from which we were birthed.

The Culture of Being Healthy

In the United States today we live in a culture frightened to the core by illness. Health is upheld as a value, and for good reason. We benefit when we honor our bodies through a good balance of work, rest, exercise, and play. We are healthier when we pay attention to nutrition, tending to the ways that we feed ourselves and our children. Preventive medicine has always been a wise course, and we are remembering its virtues.

At the same time, underneath our obsession with health is a lurking fear of death. As a culture, we tend to deny the fact that we will die, that our days are numbered. We persist in behaviors that keep us from honoring the aging process—from a perpetual depiction of lithe, too slender, almost naked young female bodies in advertising to a strange fixation on the whiteness of our teeth.

I am convinced that in part our tendencies to apply various literalisms to illness come from this distress about mortality. The underlying fear and anxiety about dying are not directly engaged, so they roil around inside us, and push us toward simplistic and impulsive solutions. But solutions are for problems; life is for living, even when the living is marked by the limitation of physical or mental impairment.

Even the church participates in the strange amnesia of forgetting that we are creatures. Our church programming endlessly cranks out events and classes geared toward ceaseless activity. We behave as if being still, reflecting, and keeping silence were not an essential part of Christian spiritual practice. We tend to encourage busyness rather than reflection, activity rather than rest in God's providence. As church newsletters tout events, congregants assume that living the life of faith means going to meetings and shoehorning more activity into an already overscheduled day.

This incessant doing tends to produce simplistic interpretations and shallow answers. It also subtly implies that if your life isn't characterized by productivity and action, you're not very valuable. However, as Roman Catholic priest and author Henri Nouwen has pointed out, the New Testament is not concerned with productivity. The New Testament is concerned with fruitfulness, an organic and mysterious bearing of life that comes from the root of our being.

RECALLING AND REMEMBERING

Within this larger context, the practice of *lectio divina* with the body, with a physical or mental malady, invites you to recall and remember. You can't rush, and you can't expect a quick-fix remedy for the dilemmas of living with illness. *Lectio divina* applied to the body invites the quiet, deep listening that leads us into the freedom of the God who brought us into being, who knit us together in our mothers' wombs. In a way, when a person begins to practice this kind of recalling, this initial reading of the text of the illness, it is not unlike being led out of captivity into freedom. In this case, the captivity is that of solutions, answers, and meanings too quickly applied to the experience of living with illness, a captivity that squelches the imagination and binds it with rules. Faithful practice of *lectio* with illness, on the other hand, allows the Holy Spirit within us to participate in the search for meaning.

This practice of recalling also may take us into memories we would just as soon not revisit. Often the experience of falling ill is deeply distressing, and the recalled images, sounds, smells, and pains may present us with feelings we would rather ignore.

There may have been moments that, in retrospect, begin to register in their full chaos and assault. It is important to remember:

1. You do not need to remember fully something that seems too fraught with emotion, particularly if you are still in a weakened state. Leave it alone until the appropriate time for engaging the memory.

2. You may want to invite a trusted friend or a spiritual director to accompany you as you recall particular moments or phases of the experience of falling ill.

3. If you feel you are ready to recall a moment in the illness that was particularly painful or wrenching, approach the recalling slowly and gently.

COMPASSION TOWARD OURSELVES

When we begin doing this practice of lectio, many of us are still vulnerable physically, psychologically, emotionally, and spiritually. So enter the process with care and compassion. As we begin to revisit those moments when we heard the physician say, "I'm sorry; the mass is malignant," or when a sudden onslaught of pain left us undefended, we encounter real fear that may have been buried or hid from our sight. We begin to pay attention to those moments when the room was spinning as we took in hard news, changing everything irrevocably. In this process we may retrieve impressions, sensory experiences, momentary glimpses that serve to guide us in living with the illness.

Isabel had been taken to an emergency room in extreme pain, and though her initial hours in the hospital were a blur, she began to recall a body-memory of a hand on her forehead. Though Isabel was not sure whose hand it was, her body remembered the touch, which gave her the gift of knowing she was accompanied even in the throes of the pain. Revisiting this memory, this page of the text of her illness, proved to be a touchstone for Isabel in the long months of recovery that followed, giving her a sense that a Presence was standing with her through thick and thin. Eventually she was led to write a note to the staff of the emergency room. Not knowing to whom specifically her thanks should be directed, she decided to thank them all, for it seemed that the one person who stood with her represented the work of the community of doctors, nurses, and technicians. Isabel's reading of this moment in the text of her illness entailed recalling those embodied memories that were directly connected to the trauma of her pain and the sudden onset of her illness. As she read this experience, she began to slowly "read, mark, learn, and inwardly digest," bringing prayer to the hours in the emergency room. She let herself be honest as she uncovered her own feelings of vulnerability and fear, realizing how stunned she was, to her very core, by the pain. All of this was read and remembered.

For Isabel, the reading, this *lectio* movement, took some months. The memories were too strong and too diffuse to be digested quickly. She did the reading with her spiritual director and with a trusted friend. As Isabel read the memories of what her body went through, a deepening tenderness and reverence for her own flesh began to emerge. With time, gratitude for her body and her life started to well up, and she found herself remembering a line from a hymn: "When through the deep waters our pathways shall lie / thy grace all sufficient will be our supply." She was able to read the text of her illness honestly, without embellishment or glossing over. She discovered that in the midst of so much crushing pain and disorientation, there were glimmers of gracious Presence.

Practice

Before beginning to recall the text of your illness, you may wish to invite a trusted friend, family member, or spiritual companion to accompany you. Though the meditations may be done in solitude, the reflection on those readings may release strong emotion. Having another person in whom you can confide and with whom you can reflect will give you support in prayer and in remembering. Choose someone who will not interfere with your own process of interpretation, and who will also courteously allow you to enter the *lectio* process gently and at your own pace. Anyone who is living with illness is slowly discovering the new identity that comes in the aftermath of physical distress. This newly emerging identity is tender and vulnerable and needs to be entrusted to persons of wisdom, kindness, and utmost compassion.

RECALLING

After I got home from my first hospitalization, I discovered that I had sore spots from being given shots that I had no memory of receiving, and I had to ask my husband what had happened. Depending on how your illness began, this may happen to you, too. Your memories may be either crystal clear or a bit hazy, and sometimes in the crush of an acute onset of illness, both the physical trauma and the pain medication may cause blank places in memory. Don't fret if there are moments—or days—you don't remember. Give your memories time to emerge.

1. As you begin the practice of *lectio*, start with the affected part of your body. If you have a chronic pulmonary disease, for example, begin by noticing your lungs and recalling the memories associated with the onset of the disease or the initial diagnosis. Breathing gently and steadily allows your focus to rest on the affected organs, limbs, and systems. Let yourself pay attention to images, memories, and impressions that come to mind, and if something in particular keeps returning to your awareness, notice it and write it down.

2. As you enter the process of recalling, note your feelings. There may be some sadness, relief, gratitude, fear, wonder, despair. Do not judge your feelings; simply allow them to be known and to be received. If you are a person for whom writing is an expressive outlet, you may want to write about your feelings. Others may wish to talk about them, or to paint

them. The point is to acknowledge the particular text of your illness, allowing yourself the space and time to discern the layers of bodily sensation, memory, and emotion. Don't hurry; don't set a deadline. Be as slow and deliberate as necessary.

READING A SCAR

If you've had surgery, the reading of the scar may be the place to start your *lectio*. Regarding the incision lets the reality of the surgery sink in. In the case of mastectomy, the incisional site is also a site of amputation. The scar itself may be read in a variety of ways. For some, it may be a sign of loss. For others, a sign of both loss *and* life. A scar is a clear sign that something has happened, that a body has been cut into and has been altered. As an outward and visible sign, the scar may intimate both wounding and healing. If you have a surgical scar, the following suggestions for reading that flesh are one way to engage this text.

1. Choose a position that will allow you to touch the scar. If it is on your back, you may want to stand or to sit on a stool. Begin by noticing your breath. Allow yourself to inhale and exhale gently, pausing for a beat at the end of the inhalation. Breathe in this manner for several minutes, praying, "My body shall rest in hope" (Ps 16:9).

2. Gently trace the scar with your fingers. Let your fingers rest on the scar tissue as you return to the gentle breathing and praying of "My body shall rest in hope." After several minutes, continue touching the scar, and listen. Notice what emotions, associations, and memories come to you. Bless the scar tissue with a simple prayer of thanksgiving for the body's ability to grow new cells: "Thanks be to God for a body that creates new tissue." You may want to sign the scar with a cross or perform another gesture, ritual, or prayer that is more fitting to your circumstance and body. The point is to become aware of the body's injury and its capacity to knit together.

3. In your journal, write about this experience. Allow yourself to read this text with care by writing about your impressions. If you found the meditation to be unhelpful, write that. If the touching of the scar made you uneasy, write that. Be honest and start where you are.

4. Offer a prayer in response to the reading of the scar.

READING A CHRONIC AILMENT

If you live with a chronic illness like diabetes or lupus or chronic fatigue syndrome, how do you begin to read its text? One way to begin is to start with a presenting physical challenge. If you are regularly administering shots of insulin, that may be the place to begin reading. If you have the troublesome symptoms of chronic fatigue syndrome, start with one symptom. Let yourself focus on this symptom, not to examine but simply to listen.

1. Following the basic pattern of getting in a comfortable physical position, breathing gently and steadily, notice your feelings toward the detail that is your beginning text. For example, how does the flesh respond to the entry of the diabetic syringe? Have you done this so long that there is a kind of familiarity or is it new enough to cause distress? Place your fingers gently on the place where you are presently administering the injections and continue to breathe gently as you pray, "My body shall rest in hope." Listen for the associations and emotions that come to you while reflecting on the dispersal of the insulin through the tiny viaducts of your body, on the minute channels that connect all of the tissues and allow the insulin to circulate. Give thanks for those systems that allow you to live with your ailment. Bless the skin through which the needle enters, using a simple prayer of your own devising.

2. In your journal, write about the prayer and the experience of noticing your body's effective dispersal of the insulin. Remember that your body has been knit together by God. Notice whatever resistances or confusions may arise. Be honest in your responses and in your prayer. If the prayer becomes "I hate this business of injecting myself with insulin," begin there. Tell yourself and God the truth.

   On the other hand, if you begin to realize that much about your flesh is marvelous, even though you live with illness, let that be the prayer. "I will thank you because I am marvelously made; your works are wonderful and I know it well" (Ps 139:14).

FURTHER SUGGESTIONS

Your body may suggest how to begin the reading of its text. Though you may think this statement is ridiculous, sometimes the presentation of an ache or a twinge or a soreness will provide a place to begin. The important thing is to begin, and to do so without presupposing the outcome. *Lectio* with a body that suffers from illness is the beginning of an extended conversation, a befriending of your flesh that has been bruised and incised. Reading your text begins with your specific illness, with your intuition and experience indicating where to start, how to pray, what ritual to employ. Above all, allow yourself to become kindly aware of your body, not only of what has been hurt but also of what is mending, healing, and working. Notice what is already present, both sickness and health. Read the full text, not the cheap summary. Read with slow and merciful care, mindful of the divine compassion that holds you in life.

SUFFERING, SPIRITUALITY, AND HEALTH CARE
–Daniel P. Sulmasy

Daniel Sulmasy, OFM, MD, Ph.D., holds the Sisters of Charity Chair in Ethics at St. Vincent Catholic Medical Centers, St. Vincent's Manhattan, and serves as professor of medicine and director of the Bioethics Institute of New York Medical College, Valhalla, New York. He is a Franciscan friar who serves as editor-in-chief of *Theoretical Medicine and Bioethics.*

There are those who say that the only proper responses to human suffering are to relieve it, where possible, or otherwise to remain silent. People who suffer, it is said, want either relief or consolation. They do not want lectures.

There is much truth to such remarks. But clinicians know the simple reality that relief is not always possible and that consolation is not always immediately apparent. In the face of this, is mute silence all there is to consolation? . . .

Pain and Suffering

Suffering must be distinguished from pain. Not all suffering is caused by pain and not all pain causes suffering. Pain is a physiological phenomenon. It results from the stimulation of certain types of nerve cells. Pain experts teach that pain signals can be distinguished into three basic types—somatic, visceral, and neuropathic. Somatic pains are from the surface of the body, visceral pains are from inside, and neuropathic pains are due to damage to nerves themselves. Psychologists and pain experts also classify pain on the basis of duration into acute and chronic. These distinctions should be readily apparent and meaningful for every clinician, but they are specifications of a variety of experiences that human beings share with most multicellular animals.

Pain is also affected by the psychological milieu in which it is experienced (something that human beings also share, to some extent, with animals). For example, it is well known that different ethnic groups have different experiences of identical painful stimuli.[1] Pain signals undergo enormously complex cognitive processing. Despite the fact that there appear to be only three basic types of pain, human beings classify their experiences of pain in rather remarkable ways—as sharp, dull, burning, aching, crampy, pressure, hankering, gnawing, and the like. And the duration of pain seems to make a difference. Acute pain that is over quickly is dealt with quite differently from pain that is of a lower level of intensity but never goes away.

Suffering, on the other hand, is something very different from pain. Suffering has less to do with the stimulation of pain fibers than it does with the experience of persons. What I mean by this is something far different from a comment about the cognitive processing of pain signals in some very broad sense. Suffering is experienced in relation to one's situation in life. One can experience pain without suffering, as an athlete in training might experience the pain of exertion toward a new limit of physical endurance, but not understand this to be suffering. Or, one can suffer without experiencing pain, as when marital discord causes immense suffering without the slightest bit of physical pain. The field of suffering is wider than pain, wider than sickness, wider even than death. As John Paul II has remarked, "What we express by the word *suffering* seems to be particularly essential to the nature of human beings."[2]

Suffering and Being Human

If suffering has more to do with the nature of being human than it does with pain per se, it follows that one must understand what it means to be human in order to understand what it means to suffer. While such a statement may seem simple, it is, in fact, very significant. To understand what it means to suffer, one must understand what it means to be human. No wonder, then, that suffering has been called a mystery. It is as deep a mystery as being human.

Even when the entire sequence of the human genome has been elucidated, only the most foolish of scientists will dare to suggest that he or she thereby has explained what it means to be human. Likewise, no one will ever be able to identify the tracks along which "suffering fibers" travel in the central nervous system, or identify the "suffering area" of the brain. The body has pain centers, but there are no suffering centers. There could be no such thing. Suffering is not a part of the brain. It is a part of the mystery of being human.

Some have thought that a distinction between merely being alive and being a person is a useful distinction in discussions of suffering, asserting that it is only persons who suffer. Prominent among these authors is Dr. Eric Cassell, who has offered a list of the characteristics that he suggests define a person. From this list, he proceeds to discuss suffering. Among the characteristics he lists as necessary ingredients for personhood are memory, relationships, personality, having a body, being aware of the future, and being oriented to the transcendent.[3]

This is not a bad list, and I deeply admire Cassell's work. But it seems to me that this sort of list leaves open the danger that some members of the human family won't measure up to Cassell's definition of a person. I think that such a list is better thought of as a list of potential spheres of human suffering. For example, if I lose my memory, on Cassell's theory I become less human. That would seem to imply that I would be less prone to suffering. But this seems wrong. It seems to me that in such a situation I would suffer greatly as a human person who has lost his memory. Similarly, in a real way, I would suffer if I were to enter into a permanent coma, even though I might be unaware of relationships or of the future, unable to express a personality, and robbed of memory in a purgatory that would leave me unable to pass over into the transcendent. If only persons suffer, and if to be a person is to have all of the characteristics on Cassell's list, then human beings in permanent comas would not be persons and could not be thought to suffer. But most people would say that there is a real sense in which a person who is in a permanent coma is suffering. A person in a permanent coma might not feel pain, but it still makes sense to say that such a person is suffering. The characteristics mentioned in lists like Cassell's had best not be looked upon as necessary characteristics for membership in the personhood "club." They are all characteristics of normal species functioning for human beings and spheres in which human beings can suffer. But it is not necessary to be possessed of all of these characteristics in order to be human. And it is not necessary that one or all of these characteristics should be functioning normally in order to say that a human being is suffering. To understand suffering, it is necessary to understand what it means to be human. No short list will tell anyone what it means to be human.

Human Being and the Transcendent

Two characteristics from Cassell's list are, if understood from a spiritual perspective, definitely constitutive of the human. These are not themselves sufficient to define the human, but they are the only two characteristics on Cassell's lists that are truly necessary. These two essential characteristics are (1) the fundamental orientation of the human species toward the transcendent, and (2) the fact that being human always means being-in-relationship. All human beings share these characteristics in radical equality, regardless of any personal powers, talents, characteristics, or circumstances. No human beings will ever lack these characteristics, no matter what should befall them. Further, these characteristics do not admit of degrees. One cannot have more or less of them.

In some ways, these two characteristics are two sides of the same coin. Understood in an explicitly religious sense, since God is the ultimate term of transcendence, orientation toward the transcendent and being in relationship with God are simply different ways to express the same phenomenon.

The relationship to the transcendent is already a given in human existence, albeit in an implicit or "prethematic" manner. And although conscious experience is not necessary in order to have this relationship, this relationship is a precondition for conscious experience. Certainly it is true that human beings can have direct access to the transcendent through religious experience, identified as such. But those who would deny that they have religious experience cannot deny any and all experience of the transcendent. This experience of transcendence comes to human beings through intellectual, moral, and aesthetic experiences, as well as through explicitly religious experiences.

To recognize any limit is to know that there is something beyond that limit. To know finitude is to know the infinite. And this is knowledge of the transcendent, even if it is never named as religious experience.

Human beings understand horizons. Visibility, for example, has its limits. But to recognize a limit implies that one knows of existence beyond the limit.

Even to ask a question is to recognize an intellectual limit. To know death is to recognize a limit as well.

Human beings also know evil. And this knowledge is only possible if one has an understanding of another transcendental category—the good. To know evil, one must know the good. To recognize injustice, one must know justice. Human beings may argue a great deal about what the good is, or about whether this or that particular state of affairs is just, or what this implies for human behavior. But all seem to acknowledge that there are such things as good and evil, just and unjust. And they seem to want to strive beyond the limits of evil. The quest for the good is a quest for ultimacy, a quest for the transcendent.

Human beings also know beauty. They can recognize the inherent unity that emerges from the particularity and diversity of a set of paint marks on a canvas. They recognize in Michelangelo's *David* something more than a hunk of marble—more, even, than the representation of a man in the marble. Such knowledge is possible only if one has had an experience of the transcendent. Arguments abound about exactly what is worthy of the descriptive adjective *beautiful*, but no one denies that there are such things as ugliness and beauty. Human beings create works of art, write symphonies, and sculpt statues. Human beings do not create works of art simply to enhance the mating process or to warn of approaching predators. Human beings seek the ultimacy of the beautiful.

All of these experiences of the ultimate *can* be ways to experience the transcendence of God. Genuine religious experience may be had either through direct experience of God or through an intellectual, moral, or aesthetic experience that culminates in the ultimacy of God. But even those who would deny the experience of God cannot deny the experience of ultimacy.

Human Being and Relationship

In Jewish and Christian thought, each and every human being is created in the image and the likeness of the transcendent God. Human beings are defined much more by this relationship with God than by any particular powers that one or another member of the species exercises. This is what gives human beings their dignity.

I frequently make the mistake, when typing, of reversing the positions of the "l" and the "a" in the word *relationship*. What appears on the page is "realtionship." I actually find this mistake instructive. Sounding out the mistake I repeatedly make suggests that relationship is "real sonship." For human beings, to be real is to be in relationship. To be real is to be a child of God, to be in relationship with God. This being-in-relationship with God is ineradicable. Human beings can ignore it in themselves or in others. They can reject it in themselves or in others. But they cannot destroy it. It is already a given in every human situation.

Human beings are also in special relationship with each other. Being human *means* being in relationship with other human beings. And if one takes seriously the revealed truth that all human beings are created in the image and likeness of

God, then one will readily understand that all human relationships reflect the one fundamental relationship that each human being has with God. This is the truth expressed by John Donne in his famous meditation: "No man is an island, entire of itself. Each is a part of the main, a piece of the whole. If a clod should be washed into the sea, Europe is the less."[4]

Thus the value or dignity of being human is not the Hobbesian notion that this is "his Price—that is to say, so much as would be given for the use of his Power: and therefore is not absolute, but a thing dependent upon the need and judgment of another."[5] Ultimate human dignity does not change with market conditions. Every human being is a child of God, made in the image and the likeness of God. The dignity of the human is based on this relationship with God as Father and, consequently, with all other human beings as brothers and sisters, equally children of the one God.

Suffering and Finitude

Taking everything I have written thus far together, I want to offer one simple insight into the spiritual meaning of suffering. I am not offering an explanation of suffering. I am not trying to explain *why* people suffer. I am simply making a suggestion about what it means to suffer. My suggestion is this: All suffering may be understood, in its root form, as the experience of finitude. Human beings are fundamentally oriented toward the infinite term of transcendence, yet aware that everything about them is radically limited. Human beings are oriented toward the truth, yet plagued by their nature as fallible, ignorant, and prone to make choices that are opposed to the truth—lying, cheating, deceiving, and exaggerating their greatness. Human beings are oriented toward the good, yet live in a world plagued by physical evils, such as pain and disease, and prone to make choices of hatred, bigotry, and selfishness. Human beings are oriented toward the beautiful, yet aware that they are not themselves totally beautiful, that they all grow old, that their beauty fades, and that they are prone to make choices of the ugly and to disfigure each other and the world. Human beings are oriented toward infinite freedom, yet live in a world in which choices are severely constrained by nature and are prone to make choices that enslave themselves and others. Human beings are oriented toward the infinite yet live in a world that is finite. They lead lives that are marked by ineluctable death and make choices that lead to finitude and to death, sometimes even killing each other and killing themselves.

Suffering is part of the nature of being human. Suffering is the experience that human beings have of knowing themselves as finite creatures who have been given the gift of a freedom that orients them to the infinite. Human beings are susceptible to suffering every time they make a choice, because to choose one thing is to give up something else. Every free choice is therefore a reminder of finitude. And to be reminded of finitude is to suffer.

Human beings are also susceptible to suffering whenever they experience pain, because pain has a way of focusing their attention on their vulnerability, making them aware of some threat to their existence, or of some rent in their bodily integrity that foreshadows the day of dissolution. Chronic pain has a way of engendering worse suffering than acute pain because the reminder of finitude is constant, not short-lived. Every pain is a reminder of finitude. And to be reminded of finitude is to suffer.

Human beings are also susceptible to suffering when their choices are constrained and controlled, because to lose control is to be reminded of one's radical insufficiency and radical dependence upon God. To be under the control of others or of natural processes outside one's will is to be reminded of one's finitude. And to be reminded of finitude is to suffer.

Finally, human beings suffer whenever they become ill because all illness smells of death, mortality, and finitude. Illness imposes limits. Illness causes pain. Those who are ill always lose some measure of control. To be ill is to be reminded of one's finitude. And to be reminded of one's finitude is to suffer.

Suffering and Health Care

The suffering of the sick and the dying is perhaps the most basic form of suffering. This is the true etymology of the word *patient*. It is from the Latin, *patiens*, "one who suffers." Every cough, every drop of blood, every wave of nausea is a reminder of finitude. Finitude is the message, and illness is the messenger.

Understanding this may help physicians and nurses in caring for patients. It may help to avert the judgmentalism of those who would complain that their patients are exaggerating their symptoms or bothering them with trivial concerns. After all, whether the patient's back pain is caused by a pulled muscle, a slipped disc, depression, or metastatic cancer, the patient, one of the not yet dead, is being reminded that the day of death is coming. On the cosmic scale, then, the significance of each patient's back pain is exactly the same. Whether it is caused by depression or by cancer, back pain implies finitude. It still evokes for each patient, in some very real way, the mystery of death.

In another sense, however, to say that the patient's suffering is a mystery is not helpful in the concreteness of daily clinical practice. What does it mean to say that suffering is a mystery? If it only means that it is something that cannot be explained, this is hardly an explanation.

I would like to avoid thinking of God as merely the answer to the questions for which I have no good reply. . . . God is not a stopgap for incomplete knowledge. The mystery of suffering can only be understood in terms of the mystery of being human. Being human inevitably involves being in relationship with the transcendent, being oriented to the transcendent, and yet possessing a knowledge of radical incompleteness and finitude. . . .

◦⟨◎⟩◦

Being Human: Love and Suffering

I will state it again: To understand the meaning of suffering, one must understand the meaning of being human. Suffering is an ineluctable part of the human condition. Just as all human beings will die, all human beings will suffer. To live a life characterized by a denial of the existence of suffering, or a life of constant effort to escape suffering, is to live a life of delusion.

The philosopher of religion John Hick asks those who would deny this fact to try to imagine a world without suffering.[6] Imagine a world in which no one who was ever shot, run over by a car, or fell from a ladder ever suffered any pain, injury, or death. Such a world would be very strange. It would be a world devoid of heroes, for instance, because there would never be any danger and therefore there would never be anyone in need of rescue. Or imagine a world in which a thief could steal a million dollars without anyone suffering the loss of a penny of it. Such a world would be absurd. Good and evil would cease to be categories by which to judge the fruits of human interactions. No one could ever possibly be wronged. Mercy would have no meaning. Justice would have no point.

In fact, it is not hyperbole to say that there is no love without suffering. To paraphrase the first letter of John, "anyone who says that he or she loves and does not suffer, is a liar."

Once again, I am not attempting to explain *why* anyone suffers. I am only acknowledging the fact that people do suffer and that physicians, nurses, and other clinicians are involved firsthand in this fact every day. Clinicians are not specially equipped to deal with suffering in ways that other human beings are not. They can treat pain and disease and a few other medical conditions that *cause* suffering, but they cannot treat suffering itself. There are no pills to treat suffering. Suffering is not a symptom. It is part of the mystery of being human. Clinicians have no direct therapy for suffering. They can only respond with human compassion toward those who are suffering, treating those conditions that give rise to suffering acutely or chronically. But when medicine, a finite art, meets its limits, all the clinician can do is to be compassionately present.

To be compassionate is to be fully human. As a finite creature oriented toward the infinite, I can only transcend my own finitude by reaching out actively, beyond the limits of my individual existence, to touch the infinite in a fellow finite creature. When I am compassionate, I transcend my own finitude and reach the infinite in the suffering other. This is where the infinite orientation of my humanity points—toward the limitless, uncharted sea of compassionate love.

This is why God, in his compassion, *had* to become human. God's infinity had to know the suffering of human finitude and still reach out beyond it to embrace the infinite orientation of his suffering creatures. Jesus understood the necessity of walking down this path no better than we do. He asked that the cup pass him by. In the end, he recognized that it could not.

Thus, I have faith that God can be found in the midst of the suffering that is the stock and trade of health care. I struggle to understand it. I am certain that I cannot explain it.

Compassion is a manifestation of love. And love, whatever else it may be, is something that involves choices. Love is the one true source of freedom in the midst of the suffering human finitude entails. Choosing between options is a condition of freedom in finitude. Every free choice involves suffering. To say yes to love involves saying no to something else. One cannot both help the homeless man who has had a seizure on the street where one is walking and get to the grocery store before it closes. One cannot be charitable toward anyone without giving something—time, effort, money, or something else. But this is the true paradox of compassionate love. By making the choice to love and facing the suffering and the finitude that love requires, one transcends finitude and embraces the ultimate freedom of boundless love.

God does not want *anyone* to suffer for the sake of suffering. But no one can avoid suffering altogether. And to make the fulfillment of one's own plans the central theme of one's life is to try to avoid the finitude, suffering, and lack of control that compassion and love demand. No physician or nurse is worthy of the name Christian if he or she continually shrinks from the suffering that compassion and love demand in response to the suffering of others. Such suffering is not a test from God, but only the simultaneous embracing of the human condition and the choice to love.

God gives everyone the freedom to choose, as well as the knowledge both that life involves choices and that choices involve suffering. Love calls forth compassionate responses to the suffering of others. Only choices that are made in love can transcend that suffering.

Suffering and Salvation

Suffering, one's own and that of others, can be the occasion of salvation. If one suffers and in that suffering experiences limitation and finitude but still manages to hold out hope for the infinite, faith in what lies beyond the horizon, and love for the God who calls everyone forth into his marvelous light (1 Pet 2:9), one is on the road to salvation. This is the way Jesus has shown. As St. Paul has written: "We are afflicted in every way, but not constrained; perplexed, but not driven to despair; persecuted, but not abandoned; struck down, but not destroyed; always carrying about in the body the dying of Jesus, so that the life of Jesus may also be manifested in our bodies" (2 Cor 4:8–11).

To relieve the suffering of another is also an occasion of salvation. But this cannot be done just with medicines. Medical treatment can eliminate some of the causes of suffering by forestalling the moment of death or by restoring some functional freedoms, but only compassionate love can overcome suffering itself. Suffering means finitude and limitation. Love means infinity and freedom. Just as Jesus did not ignore the woman who reached out to him from the faceless crowd of needy people and touched him (Luke 8:40–48), so too, health care professionals who claim to follow him cannot ignore the suffering of their patients. Christian health care professionals have a special responsibility to care for the needs of the sick, whom they have pledged to serve. Treating diseases and managing symptoms is not enough. Suffering is not a disease or a symptom and cannot be cured or eliminated by medicine. Suffering is only healed through compassionate love. In imitating the healing work of Christ, Christian clinicians enter more deeply into the kingdom of God. In following the example of the Good Samaritan, they heal with the wine of fervent zeal and with the oil of compassion.

But they are also called to humility. Medicine does not have an answer for all causes of suffering, not even all suffering of a physical nature. Medicine today does an incredibly good job of treating pain. Innovations such as the simultaneous use of multiple kinds of adjuvant pain medicines, the administration of narcotics through patches on the skin, nerve blocks, continuous infusions of medicines into the spinal fluid, and patient-controlled analgesia, in which patients can give themselves (within safe limits) extra doses of narcotics in addition to a continuous baseline infusion, are all wonderful. But they are not perfect. Most, but not all pain can be controlled. But even if it could, not all suffering is caused by pain. Feelings of fear, loneliness, embarrassment, helplessness, hopelessness, and abandonment are all aspects of suffering that morphine does not touch.

Nonetheless, health care professionals can still be healers in situations dominated by these sorts of suffering. Healing, in such situations, consists in the acknowledgment of the reality of the suffering, in expressions of empathy and compassion, in silent presence, and in the process of reminding the patient that he or she still has intrinsic dignity, still has meaning and value, even in the midst of dependency and fear. Genuine healing requires compassion. Only through compassion can one touch the infinite in the suffering other.

In a Christian context, one can appreciate that it is no accident that many of the great saints have had profound experiences of God in the midst of immense personal suffering. I, for my own part, sometimes think that I ought to take off my shoes before entering the room of a patient who is facing death with real faith, hope, and love. As a physician, I find such experiences to be encounters with the Holy.

John Paul II has written of the virtue of perseverance in the face of suffering. He writes, "[I]n doing this, the individual unleashes hope, which maintains in him the conviction that suffering will not get the better of him, that it will not deprive him of his dignity as a human being, a dignity linked to the awareness of the meaning of life."[7]

Suffering is only possible for creatures that have dignity and that search for meaning.

Suffering, Christ, and Health Care

The Gospels do not offer a neat theological answer to the problem of suffering. All that the Gospels offer is Christ himself as an example. Once again: To understand the mystery of suffering requires an understanding of the human. Suffering is part of being human. God's understanding of human suffering reaches a complete expression in the suffering of Jesus, who, as fully human, suffers like any and every other human being. In Jesus, God understands our suffering from the inside out. Jesus in the garden of Gethsemane is the God who sweats with us, bleeds with us, suffers with us. Jesus at Golgotha is the God who dies for us and ultimately rises for us. There simply is no resurrection without the cross. In Jesus, God takes on the limitations of human finitude and transcends them through divine love. He shows us the path. The way of truth and life laid out for us passes through Gethsemane and Golgotha.

Health care professionals can make the Way of the Cross every day. They see patients live out their own unique passion plays, subsumed under the passion of Christ. They see patients unjustly condemned to painful diagnoses. They see them scorned, misunderstood, unable to continue their work, abandoned, and even mocked for their infirmities. They see them fall and get up, fall and get up, and fall and get up again and again and again. They see them take up huge crosses that they do not deserve. They see people who seem to come out of nowhere to help them. They see the women, always the women, who attend to the most basic needs of the dying in their final hours and days. They hear the dying cry out in prayers of warning for all the living. They dumbly witness the physical pains of patients that sometimes seem to tear muscle and nerve away from bone. They see patients who seem fixed somewhere between earth and heaven, hanging there for what seems to be an eternity. They offer unctions that can sometimes seem as effective in the face of all this as vinegar and hyssop. They are often among those left standing, when it is finally finished, in blood and water and tears, offering faint comfort to family and friends. They send the bodies away to be anointed and buried.

But if they can see Christ in every patient's Golgotha, if they can understand that hope has more to do with the human spirit than it does with prognostication,[8] if they can see the resurrection that is promised for all who suffer in love, they will know that God is with them in their work. I pray that such insight might come to all those physicians and nurses who are confused by the suffering of their patients, fearful, and disenchanted with their work. It may be that they will learn this from some ordinary man or woman with as ordinary an occupation as a gardener, or from some stranger they meet walking along a road or on a beach, or in some experience they might have behind the locked doors of an upper room.

The Teacher of these insights awaits them. He has come for an urgent visit and has already taken a seat in the waiting room.

Notes

1. H. P. Greenwald, "Interethnic Differences in Pain Perception," *Pain* 44 (1991): 157–63.

2. John Paul II, "Salvifici Doloris," *Origins* 13 (February 23, 1984), 609–24.

3. Eric J. Cassell, *The Nature of Suffering and the Goals of Medicine* (New York: Oxford University Press, 1991), 37–43.

4. John Donne, Meditation No. 17, "Now, this Bell tolling softly for another, saies to me, Thou must die," in *Devotions Upon Emergent Occasions*, ed. Anthony Raspa (Montreal and London: McGill-Queen's University Press, 1975), 86–90.

5. Thomas Hobbes, *Leviathan*, 42, ed. Richard Tuck (Cambridge, UK: Cambridge University Press, 1991), 63.

6. John Hick, *Evil and the God of Love* (London: MacMilllan, 1966), 340–45.

7. John Paul II, "Salvifici Doloris," point 23.

8. Vaclav Havel, *Disturbing the Peace* (New York: Vintage, 1991), 181.

FOR PERSONAL REFLECTION

1. Grieving the loss of one's health or physical abilities is hard work. What has been your experience with such grief? Has it been informed by your faith? By your theology? Has it informed your faith or theology? In what way?

2. It is possible to feel more than one way about a situation—though too often, in sorting out our feelings, we try to identify the one true feeling. Early Christians used the phrase "bright sadness" to encompass joy and pain simultaneously. What are the various feelings you have had about illness? How can one's heart be enlarged to encompass all the feelings?

3. Wuellner says, "Our bodies are working with full force to preserve and keep us well, like a brave friend carrying our burden and fighting our battles. It must be allowed to do its full work without distraction. . . ." What has been your experience of caring for yourself in illness? In caring for others in their illnesses? Is there a difference? If so, why?

FOR GROUP DISCUSSION

1. Witnessing another's suffering is something most of us would instinctively rather not do. What gives a person the ability to be present to another's suffering?

2. When one is ill, a common question is: "Why is this happening?" Several answers have been alluded to: Some say God allows illness to teach us something; some say God grieves with us in illness; some believe that we

are punished by illness. To you, what is the meaning of illness? To what degree do humans invite their own illnesses? To what degree are we "innocent victims"?

3. Sulmasy says, "Human beings suffer whenever they become ill because all illness smells of death, mortality, and finitude." In what ways do our underlying fear and anxiety about mortality and death influence our experience of illness, pain and suffering?

5.
Health Care and Justice

A Litany of Penitence for Health Care
Modified from "A Lamentation" by Patricia Benner, RN, Ph.D.

God our Shalom and our Shikinah, our Healer and Reconciler, our Advocate and Comforter: Hear us as we confess to you the ways in which we have failed to live into the dream of health and salvation that you desire for us.

We have forgotten life as blessing and gift, and we seek to control it.
We confess to you, O Lord
We are quick to hide behind our expertise and to cover over our feelings. We constrain our own possibilities, preferring predictability and control.
We confess to you, O Lord
We have become invisible members of corporate systems of health as commodity, seeking to have people manage their health in order to minimize costs. We lament our invisibility while fearing visibility.
We confess to you, O Lord
We are suspicious of the possibilities of mercy and generosity, fearing that grace and forgiveness would wreck our systems of control.
We confess to you, O Lord

We fail to stand alongside the wounded and suffering, admitting our common humanity. We try to fix their wounds, their failed lifestyle, and their lack of individual control.
Have mercy on us, Lord
We no longer understand our community and our stories as sources of healing. We have lost the stories that create us, sustain us and bind us together as supplicants and celebrants.
Have mercy on us, Lord
We have sought freedom as disconnectedness and disengagement, as freedom from instead of freedom to be and to be with others. We who would bring healing and be healed have lost our place to stand.
Have mercy on us, Lord

We have used suffering as a tool of pity and a source of blame. We have experienced suffering as an embarrassment, as failure, and as a momentary breakdown in the technological promise of control. We have failed to be taught, healed and comforted by suffering.

Accept our repentance, Lord

We have made recovery into a never-ending project instead of an epiphany and a new beginning.

Accept our repentance, Lord

We have made being healthy a career, and forgotten its giftedness. We have lost our ability to rejoice in it, protect it and preserve it. We have forgotten health as blessing and gift.

Accept our repentance, Lord

Through the power of the Holy Spirit, make us anew in the image of your Son, Jesus Christ. Amen.

It is all too easy to consider health a personal venture. Seeking health can be nothing more than self-serving narcissism. But if Christianity is about anything, it is about community, about our being in life together, connected in ways deeper than our consciousness can comprehend. Christianity, therefore, needs to be about the health of the community.

Christians have an ethic about mercy and charity, caring for those on the margins of society. Religious denominations and orders have created (and still manage) health systems that give care to the poor, despite an ever more aggressive and complicated environment. Some Christian groups have formed free medical clinics to offer care to those who are medically indigent; compassionate health professionals generously staff these clinics.

As wonderful as charity and mercy are, they must be matched by justice. We Christians have found it too easy—maybe even a bit self-serving—to put a finger in the dyke by having soup kitchens in the church or by sending volunteers to help with an immunization program. These are good, maybe even noble enterprises, but they do not change the system. They cannot enlarge the system enough to make room for all the disenfranchised and marginalized people who need both health care and empowerment.

One has to wonder: "What would Jesus do?" I don't think he'd set up shop as a healer, dispensing cures one-by-one. I do think he would rail against a system that allows the rich to purchase extravagant procedures and leaves hardworking people without access to health care for themselves or their families. I believe Jesus would call for justice.

Patricia Benner's "A Litany of Penitence for Health Care" has struck some as too negative. But a lamentation is not about offering solutions; it's about naming pain. Health care professionals and laity share sadness at the failure of the current health care delivery system. Too often it is not about health, but illness; it is not about care so much as cure; it often fails to deliver on its promises; and it is hardly a system at all. Just what is the current system like? "Fact or Fiction: What do you really know about U.S. health care?" will expose facts we seldom consider. Abigail Rian Evans offers the background to our current dilemma, and the words from several Christian denominations call for solutions.

FACT OR FICTION: WHAT DO YOU *REALLY* KNOW ABOUT U.S. HEALTH CARE?

Test your knowledge of the present state of health care in America by considering these facts and fictions. It is excerpted from *Seeking Justice in Health Care: A Guide for Advocates in Faith Communities* published by the Universal Health Care Action Network (UHCAN) in Cleveland, Ohio. It was developed to support the efforts of members of faith communities working for health care for all. UHCAN can be contacted by telephone at 216-241-8422 x 15, email at <faithproject@uhcan.org> or through their website at www.uhcan.org.

ACCESS TO HEALTH CARE

Fiction: Anyone with a steady job can get insurance.

Fact: Nearly 70% of the uninsured live in families with at least one full time worker. As costs of premiums continue to rise, more and more employers are dropping employer-sponsored coverage, reducing dependent benefits, or shifting enough costs to the employees to make premiums unaffordable for low wage workers.

Fiction: The law says that anyone can receive the health care they need in hospital emergency rooms.

Fact: The Emergency Treatment and Active Labor Act of 1986 (EMTALA) requires hospitals to provide appropriate care, including admission, to anyone who goes to an emergency room with a *life-threatening condition*. Beyond that, there is no mandate for follow-up care, including providing any prescribed medications.

Fiction: Anyone can buy insurance. It's just a matter of choosing to purchase insurance rather than luxury items.

Fact: Numerous factors, including age, pre-existing conditions, and place
            of residence, often make it impossible for some persons to purchase
            affordable insurance. Pre-existing conditions also can make it
            impossible to purchase insurance at any cost.

Fiction: Since everyone can get emergency care, being uninsured doesn't really
            make a big difference in health outcomes.

Fact: Being uninsured is the 7th leading cause of death in the U.S., killing
            more people than kidney disease, liver disease and AIDS combined.
            It is estimated that 18,000 people in the U.S. die prematurely each year
            because they do not have insurance.

Fiction: With CHIP/SCHIP all children are insured.

Fact: About 10 million children remain uninsured. To receive the CHIP
            funds, states have to match the federal dollars, and some have
            chosen not to fund as much coverage as is needed.

NEEDED PRESCRIPTION DRUGS

Fiction: Most people have prescription drug coverage in their insurance policies.

Fact: Nearly 1 in 4 people in the U.S. do not have prescription drug coverage.

Fiction: Lowering prescription drug prices will compromise the development
            of new drugs.

Fact: Research and development (R & D) dollars are considered part of drug
            companies' expenses. Profits—up to 6 times higher for pharmaceuti-
            cals than for other Fortune 500 companies—are unrelated to research
            and development. In addition, considerable funding for R & D is
            provided by the federal government.

Fiction: What's wrong with direct-to-consumer drug advertising? Everybody
            does it!

Fact: Only two countries (the U.S. and New Zealand) permit direct-
            to-consumer drug advertising. Pharmaceutical marketing and admin-
            istration can be as high 25-30% of drug revenues, often exceeding
            research and development spending.

Fiction: The drugs we can purchase from other countries just aren't safe.

Fact: Many of the drugs available for purchase from other countries were
           actually manufactured in the U.S. They're just cheaper because other
           countries negotiate lower wholesale prices with drug manufacturers.

COSTS OF HEALTH CARE

Fiction: U.S. health care is expensive, but we get what we pay for.

Fact: Actually, we spend over $5,000 per capita for health care in the U.S.—
           twice as much as any industrialized country that provides universal
           health care. But life expectancies are lower and rates of disease higher
           than in many countries that spend a lot less.

Fiction: Universal health care would raise taxes and cost too much.

Fact: Numerous studies have shown that there already is enough money
           in the system to pay for universal health care. While taxes *might* be
           higher, that increase could be offset by system-wide savings through
           administrative and clinical efficiencies.

HEALTH CARE IN CRISIS
–Abigail Rian Evans

Abigail Rian Evans, Ph.D., is an ordained minister in the Presbyterian Church (U.S.A.)
who began her work in Brazil as a missionary and faculty member at a seminary.
Before joining the faculty at Princeton Theological Seminary as professor of practical
theology, she was the director of National Capital Presbytery's Health Ministries, an
organization she founded. She has also served as director of new programs and as
senior associate at the Kennedy Institute of Ethics at Georgetown University.

Failure of Systematic Health Care Reform

Despite the numerous reasons for the Clinton health care reform bill's
failure and the disaster of managed care, there are systematic reasons why health
care reform is floundering in the United States and in the United Kingdom. The
first reason is *moral weakness*. Fundamentally, one must ask: Is health care reform
or societal reform needed? Are there sufficient shared values, inclusive behaviors,
and communitarian goals? Or do autonomy and individual rights so rule the day
that society is not willing to give up a little so that others will have something? Is
there a willingness to share? Is a communitarian or even a utilitarian ethic (the
greatest good for the greatest number) a possibility, or is this a manifestation of

some Darwinian morality of the survival of the fittest? Are justice, equality, and liberty empty ideals, or do they form the basis of health care reform?

The way chosen to care for poor, elderly, and disabled persons is a measure of our moral fiber. What sacrifices are people willing to make for the welfare of others? Health care strikes at the heart of the moral nature of society, as Peter Draper pointed out was the case in England after the war. British society was committed to providing universal health care for all citizens based on the sacrifices they had made during the war. The country had pulled together, and a moral commitment was made to care for everyone. Will Americans rise to the challenge of health care for all? Perhaps the words of Winston Churchill are apt: "You can always count on the Americans to do the right thing—but only after they have tried everything else first."[1] We are now trying everything else.

The second reason that health care reform is not moving forward is the *lack of a consensus*. Bioethicist Madison Powers asserts that the consensus for health care reform is pervasive but shallow.[2] Perhaps there is a shared dissatisfaction rather than a shared vision. Voters in the late 1990s evidenced some willingness to change but to what was not always clear.[3]

Sixty-six percent of Americans named cost as the main problem facing health care in the United States in the 1990s.[4] Among the five health-system reform issues suggested, 82 to 84 percent of Americans said being able to choose their own doctor without paying extra and "having access to the latest technology" were most important. More than three-quarters of those surveyed favored providing health insurance through large groups that could bargain with hospitals and doctors for better rates, limiting the prices that doctors, hospitals, and drug companies could charge, and requiring most businesses to pay for employees' basic health insurance.

There was a strong consensus on the importance of comprehensive coverage of health needs so that not just physical but mental illness would be treated and paid for. More than two-thirds favored using government money to provide mental health care to all who need it. In addition, those Americans polled wanted to require insurance companies to provide coverage for chronically ill people at the same price charged for healthy people. On the other hand, less than one-third favored requiring workers who receive health benefits from their employers to pay income tax on the benefits. And almost half said that their support for health care reform would decrease if it increased their taxes.

The third reason that health care change is difficult is the activity *of so many special interest groups*, including the 11 million people who have jobs in the health care industry. Debates also rage between pro-life and pro-choice groups about whether abortion should be in or out of the core benefits package. The effect of pluralism in today's society is to slow down any drastic changes. The United States appears to be a collection of special interest groups lacking a true sense of being a nation.

The fourth reason health care reform is floundering is the *complexity of the issues*—health care needs are vast in scope and are viewed as a fundamental right. How much is really understood about health care costs, patient-physician relationships, or the best health care plans? How does one address an industry in the United States that represents more than $900 billion in expenditures or a medical delivery system in the United Kingdom that is rooted in a government-instituted system?

The last reason that health care reform is ineffective is its *overreliance on the medical model of health care*. This has caused a neglect of preventive health care and the lack of incorporation of complementary health care practices, including spiritual resources and religious beliefs and practices. Rearranging the delivery system rather than changing what is delivered inhibits real change and reform. This reality is clearly observed in the latest US attempt at health care reform under the banner of managed care. Managed care is not systematic reform but supposedly an attempt to control costs. In its first decade, managed care has not succeeded in this goal. Even when there was some reduction of hospital costs, any savings achieved, rather than providing benefits for those who had no health care, filled the bank accounts of health corporation executives or stockholders.

It may be instructive to discuss managed care in some detail to illustrate the need for a fundamental reenvisioning of the health care system. Our assumptions about health, healing, and healers need to be radically changed.

The Rise of Managed Care

Examined in the best light, managed care has operated from three basic ethical principles: beneficence (improve quality); non-maleficence (reduce harmful care); and justice (decrease the cost of care). Managed health care emerged in the 1990s as an attempt to answer the problem of excessive costs in the US health care system. The hope was that by treating the caring profession as a business rather than a service, bottom-line discipline would bring runaway costs under control. The first question is whether or not commercial principles can be applied to the provision of medical care. The changes in health care delivery are exemplified by the health insurance industry, which created a new method of delivering health care. A wide range of groups emerged to "manage" care, that is, managed care organizations (MCOs), health maintenance organizations (HMOs), preferred provider organizations (PPOs), point of service groups (POSs), independent practice associations (IPAs), insurance reviewers, hospital administrators, institutional managers, and the purchasers of groups needing care who run the health care corporations.[5]

The difference between HMOs and PSOs (provider-sponsored organizations) is ownership. HMOs are usually owned by insurance companies, while PSOs are owned directly by doctors and hospitals. At the end of the 1990s about 14 percent of the nation's more than six hundred licensed HMOs were actually PSOs, according to the Blue Cross/Blue Shield Association. Naturally, the insurance industry tried to keep physicians and hospitals from the lucrative health care market.

HMOs and PSOs both provide medical care to their members for a flat fee regardless of how much care a member uses. To make a profit, they bet that high costs incurred by one member will be offset by the low costs of other members. They risk losing money if their costs exceed their income, so the goal is to exclude persons who are too sick.[6]

Whatever the type, managed health care functions as individual, profit-driven corporations whose product is medical care. The vocabulary used by these organizations reflects their corporate image: the "consumer" (formerly the patient), the "provider" (the physician and other health care professionals), the "insurer" (the reimburser for any care), the "buyer" of health services (most often the large employer organization). A certain dollar amount is negotiated for health care for a certain number of patients whether the care is given or not; the provider shares with the insurer any financial risk for the actual costs of care.[7] And despite the observation by some health industry analysts that managed care heralded an alternative to the medical model, it fits squarely within that model. The managed care system does not attempt to redefine health and sickness but accepts the existing definitions. Exclusion of coverage is based not on new defini-tions but on cost savings. Managed care differs from the medical model only because it has weakened the authority of physicians by the primacy of the dollar.

To understand the history of managed health care, one must grasp the context in which it first emerged in the early 1930s when physicians controlled the economic power of medicine. In the mid-twentieth century, wealth, power, and trust were given to the doctors. Each year brought better coverage and more treatments. Beginning in the 1970s, there was a breakdown of the payer-provider contract. A resistance to runaway costs developed that gave rise to managed care; in many ways, economics changed health care. Patients were billed directly by their doctors an amount that rested largely on the conscience of the physician. If the patient was poor or otherwise burdened, the doctor might waive the bill and increase the amount charged for richer clients. That was called fee-for-service. In most instances, the more medical care delivered, the higher the physician's income; thus, the incentive was for maximum procedures and tests. In its best manifestation, however, the patient's good was primary.

Against this backdrop, the first third-party payment system began at Baylor University for public school teachers, a well-organized identifiable group who could not depend on the charitability of physicians to meet medical costs on modest salaries. Insurance companies began paying teachers' bills, but the amount was still determined by the doctors. As the third-party payment system spread to other sectors of the population, insurance companies gradually dictated to doctors what would be paid for their services. Blue Shield started by covering the costs of surgeons and other hospital-based specialists until it had enrolled 15 million members in 1950; by 1962 with 56 million members, it became Blue Cross/Blue Shield.[8]

Despite this growth, insurance coverage was still spotty and uneven in the early sixties. Twenty-six percent of the population had no health insurance; and only 27 percent of the money that Americans spent on health care was paid for by insurance companies.[9] The average private health care expense of aged persons was 80 percent more than that of the population as a whole, and insurance paid only one-sixth of it.[10]

It is not surprising that insurance coverage was less than satisfactory, given its lackluster record of government support. In the 1940s, Roosevelt deleted the section on health care coverage for the aged from the Social Security Act because of the fear that the Social Security Act itself might fail. National health insurance was uniformly rejected. President Truman advocated health insurance for the aged under the umbrella of Social Security in 1951, which also failed. It was not until 1965, under the Johnson administration, that Medicare for the aged and a Medicaid program for the poor were passed. These initiatives, however, had start-up problems with uneven and incomplete coverage.

In this climate, Henry Kaiser launched what is now the most common type of managed health care system, known as the health maintenance organization, in 1942. HMOs took health insurance a step further by blending insurance and provision of treatment itself. The original prepaid group plans were nonprofit and covered all health needs for a flat monthly fee; money saved from unnecessary procedures was recycled to better preventive care.[11]

However, the growth of managed health care as an industry was practically nonexistent as long as physicians had the economic role and the clout to dominate medicine on the basis of fee-for-service. As insurance companies began wresting economic control away from physicians, they were simultaneously confronted by the alarmingly high increases in the cost of health care exemplified by the medical model.

The Growth of Managed Health Care

The tremendous growth of managed care in a very short time demonstrates just how profitable the promise of cutting medical costs can be. During the Nixon administration, prepaid group models were transformed into health maintenance organizations. At that point the federal government began helping new HMOs. By the 1980s, many HMOs were profit-making companies.[12] The percentage of the population covered by managed care grew from about 15 percent in 1985 to almost 50 percent in 1995.[13] More than 13 percent of the 38 million Medicare beneficiaries were in HMOs. Congress and the administration wanted to increase Medicare participation in managed care and to offer a broader choice of systems. By 1998, 85 percent of working Americans were covered by managed care[14] and the total number of persons enrolled in HMOs was 70 million.[15] (Note: HMOs are a subset under managed care.) In the 1970s only 6 million people considered managed care an option, prompting one social pundit to note, "This may be the only US industry to go from being considered a communist plot to a capitalist conspiracy in a little over a decade."[16]

Of the 1,500 managed care plans in place in the late 1990s, up to 30 percent of the profits went into the pockets of investors. The total compensation package of a typical managed health care corporate CEO was more than $1 million. Annual salaries built into the packages were also impressive and on the rise. One example was the $3.6 million in salary and bonus paid to Malik Hasan, an entrepreneurial doctor, in 1994. His $5 million or so in stock options was compensation over and above his salary.[17] So attractive was the margin of success that an entire new group of research organizations sprang up around the managed health care field just to monitor it for newcomers or improve the competitive edge for participants. Minnesota-based InterStudy, for example, "maps" the managed care marketplace with research reports that pinpoint HMO enrollment by "product type, penetration, financial measures, premiums and reimbursement methods" in more than three hundred metropolitan statistical areas. The reports sell from a few hundred to thousands of dollars.[18] One cannot help comparing the current entrepreneurial zeal of the managed care field to the market research firms that proliferated in the wake of the technology boom during the go-go years of the seventies.

Assessment of Managed Health Care

After an impressive decade of explosive growth that has succeeded in curbing a steep rise in medical costs, managed health care organizations are now on the receiving end of a frontal attack from critics who charge HMOs with nothing less than raping US health care for their own profit. The financial risks for health care costs have been shifted from the insurance company to the physician with incentives to restrain costs. In the last six years the number of doctors has increased by 20 percent, while the number of health care managers has increased by 683 percent in the last fourteen years.[19] The quickest way to make money is to avoid treating sick people.[20] Physicians such as Ronald Glasser, who wrote a scathing critique of managed care, believe that the wellness craze is obscuring the real threat of illness.[21] Balance sheets seem to be the top priority. The applause for the progress of managed care firms may still be ringing on Wall Street, but the needs of the 40 million uninsured Americans who cannot afford any form of health care remain unaddressed. Anecdotes abound among HMO enrollees about denial of treatment, limits on hospitalization and choice of physicians, greedy health care plan executives, and a system cutting corners for profit.

Where previously doctors believed it was unethical to advertise, HMOs in the late 1990s competed aggressively for the $80 billion-a-year market, with advertising slogans such as, "You'll feel better with us," and "Be Happy, Be Healthy." Managed care organizations claimed to be primarily interested in patients' welfare, but doctors and patients alike attested otherwise. Most opinion polls in 1996–97 reflected high dissatisfaction by participants in managed care plans. Eighteen percent of *Consumer Reports* readers polled went outside their HMO plan to obtain the care they needed, paying the costs out of pocket.[22] Still, ambiguity predominates when assessing the managed care field in light of the overall state of the nation's health care system. Studies by E. Harris Associates and the Robert Wood Johnson Foundation show that while 53 percent of respondents felt the health care system was getting worse, managed care as a corrective measure got favorable marks from 59 percent of the respondents.[23] However, the poll does not explain what is meant by "good" in the assessment of HMOs. In a September 1998 poll, two-thirds of Americans surveyed said they had some problem with their health care system.[24] However, some flagship health care systems, such as Advocate Health Care, which represents a merger of the United Church of Christ and Lutheran Health Care Systems, are first-rate in their vision for health care and for a more inclusive delivery system. As an integrated delivery system, it can respond more holistically to people's health needs.

Changes in the Physician-Patient Relationship

The crucial question that must be asked is whether a health care policy should be cost-driven or care-driven. Who is protecting the traditional ethics of the primacy of patient care? HMOs now talk of lowering the percentage of income that goes for patient care, which is going against everything we believe about health care.[25] Doctors can no longer prescribe what is best for the patient, but only what is covered. Drive-through deliveries, which limited post-delivery hospital stays to twenty-four hours, and the gag rule, which prohibited doctors from mentioning treatment options that were not covered under a patient's HMO, were just the more sensational fallout of the managed care system. An interesting footnote must be added to this practice: Congress passed legislation in 1996 requiring health plans to give new mothers at least two days in the hospital.[26] Some have even quipped that the doctor's office is now known as the insurance company's waiting room.[27]

HMOs pressured doctors to reduce the time allotted to each patient from fifteen to ten minutes. They reward them for "cost-effective medicine"[28] for good reason: one of the problems with the new system is that physicians accustomed to fee-for-service do not know how to do cost-effective patient management. The managed care physician is open to malpractice suits since the system is set up to reward doctors for delay in treatment. In addition, while patients value care by a known physician with whom trust can be developed, patients are forced to relate to a group of doctors. Moreover, doctors can no longer simply refer their patients to the best specialists but must comb through authorized lists to see who is on the list, which may already be outdated.[29] Many doctors spend their time quieting patients' anger at the policies of HMOs. Outside their office doors in the hallways, hospital personnel are consumed with conversations about mergers and acquisitions. Patient care seems to be the last item on the agenda.

The patient-physician relationship, the quality of care versus cost containment, patient choice versus organized health care groups—all constitute key ethical conflicts in managed care today. One of the fundamental issues raised by managed care is whether a patient's interests can trump all other needs or whether they should be weighed against competing claims of other patients, payers, society, or even the doctor. The patient does have a fundamental right to participate in sharing the goals and methods of care. The marketplace is not the appropriate arena for patients weakened by illness who cannot defend their rights or negotiate their needs. In fact, now at the end of the twentieth century, a new patient bill of rights and radical reform of managed care are already in process, with more than fifty bills presented.[30]

Older physicians who have practiced under a patient-centered model are especially concerned about the divided loyalties that managed care plans generate, even though these may arise in any contract or covenant relationship. Yet self-interest appears to be rewarded in a way not hitherto seen in the patient-physician relationship. The very structure of managed health care encourages a built-in conflict with the doctor's first obligation to the patient; the good of all the other patients served by the plan and the good of the organization may trump the individual patient's needs. Using corporate terms such as "fund holder" to refer to doctors in the United Kingdom, for example, will begin to shape the reality of who doctors are. When there is a conflict between various obligations, the doctor's first covenant should be with the individual patient who trusts that the doctor will do what is best for his or her health.

It is true, of course, that a physician who accepts employment in a managed care plan incurs an obligation to serve the goals of that organization. In 1998, only 19.9 percent of doctors practiced outside HMOs.[31] However, they are ultimately placed in an ethically untenable position if they cannot meet their primary obligation to the patient. The requirements of the plan could render the doctor powerless to intercede on behalf of the individual patient. Even worse, from the perspective of Edmund Pellegrino, a renowned physician-educator, are incentives and disincentives based on the belief that if all persons serve their own self-interests, the good of the whole will be met. In medicine, the doctor's self-interests, however legitimate, should never be met to the detriment of the patient.[32]

Many observers fear that the role of the physician to protect the good of the patient will be lost in all the debates. As an initial response, forty states have introduced more than 350 bills to regulate managed care programs; thirty-four of these bills have passed.[33] This points the nation to the red flags that need to be raised about managed health care concerning the quality of care, the speed of care, the qualifications of the doctors, the availability of care, and the cost. The effects of the legislative action will be far-reaching. As a *Time* magazine article pointed out, "managed health care [is] not just cutting costs but changing in a fundamental way how doctors view patients, and perhaps how patients should view their doctors."[34] Doctors become "gatekeepers," determining what specialist services and procedures a patient may receive. Patients become "covered lives" whose health needs are measured by what is reimbursable. Corporate managers decide who gets treated and who does not, based on costs.

Managed care challenges the basic tenets of US medicine—the freedom to choose one's own doctor and the autonomy of physicians to order care as they see fit. Many prominent physicians are afraid that doctors will be reduced to "case managers," "fund holders," or "clinical economists."[35] Primary care physicians become the principal targets for manipulation by managed care because their role is to contain costs. The burden rests with the generalists, who as the "ethical gatekeepers" must resist the pressure to become marginal specialists as managed care generally rewards fewer referrals to specialists.

It seems that a doctor can serve the patient's interest only until it conflicts with the managed care plan's guidelines. If the patient's interest holds sway, what happens to cost containment? Reasonable salaries for service rendered should be the practice of physicians; yet their salaries represent more than 18 percent of health care costs in the United States today. As a citizen, the physician is bound to use society's resources wisely and well. Ordering unnecessary tests simply to avoid malpractice suits is not good stewardship. However, requiring advance directives to avoid "unnecessary and futile treatments" because they are not reimbursed was not the intent of living wills. It is true that patients may no longer be pressured by doctors to undergo prolonged testing against their will, but commitment to patient education and choice should not be driven by market concerns.

Another pressing concern is the quality of doctors in HMOs. Are they the best trained, experienced, knowledgeable, and patient-centered doctors available? There is no reason to believe they are better or worse than other certified and licensed physicians, since belonging to a managed care plan is more and more the only option for a doctor. Some industry observers have even gone as far to say that credentialing is totally useless. Only 1 percent of the doctors are not re-credentialed when evaluations for their continuance with the health care company are done. In fact, the major reason for dropping doctors seems to be their ordering too many procedures or medications for their patients, hence pushing up the cost. This "deselection" process, as it euphemistically is labeled, has become such a threat that new laws providing doctors with hearings in such cases are being considered.[36]

Cost Containment Is a Myth

In assessing the various pros and cons of a managed health care system, one comes to the core question that underlies the raison d'être of HMOs: Do they, in fact, save money? The government reported in 1996 that the rise in health care costs measured in double digits through the early 1990s had shrunk to a 6.4 percent increase. During 1994 there was the slowest growth rate in three years, and costs were expected to grow no more than that in 1995.[37] However, 1998 projections were that health care costs will reach $2.1 trillion—i.e., they will double—by 2007.[38]

Furthermore, 1996 figures indicated that doctors' earnings rose nationally by 6.7 percent, and projections for 1997 and 1998 were that medical care supplies, equipment, and services would increase at 5 to 7 percent annually compared with 2 to 4 percent a year in 1995 and 1996. Health insurance was also projected to increase; however, it is important to note that while HMOs will increase on the average 4 to 10 percent, traditional indemnity insurance will rise by 7 to 15 percent.[39] Yet the savings by HMOs are not being passed on to the patients, who are spending more for out-of-pocket expenses. In 1996, the average person spent $3,759 out of pocket; in 2007 this same person will spend $7,100.[40] Some believe that any savings generated by managed care will go to pay shareholders dividends and not to expand services to the uninsured.

The effects of managed care must be watched for possible neglect of persons who already do not have access to health care and for diminished employment opportunities for all health professionals. Adverse selection, risk adjustment, and outcomes measurement as the guiding methods in managed care will result in neglect of persons with chronic illness.[41] There is little doubt that health care companies will continue to increase their profits on an unprecedented basis. Wall Street is bullish on the prospects of health care companies, now that national health reform poses no threat to corporate profits. In 1995, for-profit chain mergers included almost $50 billion in transactions, and three of the largest deals involved Columbia/HCA, which was under investigation during 1997–98 for its questionable practices.[42]

These huge profits might be acceptable if personal health care costs were less. To determine cost-effectiveness of managed care, one must understand how the system works. Doctors are paid in various ways: as employees, as groups of doctors, or through multi-plan contracts with multi-specialty groups. In one type of plan, physicians receive a salary, but an important part of their income comes from bonuses or other monetary incentives that depend on how well the group does financially. This kind of capitation schema gives doctors incentives to order fewer tests and to defer patient visits; it is the opposite of fee-for-service medicine. With managed care, doctors are paid more for doing less. The system offers perks to physicians for cutting costs, which results in robust profits for the plan and slim treatment for the patients. Corporate cost control means minimizing benefits delivered to members unless they are willing to pay a premium.

Indeed, so "multitiered" is the system that much time is lost on the job for US citizens as they try to navigate the health care system and get reimbursed for benefits given. Causing downtime on the job because of the complexity of the system is only one troubling side effect that makes it difficult to assess the overall cost-effectiveness of managed care. Nurses and other health care professionals may receive pay reductions or even lose their jobs to provide the profit margin for the large corporations. When Mann County General Hospitals in California converted to private hospitals, 540 registered nurses lost their jobs while the hospital reported a profit of $5.6 million.[43] Nurses' and nursing assistants' percentage of annual pay for total hospital costs continued to drop—hovering around $38,000 average annual salary for registered nurses[44]—while hospital CEOs averaged $235,000.[45] One big concern about the impact of managed care is that hospitals will be squeezed so badly they will no longer be able to support research, education, community programs, or free care for the uninsured.[46]

Especially disturbing is the method HMOs use when they do not want to pay for a service. This method is called "rationing by inconvenience"; appeals and grievances go unanswered.[47] This jams the nation's legal dockets, wastes the time of judges, and makes lawyers richer. Based on past experience with HMOs, some believe that managed care does not save money because of the additional costs for multilevel bureaucracy, marketing and advertising costs, and so forth.

Gatekeepers May Not Save Money

Critics of HMOs claim that the gatekeeper general practitioners are costing the health care system millions of dollars because of ineffective office visits and physical therapy. To date there are no clear studies proving that HMOs are more expensive. However, a CAPP Care study shows that gatekeepers increase other primary care and specialist utilization; hence, using gatekeepers may actually be more expensive.[48]

As gatekeepers refer patients to other health care specialists, economics drive some managed care decisions and reward doctors for limiting utilization of specialists. One study by the U.S. General Accounting Office found that little empirical evidence exists on the cost savings of managed care.[49] Premiums for both types of health care plans have been rising at the same rate. Furthermore, some patients' care is better managed by a specialist; for example, advanced rheumatoid arthritis could be more economically managed by a rheumatologist. Some people believe that technology drives costs high. However, for example, if all transplants in the United States were halted, there would be a savings of only $300 million a year, a few hundredths of 1 percent of the total annual health expenditure.[50]

In a 1990 survey of Washington State specialists, 93 percent believed that gatekeeper-based plans would lead to patient dissatisfaction about lack of direct access to specialists; 81 percent predicted that necessary tests would not be performed; and only 7 percent believed that quality of care of the specialists would improve.

"Gatekeeper" may be too adversarial a term because in many cases a general practitioner can manage a problem just fine. The patient does not realize this and thinks he or she needs a specialist. A coordinator can play an important role by overseeing a patient's care. One solution to the financing problems is to also capitate specialists. Thus, the rationing is not simply in the hands of the general practitioners. There certainly seems to be a trend toward reduced hospital days, which is in most instances a cost savings. For example, in California, five physician groups alone had reduced the number of hospital days by an average of almost 30 percent from 1990 to 1994.[51]

Another cost-containment measure concerns medications. Drugs are now more often prescribed based solely on whether there is a generic drug or whether a discount is offered by a patient's HMO. Of course, a reduction in drug prescriptions could be good since there is growing literature about fatal drug interactions and addiction to prescription drugs. Nevertheless, drug prescriptions should be based on the patient's good, not on cost.

Mental health benefits have long been curtailed in most health care plans. Of the insured population, including Medicare, 48.7 percent are enrolled in managed behavioral health programs, which is the designation for mental health care.[52] A review of articles about mental health care under the new managed care plans shows that most mental health practitioners say there is poorer care for chronically, seriously mentally ill persons and no care at all for "worried well" persons. For the latter group, the care could prevent them from becoming chronically ill in the first place. Initially, the inclusion of mental health benefits in the Clinton plan's core benefits package was assured only when the vice president's wife, Tipper Gore, became an aggressive spokesperson for their importance. In HMOs one sees the use of effective medications, the substitution of day hospitals for residential hospitals, and shorter courses of therapy. The effectiveness of these approaches to mental health care is too soon to call.

Preventive Care Is Offered but Limited

HMOs are supposed to invest in preventive care. Immunization rates at HMOs are high, ranging from 60 to 85 percent of patients needing them. However, HMO businesspersons find that broad preventive care does not pay off in their quarterly and annual bottom-line calculations. Of course, in the long haul preventive care can reduce health care costs.

When routine assessments are made and patients are enrolled in wellness programs, Americans may see managed care at its best. If Blue Cross/Blue Shield associations added routine, periodic screening for diseases to their coverage, premiums would increase by $7.50 monthly for families. The screening package in many HMOs includes tests for breast, colon, cervical, and lung cancer; heart disease; hypertension; diabetes; thyroid disease; and osteoporosis. Nationally, routine preventive services would add about $3 billion to the nation's health care bill. Under Medicaid all states cover preventive services for children. Nineteen states cover preventive services for adults.[53]

The most important question is this: Is cost containment a moral goal in and of itself if needed health care is expensive? Physicians such as Pellegrino believe their goals are mutually exclusive. Economic constraint is not in and of itself morally justified. Philosophers such as Daniel Callahan would take issue with this analysis. Callahan suggests in *Hard Choices* that allocation of scarce health care resources is a moral act.

Notes

1. Editorial, *Times* (London), April 21, 1996, CC3.

2. Madison Powers, "Justice and the Market for Health Issues: Current Proposals for Securing Access to Health Care" (paper presented at the Kennedy Institute of Ethics, Washington, D.C., March 21, 1991).

3. "AMA/Gallup Survey Reveals Public's Attitudes on Health System Reform," *Michigan Medicine* 93, no. 6 (June 1994): 15–19.

4. Ibid., 16.

5. Martina Darragh and Pat Milmoe McCarrick, "Managed Health Care: New Ethical Issues for All," *Kennedy Institute of Ethics Journal* 6, no. 2, Scope Note 31, Baltimore: Johns Hopkins University Press (June 1996): 189–92.

6. Larry Lipman, "The Medicare Battle Rages On," *Trenton Times*, April 4, 1997, A13.

7. Ibid., 2.

8. Charles Andrews, *Profit Fever: The Drive of Corporatized Health Care and How to Stop It* (Monroe, ME: Common Courage Press, 1995), 5.

9. Ibid., 7.

10. Ibid., 11.

11. Robert Kuttner, "Mutant HMOs," *Washington Post*, January 1, 1997, A19.

12. Ibid.

13. Susan Dentzer, "Shedding Light on Managed Care," *U.S. News and World Report*, May 6, 1996, 120.

14. Associated Press, "Health Care Spending Projected to Double in Decade," *CNN Interactive*, September 14, 1998, http://cnn.com/HEALTH/9809/14/health.care.spending.ap.

15. George Anders, "The Outlook for HMOs," *Frontline Online*, April 14, 1998, http://www.pbs.org/wgbh/pages/frontline/shows/hmo/etc/outlook.htmI.

16. Dentzer, "Shedding Light on Managed Care," 120.

17. George Anders, "A Profile of Malik Hasan," *Frontline Online*, April 14, 1998, http://www.pbs.org/wgbh/pages/frontline/shows/hmo/hassan/profile.html.

18. InterStudy Publications, *Publications and Services Catalog* (Winter 1996), 3–7.

19. Ronald J. Glasser, MD, "The Doctor Is Not In," *Harper's Magazine*, March 1998, 39.

20. Stuart Auerbach, "Managed Care Backlash," *Washington Post Health*, June 25, 1996, 12–15.

21. Glasser, "The Doctor Is Not In," 40.

22. Nationally, out-of-pocket health expenditures totaled $174.9 billion in 1994. See Bureau of the Census, *Statistical Abstract of the United States*, 1996, 112.

23. Auerbach, "Managed Care Backlash," 14.

24. "Poll: American Anxious about Health Care System," *CNN Interactive*, February 28, 1998, http://cnn.com/HEALTH/9802/28/health.poll.

25. Glasser, "The Doctor Is Not In," 37.

26. Kuttner, "Mutant HMOs," A19.

27. Ibid., 35.

28. InterStudy Publications, *Publications and Services Catalog*, 5.

29. Amitai Etzioni, "One Fuming Physician," *Washington Post*, September 17, 1995, C3.

30. "A Bill of Health," *Online News Hour*, February 5, 1998, http://www.pbs.org/newshour/bb/health.

31. Glasser, "The Doctor Is Not In," 78.

32. Edmund Pellegrino, "Managed Care and Managed Competition: Some Ethical Reflections," *Calyx* 4, no. 4 (1994): 1–5.

33. Auerbach, "Managed Care Backlash," 15.

34. Erik Larson, "The Soul of an HMO," *Time*, January 22, 1996, 45.

35. Edmund Pellegrino, "Words Can Hurt You: Some Reflections on the Metaphors of Managed Care" (First Annual Nicholas J. Pisacano Lecture), *Journal of the American Board of Family Practice* (November-December 1994): 505.

36. John H. Fielder, "Disposable Doctors: Incentives to Abuse Physician Peer Review," *Journal of Clinical Ethics* 6, no. 4 (Winter 1995): 331.

37. Auerbach, "Managed Care Backlash," 14.

38. "Health Care Spending Projected to Double in Decade."

39. Judi Hasson, "Doctors' Incomes Up 6.7 Percent after '94 Drop"; Hasson and Steven Findlay, "Signs Hint at Higher Health Costs," *USA Today*, December 20, 1996, 1, 3A.

40. "Health Care Spending Projected to Double in Decade."

41. Steven A. Schroeder, "Cost Containment in U.S. Health Care," summary in Darragh and McCarrick, "Managed Health Care," 189–92.

42. Laurie Zoloth-Dorfman and Susan Rubin, "The Patient as Commodity: Managed Care and the Question of Ethics," *Journal of Clinical Ethics* 6, no. 4 (Winter 1995): 347.

43. Andrews, *Profit Fever*, 24.

44. Don Colburn, "Nurses' Jobs Are Changing or Disappearing," *Washington Post Health*, November 22, 1994, 8.

45. Andrews, *Profit Fever*, 24.

46. Darragh and McCarrick, "Managed Health Care," 191.

47. David Azevedo, "Rationing: America—From De Facto to Explicit," *Medical Economics*, May 24, 1993, 184–90, 196–99.

48. David Azevedo, "Are We Asking Too Much of Gatekeepers?" *Medical Economics*, April 11, 1994, 126, 128, 130–32, 134–37.

49. Ibid., 128.

50. Azevedo, "Rationing," 187.

51. "How Good Is Your Health Plan?" *Consumer Reports*, August 1996, 36.

52. Sharon J. Jackson, "Why Managed Care, Why Now?" *Journal of the California Alliance for the Mentally Ill* 7, no. 1 (April 1, 1996): 6.

53. Associated Press, "Coverage of Preventive Care Endorsed by Health Insurer," *Washington Post*, June 19, 1991, A3.

DENOMINATIONS SPEAK OUT ABOUT APPROPRIATE HEALTH CARE

Evangelical Lutheran Church in America

The following is excerpted from "Caring for Health: Our Shared Endeavor," a social statement of the Evangelical Lutheran Church in America on health, healing and health care. It was adopted by the eighth biennial Churchwide Assembly in 2003. The complete document is extremely comprehensive and reflects the serious work this denomination has invested in health. The statement in its entirety is available online at www.elca.org/dcs/socialstatement/healthcare.html.

Health is central to our well-being, vital to relationships, and helps us live out our vocations in family, work, and community. Caring for one's own health is a matter of human necessity and good stewardship. Caring for the health of others expresses both love for our neighbors and responsibility for a just society. As a personal and social responsibility, health care is a shared endeavor. . . .

THE CHURCH AND THE HEALTH CARE CRISIS

The Christian Church is called to be an active participant in fashioning a just and effective health care system. Responding to those who were sick was integral to the life and ministry of Jesus and has been a central aspect of the Church's mission throughout its history. Health care and healing are concrete manifestations of God's ongoing care for and redemption of all creation.

We of the Evangelical Lutheran Church in America have an enduring commitment to work for and support health care for all people as a shared endeavor. Our commitment comes in grateful response to God's saving love in Jesus Christ that frees us to love and seek the well-being of our neighbor. It is shaped by the witness of Scripture—including the ministry of Jesus—and the Lutheran Confessions, together with the Christian Church's historical and contemporary ministry in healing and health. Our commitment draws upon God-given abilities to understand our situation and discern our response.

As members of the Evangelical Lutheran Church in America, and as a corporate body, we support:

- a comprehensive approach to health care as a shared endeavor among individuals, churches, government, and the wider society;

- a vision of health care and healing that includes individual, church, and social responsibilities;

- a vision of a health care system that is based on understanding health, illness, healing, and health care within a coherent set of services;[1]

• equitable access for all people to basic health care services and to the benefits of public health efforts;

• faithful moral discernment guiding individual participation and public policy making in health care services.

God continues to call the Church—its institutions and believers—to work in society for individual and collective actions that promote health and ensure care for those who suffer. Understanding health care as a shared endeavor compels the Church and all people of good will to join in efforts for change. . . .

THE CHURCH'S MINISTRY

A ministry of healing is integral to the life and mission of the Church. It expresses our faith in the power of God to create and to save, as well as our commitment to care for our neighbor. The Holy Spirit empowers us so that we can care for all people as God's children and seek their healing. The Church promotes health and healing and provides health care services through its social ministry organizations and congregation-based programs. The Church's ministry may offer healing or forms of health care in ways not found or adequately addressed within a health care system. The Church also supports the just obligations of a society to serve those who are often left out and to be present with those who suffer. Because it originates from and carries out Christ's healing work, the Church's ministry is freed to contribute to the health care system as well as to address its injustices.

CONGREGATIONS

Worship stands at the center of the congregation's ministry of healing. Holy Communion strengthens, sustains, and refreshes us and heals the troubled conscience of believers through the gift of grace. The preaching and hearing of the Word enliven us by the promise of reconciliation with God through Christ. The liturgy provides a structure of meaning that nourishes and sustains. Music and hymns often bring comfort and healing to those who are suffering. Education and pastoral care equip people to understand better and cope with illness within the biblical story of God's salvation. Congregations provide people with acceptance, support, and community, listening to those who are ill and bringing their suffering, injustices, and concerns to God in prayer. Congregations hold up these dimensions of healing in all aspects of their life together and in special liturgies of healing.[2] They make special provision for those who are ill to hear the Good News and receive Holy Communion. Members visit the sick and dying; they encourage and pray for those who are in health care occupations or are voluntary caregivers. Some congregations develop specific health ministries that include counseling centers, health care advocacy, and congregational health ministry teams. Parish nurse ministries provide for wellness programs, including health screening and health education. As part of their ministries of health and healing, congregations can also:

- inform themselves of global health concerns and support global ministries of health;

- provide members with education and opportunities for deliberation and advocacy about health issues;

- ensure full participation of all people in the life of the congregation by removing physical and other barriers;

- help people evaluate avenues of care and treatment, whether those of standard Western medicine, various complementary systems, or those based in religious claims or faith communities, and to distinguish between means that are appropriate and beneficial and those that are potentially inappropriate or exploitive;

- seek ways to collaborate with and support our church's social ministry organizations;

- provide physical access and other vital links between people and the health care they need, especially in rural communities and inner cities;

- strengthen efforts to be places where people seek help in times of crisis or need, where spiritual needs are understood and met, and where traditions are honored and shared;

- pay particular attention to the health of all staff, providing a working environment that is physically and emotionally safe and supportive, as well as a work schedule that allows for adequate recreation and stress reduction;[3]

- ensure that all paid staff of the congregation have access to health care services;

- inform themselves of global health concerns and support global ministries of health. . . .

TOWARD A BETTER SYSTEM OF HEALTH CARE SERVICES

A health care system should have the explicit purpose of: promoting and improving the health of all people; reducing the impact and burden of illness, injury, and disability; and promoting healing, even when cure is not possible. Too often, however, the various sectors of health care and health promotion are fragmented and disjointed. This inhibits equitable access to health-related services and good quality care, especially when individuals are unable to obtain the treatment they need. This system should be coherent, with the different services being functionally interrelated and mutually accountable. No one group—public or private—can design the structure or financing of such a system alone; representatives of all groups that provide services and financing must together seek a solution that enhances interdependence.

Health care as a shared endeavor entails a comprehensive and coherent set of services of good quality care throughout one's life span. At a minimum, each person should have ready access to basic health care services that include preventive, acute, and chronic physical and mental health care at an affordable cost.[4] The United States does not currently have a health care system that is capable of care for all people. Significant changes in financing and structure are therefore required. Discerning what these changes might entail within the limits of what is economically and politically feasible needs to be worked out as a shared endeavor in the democratic process.

Without attempting to describe all components and attributes of a system in detail, the following highlights some particular concerns that require our attention.

PUBLIC HEALTH SERVICES

Health as a shared endeavor makes public health services, which focus on the population as a whole, the foundation for any health care system. We urge renewed political and financial support for services undertaken on behalf of the entire community to prevent epidemics, limit threats to health, promote healthy behavior, reduce injuries, assist in recovery from disasters, and ensure that people have access to needed services. Governments have an obligation to provide or organize many of these services, but all services depend on active collaboration with the entire community.

Since threats to health do not respect national boundaries, nations and international organizations must cooperate in public health efforts. In facing this global challenge, the United States government and non-governmental organizations have responsibility to work with others in such areas as securing clean water and sanitation, overcoming hunger and malnutrition, preventing and combating infectious diseases, responding to disasters, and providing health services for women, men, and children who live in poverty. . . .

MOVING TOWARD JUST ACCESS

While the mandate for equitable access to health care for all is clear and com-pelling, questions about the best organizational and financing mechanisms for achieving it leave room for legitimate disagreement in this church and in society. Because health care is one vital social good among many, people also legitimately differ over how to balance expenditures for health care with other social goods.

Our obligation could be met through any one of several combinations of personal, market, and governmental means, although none of these means alone can provide equitable access to health care. Taking personal responsibility for one's health and the health of others can meet some health care needs and provide care in important ways; however, many people are left without adequate care due to uneven distribution of health care and wealth. Markets of health care services may contribute to improved quality and efficiency, but they also may contribute to increased costs, unequal access, and both over- and under-treat-ment. Governments are shaped by political pressures and often function with inefficiencies; yet as representatives of all citizens they have a particular responsi-bility to ensure society's obligations to promote the general welfare. This includes such areas as security, education, and health care. Public health measures ensuring safe water and food or preventing and limiting outbreaks of infectious diseases are so "communal" that they can be done well only from a governmental base with adequate tax dollars.

As the guarantors of justice and promoters of the general welfare, govern-ments also have the unique role of ensuring equitable access to health care for all. This role does not necessarily entail a specific governmental program or one approach to health care coverage. It does mean, however, that governments have the obligation to provide leadership and coordination in balancing competing private and social interests in moving toward the goal of equitable access to health care. In ways that are fair in both process and outcome, citizen representatives in government must take on the challenging task of defining the level of health care services to which each person should have access.

MEETING OUR OBLIGATIONS

Achieving these obligations of love and justice requires sacrifice, goodwill, fairness, and an abiding commitment to place personal and social responsibilities of love and justice above narrower individual, institutional, and political self-interests. For some people, this may mean paying more in taxes or in direct payments to assure that everyone has care. As difficult as this may be, citizens should not shrink from these moral challenges. We urge all people to advocate for access to basic health care for all and to participate vigorously and responsibly in the public discussion on how best to fulfill this obligation. The chronic failure of our society to provide its members access to basic health care services is a moral tragedy that should not be tolerated.

Alongside the pursuit of justice, we in the Evangelical Lutheran Church in

America recognize the biblical obligation that each person in society is responsible for the neighbor. No one of us is free to pass by "on the other side" (Luke
10:31–32) and assume that governments and other parties will take care of all
obligations for health care. We therefore seek to participate in and supplement
health care services out of love for all people who are in need (Matt 25:36). All
people of good will should be concerned especially to attend to the health care
needs of those who, for whatever reason, lack adequate care or are marginalized
in society. People without power and status such as the poor and needy, widows
and orphans, and the incurably ill were the focus of attention of the biblical
prophets (Isa 10:2) and of the healing ministry of Jesus (Matt 4:23). . . .

Notes

1. For a description of "a coherent set of services," see "Toward a Better System of
Health Care Services" found in the full document.

2. *Occasional Services: A Companion to Lutheran Book of Worship* (Minneapolis:
Augsburg Publishing House, and Philadelphia: Board of Publication, Lutheran Church in
America, 1983) offers, "The Service of the Word for Healing," pp. 89–98. *Life Passages:
Marriage, Healing, Funeral. Renewing Worship, Vol. 4* (prepared by the Evangelical Lutheran
Church in America for provisional use, 2002, administered by Augsburg Fortress), offers a
rite for "Healing," pp. 23–39.

3. Division for Ministry and Board of Pensions, *Ministerial Health and Wellness 2002*
(Chicago: Evangelical Lutheran Church in America, 2002).

4. More specifically, such a set of basic services likely will include: primary care
services (including a relationship with a provider, routine well-child and well-adult
examinations and prevention, age-appropriate screening for disease, treatment for acute
problems, coordinated referral for more complex levels of care); dental care; in- and
out-patient care for acute and chronic physical and mental illness; emergency care; treatment for substance abuse; and appropriate complementary and supportive services.

American Baptist Churches

This statement is a resolution adopted by the General Board of the American Baptist
Churches in 1992 entitled "Health Care for All" (General Board Reference # -
8193:11/91). It was reviewed and modified by the Executive Committee of the
General Board in 1993, 1994, and 1998.

Healing is a significant sign and metaphor of biblical faith. The prophets of
the Old Testament and Jesus himself were healers. Physical well-being was valued
for its own sake as well as a sign of hope for the day when everyone would share
equally in the blessings of shalom.

Many of Jesus' miracles were miracles of healing. He touched and healed
lepers, restored sight, caused the lame to walk and renewed the life of the woman
who had suffered for years with a flow of blood. Christ's example (Mark 6:53–56)

has inspired countless Christian health care workers including those serving as missionaries. Clearly, we have understood Jesus' concern for physical well-being as a commission to carry on that work of healing.

Today in the United States we have a health care system that is in crisis. Health care providers, health office workers, health support staff, insurers, and payers form a patchwork system without any coordination based on policy.

Health statistics tell an ugly story. At any given time about 35 million people in the United States, one-seventh of the population, have no health care coverage. They are not covered by private insurance, employer-based insurance or government programs. Another 60 million people, including a large proportion of the elderly, do not have adequate coverage.

In the United States we pay more for health care than other industrialized nations and get less for our money. The Department of Health and Human Services estimates the total cost of health care in the United States in 1992 to exceed $800 billion, 13 percent of the gross national product. These dollars and percentages are rising daily.

Many people do not have health insurance and therefore go without basic health care. They see physicians less often and die younger than those with insurance. Even people with apparently good health insurance coverage have hidden vulnerabilities when faced with paying for expensive medical conditions. Catastrophic accidents or chronic long-term needs can bankrupt a family.

Efforts at shifting costs among government agencies, private insurers, and individual payers drain enormous amounts of energy and attention, and create enormous additional bureaucratic and regulatory costs beyond the costs for the health care itself.

Powerful forces seek to preserve the status quo, but we as American Baptists, like many other citizens and public officials, believe that the time has come for significant change.

Three general approaches dominate the national debate on universal access to health care. One would merely seek to reform current health insurance programs. The second is an aggregate of proposals under the umbrella term, "managed competition." The third, the "single-payer" approach, is a publicly financed system based on taxes with benefits paid by the government and with services delivered by the government and with services provided by a mix of private and public providers, as Canada does. All have negatives as well as benefits.

In accordance with our 1975 Policy Statement on Health Care, we believe that health care should be viewed as a right, not a privilege, and that the basic goal for health care reform should be universal access to comprehensive benefits.

Therefore, as American Baptists, we urge the President and Congress to work together expeditiously to enact a major program of health care reform that will extend health care coverage to every person in the United States.

We seek a national health care system that:
• Serves everyone in the United States

• Provides comprehensive access, care, and services

• Is sensitive to the needs and rights of health workers, patients, and their cultures

• Promotes health awareness, disease prevention, nutrition, fitness, and safety

• Slows the upward spiral of costs

• Draws financial support from the broad base of the entire nation

• Reduces unnecessary administrative costs

• Reduces inappropriate medical procedures

Episcopal Church

The following is excerpted from the Report of the Standing Commission on Health that was distributed to the General Convention of the Episcopal Church in 1994. The Commission members included bishops, lawyers, priests, physicians and other health care professionals.

CHRISTIANS AND THE FORMATION OF PUBLIC POLICY ABOUT HEALTH CARE

The Baptismal Covenant in The Book of Common Prayer includes two questions, put to those who seek to commit themselves to Christ by baptism, and to those who renew their baptismal vows:

"Will you seek and serve Christ in all persons, loving your neighbor as yourself?"

"Will you strive for justice and peace among all people, and respect the dignity of every human being?"

The answers to those questions are the same: "I will, with God's help." To say, "I will," to those central questions of faith is to be summoned into the realm in which social policies are made, the realm where the commonwealth is shaped. Very many others occupy that realm: Politicians and economists, clinicians and surgeons, insurance executives and benefit managers, social philosophers and professional ethicists. It is essential that those who mean to be true to their baptismal vows join that large and diverse company and give voice to the imperatives of Christ the Healer. Absent their voices, the decisions about health care in our nation may be left to those for whom health care is a mere commodity, and those in need of it considered to be only consumers.

THE BIBLICAL IMPERATIVES

To find a response to the question, "Why should Christians concern themselves with issues of health care?" one need only refer to the Bible. There is a sense in which the whole of the biblical story, from the third chapter of Genesis forward, is the tale of the Creator seeking to mend the broken creation. Moreover, as the texts reveal, God persistently calls men and women to join in the work of mending the creation, to be themselves healers, both of individuals in need and of the social order.

In Jesus Christ, the sign of God's presence as healer in the world's life is supremely expressed. In Jesus of Nazareth is the full disclosure of the divine intention to seek out the weak and the sick and the outcast and to heal them, restoring them to the communities where they belong. In the healing presence of Christ there is the proclamation that God heals, and also that God *reigns*. The Gospel accounts include the mandate of Jesus to his followers that they go into the world to "heal the sick" in his name. As they go, they become signs of the inbreaking of the rule of God. In the summary of his teaching, Jesus says of the true servant of God, "When I was sick you came to my help." As the story of Peter and John healing a crippled beggar in Acts 3 illustrates, the infant Christian community saw the care of the sick as among its principal works of ministry. What is plain from the biblical texts is that Christ the Healer charges those who would follow him with the works of consolation and comfort, of sacrifice and compassion and healing. The community of the baptized is empowered by the presence of the healing Christ. Each individual Christian, organically joined to Christ in baptism, is equipped to function as a healer in his name. These works were not just good undertakings of individuals, but of a people fortified by the *community* of faith, in which each received according to need (Acts 2:45).

THE CHURCH AS THE EVIDENCE OF THE HEALING PRESENCE OF GOD IN THE WORLD

Christianity brought into the world what one commentator has described as "the most revolutionary and decisive change in the attitude of society toward the sick. . . . It addressed itself to the disinherited, to the sick and afflicted, and promised them healing. . . . It became the duty of the Christian to attend to the sick and the poor. . . . The social position of the sick . . . became . . . a preferential position" (Henry Sigerist, quoted in *Health/Medicine and the Faith Communities*, M. Marty and K. Vaux, eds., Fortress Press, 1982, 110). Across the centuries of the Common Era, there are very considerable evidences of Christians caring for the sick, honoring them as they ministered to their needs, risking illness themselves by exposure to victims of plagues. By the early medieval period, the centrality of the ministry to the sick appears in *The Rule of St. Benedict*: "Before all things and above all things care must be taken of the sick . . ." (Chapter 36). From this conviction, especially as it was manifest in the monastic orders, hospitals were born. These were meant as signs and emblems of the presence in the world of

Christ the Healer. Indeed, the sick themselves were seen as evidences of the presence of the suffering Christ, such that in certain parts of western medieval Christendom the sick were declared as an "ordo" of ministry, a distinct category of sacred ministers along with catechumens, widows, and so on.

Anglicans, of course, inherit this tradition, and nowhere is it more apparent than in the service for the "Ministration to the Sick" in The Book of Common Prayer. The three-part service—The Ministry of the Word, The Laying on of Hands and Anointing, and Holy Communion—asserts that God is present, in and for and to the sick person. The sign of unction is primarily the sign of God's presence, just as the proclamation of the Word and partaking of the bread and wine are signs of a present, restorative God. As hands are laid upon the sick one, the priest beseeches "our Lord Jesus Christ to sustain you with his presence."

So it is that the participation of Christians in the public dialogue about what constitutes sound and appropriate and equitable health care is sponsored by the determination that it is a Christian calling to represent the healing power of Christ in the midst of the world's life.

PRECEPTS TO GUIDE A CHRISTIAN APPROACH TO HEALTH CARE

The fundamental assumption of the Christian approach to the issues of health care is that human life is of infinite value, that every individual is of irreplaceable worth. This conviction is derived from the Christian doctrine of creation. It declares that because it is of God, all creation is good and that humankind is the apex of the divine work, the masterwork of God. God entrusts the created order to human beings, at the same time blessing them, in the words of a eucharistic prayer, with "memory, reason, and skill," making them stewards of creation. That trust requires that all life be treated with reverence, but that human life has the highest claim. The incarnation of God in Christ, in Jesus the God-human, puts a seal upon that claim. To be obedient to the baptismal promise to "seek and serve Christ in all persons" is to acknowledge the infinite sanctity of every human life. Acknowledging the sanctity of life, however, does not mean honoring life in a merely vitalistic definition. What is to be acknowledged and honored is the sacred gift of selfhood. When that sacred, personal reality is gone, life in the sense in which God gives it is also gone. Determining the presence or absence of selfhood is not an easy undertaking. It is clear, in the Christian—and specifically in the Anglican—tradition, that such decisions belong to the community. Hard choices about the continuation or discontinuation of medical treatment, for example, need to be made by means of dialogue among the patient (if possible) and the patient's family and the physician and nurses and all other relevant parties. Those difficult choices need to be made in the light of the good stewardship and allocation of resources to which Christians are called.

The Christian view of the value of human lives leads to a determination to build a social order in which each person is cared for according to his or her needs. That distinguishes the Christian social view from one that would serve each individual according to his or her assets, or serve each according to some definition of "societal worth."

At present, in the matter of the distribution of health care assets in American society, very many with need are unserved or underserved. Where Christians would contend that *need* alone is the criterion for receiving health care, the present society distributes health care according to the *assets* of the recipients. Those who can pay (or are insured) are cared for, and those who cannot, go without. At the same time that a large segment of the population is made to go without adequate health care (approximately 36 million uninsured Americans in 1992), large sums are spent by the whole society to provide for those who can afford it. There is a striking equality among the sick. As one contemporary ethicist has put it, "When we are sick, we are as human beings on a level playing field in a way characteristic of few other circumstances" (Philip Turner). That such fundamental human equality is addressed in unequal ways constitutes a failure of justice that strikes at the heart of Christian convictions about human worth. In the Baptismal Covenant the worth of every individual in the eyes of God is firmly established, as it is again in the Burial Office, where the same pall lies upon the casket of people of every kind and condition.

CHRISTIANS AND THE MAKING OF PUBLIC POLICY IN THE HEALTH CARE FIELD

Christians, and those in the Anglican tradition in particular, can bring to the public discussion and the making of public policy certain perspectives that are capable both of elevating the discourse and of bringing it into line with the reality of human existence.

Episcopalian Christians can, for example, stand fast against what one commentator has called, "a Promethean vision of medical possibilities" (D. H. Smith). That is a vision that characterizes some approaches in American medicine and it fails to account for finitude and the truth that "ultimately all medicine is palliative." It is a vision that is blind to the inevitability of suffering and death, realities that are at the heart of the Christian diagnosis. "The brokenness of life—of healer and patient—is there for anyone with eyes to see" (Smith, *Health and Medicine in the Anglican Tradition*, Crossroad, New York, 1986, 7).

The truth that life is limited is joined by the fact that there are limitations of all kinds in the world, including limitations of health care resources. Issues arising out of the way in which those resources are distributed—to high technology neo-natalogy units or to programs in pre-natal care among the undereducated poor, for example—are issues in which people of conscience, and especially people of Christian conscience, should have important things to say.

Essential to the discussion and to the making of health care policy is the need to agree upon the common good. Christians must approach that definition, not as utopians, but, recognizing that, as Dean Turner has put it, "We wait with eager longing in a world that cannot yield all we want it to. In public policy, we can only hope for a good enough society." The resurrection of Christ is the sign that the ultimate outcome is God's and *also* the holy encouragement to Christ followers to strive mightily for a social order that is grounded in righteousness.

Whatever the definition of the "good enough" society turns out to be in this country, some elemental objectives for an approach to health care are clear:

- That universal access to quality, cost effective, health care services be considered necessary for everyone in the population, including those requiring long term care.

- That "quality health care" be defined so as to include programs in preventive medicine, where wellness is the first priority.

- That "quality health care" include interdisciplinary and interprofessional components to insure the care of the whole person—physiological, spiritual, psychological, social—in the community in which that person lives.

- That "quality health care" include the balanced distribution of human resources and not merely of financial resources, so that no region of the country is underserved by health care professionals, including primary care providers and nurses.

- That "quality health care" should include the treatment of incurably ill persons such that pain and distress are relieved even if life is shortened. Followers of the crucified and risen Christ do not place highest value on mere biological existence.

CONCLUSION

As stated at the outset, it is the hope and expectation of the Standing Commission on Health that these observations, including the five basic principles at the end of the document, become the basis for discussion and debate within the Episcopal Church. That proceeding should include attempts to refine the broad statements of this essay and begin to address the particular questions posed, for example, by the tension between the development of high-technology medical remedies and the crying need for primary care among large segments of the population.

United States Conference of Catholic Bishops

The following statement is excerpted from "A Framework for Comprehensive Health Care Reform: Protecting Human Life, Promoting Human Dignity, Pursuing the Common Good," a resolution of the United States Conference of Catholic Bishops dated June 18, 1993.

CRITERIA FOR REFORM

Applying our experience and principles to the choices before the nation, our bishops' conference strongly supports comprehensive reform that will ensure a decent level of health care for all without regard to their ability to pay. This will require concerted action by federal and other levels of government and by the diverse providers and consumers of health care. We believe government, an instrument of our common purpose called to pursue the common good, has an essential role to play in assuring that the rights of all people to adequate health care are respected.

We believe reform of the health care system which is truly fundamental and enduring must be rooted in values that reflect the essential dignity of each person, ensure that basic human rights are protected, and recognize the unique needs and claims of the poor. We commend to the leaders of our nation the following criteria for reform:

- *Respect for Life.* Whether it preserves and enhances the sanctity and dignity of human life from conception to natural death.

- *Priority Concern for the Poor.* Whether it gives special priority to meeting the most pressing health care needs of the poor and underserved, ensuring that they receive quality health services.

- *Universal Access.* Whether it provides ready universal access to comprehensive health care for every person living in the United States.

- *Comprehensive Benefits.* Whether it provides comprehensive benefits sufficient to maintain and promote good health; to provide preventive care; to treat disease, injury, and disability appropriately; and to care for persons who are chronically ill or dying.

- *Pluralism.* Whether it allows and encourages the involvement of the public and private sectors, including the voluntary, religious, and non-profit sectors, in the delivery of care and services; and whether it ensures respect for religious and ethical values in the delivery of health care for consumers and for individual and institutional providers.

- *Quality.* Whether it promotes the development of processes and standards that will help to achieve quality and equity in health services, in the training of providers, and in the informed participation of consumers in decision making on health care.

- *Cost Containment and Controls.* Whether it creates effective cost containment measures that reduce waste, inefficiency, and unnecessary care; measures that control rising costs of competition, commercialism, and administration; and measures that provide incentives to individuals and providers for effective and economical use of limited resources.

- *Equitable Financing*. Whether it assures society's obligation to finance universal access to comprehensive health care in an equitable fashion, based on ability to pay; and whether proposed cost-sharing arrangements are designed to avoid creating barriers to effective care for the poor and vulnerable.

KEY POLICY PRIORITIES

We hope Catholics and others will use this criteria to assess proposals for reform. In applying these criteria, we have chosen to focus our advocacy on several essential priorities:

Priority Concern for the Poor/Universal Access: We look at health care reform from the bottom up, how it touches the unserved and underserved. Genuine health care reform must especially focus on the basic health needs of the poor (i.e., those who are unable through private resources, employer support, or public aid to provide payment for health care services, or those unable to gain access to health care because of limited resources, inadequate education, or discrimination).

When there is a question of allocating scarce resources, the vulnerable and the poor have a compelling claim to first consideration. Special attention must be given to ensuring that those who have suffered from inaccessible and inadequate health care (e.g., in central cities, isolated rural areas, and migrant camps) are first brought back into an effective system of quality care. Therefore, we will strongly support measures to ensure true universal access and rapid steps to improve the health care of the poor and unserved. Universal access must not be significantly postponed, since coverage delayed may well be coverage denied. We do not support a two-tiered health system since separate health care coverage for the poor usually results in poor health care. Linking the health care of poor and working-class families to the health care of those with greater resources is probably the best assurance of comprehensive benefits and quality care.

Respect for Human Life and Human Dignity: Real health care reform must protect and enhance human life and human dignity. Every member of the human family has the right to life and to the means that are suitable for the full development of life. This is why we insist that every human being has the right to quality health services, regardless of age, income, illness, or condition of life. Government statistics on infant mortality are evidence that lack of access and inadequate care are literally matters of life and death. The needs of the frail elderly, the unborn child, the person living with AIDS, and the undocumented immigrant must be addressed by health care reform.

Neither the violence of abortion and euthanasia nor the growing advocacy for assisted suicide is consistent with respect for human life. When destructive practices such as abortion or euthanasia seek acceptance as aspects of "health care" alongside genuine elements of the healing art, the very meaning of health care is distorted and threatened. A consistent concern for human dignity is strongly demonstrated by providing access to quality care from the prenatal period throughout infancy and childhood, into adult life and, at the end of life, when care is possible even if cure is not. Therefore, we are convinced it would be a moral tragedy, a serious policy misjudgment, and a major political mistake to burden health care reform with abortion coverage that most Americans oppose and the federal government has not funded for the last seventeen years. Consequently, we continue to oppose unequivocally the inclusion of abortion as a health care benefit, as do three out of four Americans (cf. April 6, 1993 *New York Times* poll).

As long-time advocates of health care reform, we appeal to the leaders of the nation to avoid a divisive and polarizing dispute which could jeopardize passage of national health reform. We strongly believe it would be morally wrong and counterproductive to compel individuals, institutions, or states to pay for or participate in procedures that fundamentally violate basic moral principles and the consciences of millions of Americans. The common good is not advanced when advocates of so-called choice compel taxpayers to fund what we and many others are convinced is the destruction of human life.

Pursuing the Common Good and Preserving Pluralism: We fear the cause of real reform can be undermined by special interest conflict and the resistance of powerful forces who have a major stake in maintaining the *status quo*. It also can be thwarted by unnecessary partisan political combat. We believe the debate can be advanced by a continuing focus on the common good and a healthy respect for genuine pluralism. A reformed system must encourage the creative and renewed involvement of both the public and private sectors, including voluntary, religious, and nonprofit providers of care. It must also respect the religious and ethical values of both individuals and institutions involved in the health care system. We are deeply concerned that Catholic and other institutions with strong moral foundations may face increasing economic and regulatory pressures to compromise their moral principles and to participate in practices inconsistent with their commitment to human life. The Catholic community is strongly committed to continuing to meet the health needs of the nation in a framework of genuine reform, which respects the essential role and values of religiously affiliated providers of health care.

Restraining Costs: We have the best health care technology in the world, but tens of millions have little or no access to it and the costs of the system are straining our nation, our economy, our families, and our Church to the breaking point. We insist that any acceptable plan must include effective mechanisms to restrain rising health care costs. By bringing health care cost inflation down, we could cut the federal deficit, improve economic competitiveness, and help stem the decline in living standards for many working families. Without cost containment, we cannot hope to make health care affordable and direct scarce national resources to other pressing problems that, in turn, worsen health problems (e.g., inadequate housing, poverty, joblessness, and poor education).

FOR PERSONAL REFLECTION

1. What did "Fact or Fiction: What Do You Really Know About U.S. Health Care?" reveal to you?

2. In what ways has the current health care delivery system worked well for you? Has it ever failed to live up to its potential for you personally? If so, what has the impact of this been in your life?

3. If you were asked to help write a position statement on health care for your faith community, what would you include? How would you support the statement theologically?

FOR GROUP DISCUSSION

1. It is apparent that there is no easy solution to the health care crisis in America. Ask each member of the group to jot down what he or she wants in a "re-formed" system. Share those hopes using a round-robin format. Discuss these hopes, looking for commonalities. Then seek to come to consensus on the top five priorities.

2. Evans suggests that the first reason that health care reform is floundering in the United States is "moral weakness," questioning whether "autonomy and individual rights so rule the day that society is not willing to give up a little so that others will have something." In what ways does that thought resonate with your thoughts? Can you envision our society accepting change in health care? What should the church's role be in health care policy?

3. Statements about health care reform gleaned from several church groups have been included in this book. Prior to reading them here, had you been aware of these statements? How have you experienced the Church's response to those marginalized by the health care delivery system? Have you found those responses satisfactory? In what way do "Faith-Based Initiatives" enhance and/or compromise the mission of the Church?

6.
Health Ministry and the Parish

Where Cross the Crowded Ways of Life
–Frank Mason North

Where cross the crowded ways of life,
Where sound the cries of race and clan,
Above the noise of selfish strife,
We hear thy voice, O Son of Man.

In haunts of wretchedness and need,
On shadowed thresholds dark with fears,
From paths where hide the lure of greed,
We catch a vision of thy tears.

The cup of water given for thee,
Still holds the freshness of thy grace;
Yet long these multitudes to see
The true compassion of thy face.

The church has too long settled for health promotion and health care as the purview of the health care delivery system. It's time to reclaim health ministry at the congregational level. It's time for people to see, incarnated in the neighborhood church, "the true compassion of [Jesus'] face."

I've heard it said that ministry is what we do with our spirituality. Health ministry is what we do with our spirituality of the body, our theology of the body. A spirituality of health cannot remain in the realm of head, but must work itself into our fingers and feet. Acting on beliefs changes the congregation.

It doesn't take much. Maryfran Crist, a nurse practitioner, describes her small Midwest Episcopal congregation as "The Little Church That Could." With an average Sunday attendance of twenty-one and average parishioner age of seventy, the congregation's first response to developing a health ministry was "We're too small and we're too old." Yet after months of reflection and discussion, they saw possibilities. Four years later, the congregation has an active health ministry. They have, among other things, done the following:

- Built a two-level ramp, with the help of Lutheran Brotherhood, to make the space handicap accessible.

- Moved coffee hour upstairs to the back of sanctuary so that all may gather (and they even remembered to have a high chair available).

- Started monitoring parishioners' blood pressures every three months.

- Begun serving a simple, free, community meal at the end of the month when Social Security funds are running low.

- Invited Head Start to use the facilities for health screening each summer.

- Introduced the anointing of the sick at Sunday services, and

- Instituted a weekly Bible study and Eucharist at the nearby elderly high-rise once a week, where many are essentially homebound.

Spiritual healing has a long tradition of the church. Much has been written about spiritual healing, and though that is important, our limited space in this volume keeps us from doing it justice, so it's not specifically addressed here. Suffice it to say that, despite our twenty-first century embarrassment at Jesus' simplicity of healing, contemporary research has shown that prayer works. Maybe prayer, anointing, and the laying-on-of-hands creates the environment for healing to take place. After all, isn't that all that surgery and medicines really do?

Consider the stories, ideas, tools, and exercises on the following pages, and let them spark your imagination for health ministry in your congregation.

COMMON QUESTIONS ABOUT PARISH HEALTH MINISTRY
—Jean Denton

Jean Denton, RN, MA, is a founding member of Health Ministries Association, an interfaith organization that serves members as they work toward integration of faith and health. She has consulted with congregations and dioceses, taught, written, and led workshops about establishing congregationally based health ministry.

What Is Health Ministry?

Health ministry in a local congregation is an intentional ministry focusing on both healing and health, combining the ancient traditions of the Christian community and the knowledge and tools of modern health care. Health ministry embraces the body as integral to who we are as persons, and bears witness to God's creative and redeeming work for the whole person. Health ministry encourages health through:

- Integration of body, mind, and spirit;

- Increased self-knowledge;

- Personal responsibility; and

- Interdependence among the faith community.

INTEGRATION OF BODY, MIND, AND SPIRIT

Every human being is a trinity in unity, reflecting the relationships inherent in our Trinitarian God. Body, mind, and spirit are so intricately woven together that a person cannot be divided mind from body or body from spirit without losing his or her essence. Yet the current health system inadvertently pulls people apart. Health care systems address biological concerns, often quite well, but the health care system is much less comfortable when a patient asks, "Why did God let this happen to me?"

The church, on the other hand, is often uncomfortable with the biological side of life, and thus also bears some responsibility for dividing the integrity of mind, body, and spirit. Spurred on in its early history by the heresies of Gnosticism and Manichaeism, the church has split the spiritual (the "truly" good) from the physical (that which is passing away). The eighteenth-century philosopher René Descartes further articulated this split, and unfortunately, the church seems to have listened more keenly to Descartes than to Jesus on this point. Today's church is still uncomfortable in dealing with issues of the body. Health ministry seeks to weave together "cure of body" with "cure of soul."

INCREASED SELF-KNOWLEDGE

Health ministry takes seriously the importance of knowing oneself—of identifying patterns of behavior that have become unexamined habits, learning ways the body responds to exercise and food, and becoming skilled at recognizing responses to illness. Health ministry also takes seriously the importance of knowing the wisdom of the Christ in matters of health and health care.

PERSONAL RESPONSIBILITY

As amazingly created beings, we bear responsibility to do our part to seek, attain, and maintain health, all the while knowing that none save God is ultimately responsible for our welfare. We know ourselves to be granted the power and the authority to be co-creators with God, and to be answerable for our stewardship of that tiny piece of creation that is ourselves. We bear responsibility for the health of the community as well, understanding health to be a corporate as well as a personal matter.

INTERDEPENDENCE AMONG THE FAITH COMMUNITY

We know health to be a community affair. Health is a social experience, from establishing behavioral norms to sharing costs of medical care. The Christian community has the opportunity to walk with members who are not well, to learn from both receiving and giving care to one another, and to encourage one another in healthy lifestyles. Christians might look at health as we look at salvation—it is both personal and communal. It is the community that carries the individual through illness and suffering, and it is community that supports and encourages well-being.

What Is Parish Nursing?

Parish nursing is caring for health of mind, body, and spirit by combining the knowledge and skills of nursing practice with an understanding of the spiritual and religious beliefs that underlie health. Parish nursing is practiced in the local community of faith. With one foot in the spiritual world of the church and one foot in the physical world of medicine, the parish nurse addresses the relationship between the invisible and the visible. The nurse links these spheres in translating jargon (sometimes medical and sometimes ecclesiastical), forging connections, and facilitating the parishioner's more complete understanding of his or her health experience.

Parish nurses are registered nurses who have been formally educated through a course of study offered by a university or seminary. The parish nurse engages in several functions:

- Integrating faith and health within the parish community;
- Counseling parishioners on questions of personal health;
- Acting as a health educator;
- Acting as a referral agent;
- Coordinating volunteers;
- Developing support groups; and
- Advocating for individual and community health.

The parish nurse is a nurse of the church, not simply a nurse *in* a church. She is not transplanted from the hospital or clinic to perform the same tasks, and she does not attempt to replicate existing services available in the community. Many agencies are already providing nursing care in the home—changing dressings, drawing blood, monitoring intravenous feedings, for example. (Most, though certainly not all, geographic locations have doctors and clinics available for treatments.)

The practice of the parish nurse is broader than the general public usually imagines a nurse's role to be. Under the Nurse Practice Act (which differs somewhat from state to state), the registered nurse has several responsibilities. Some are delegated functions, tasks done under the supervision of a physician. Often these are invasive procedures, and they are often the first tasks people think of when they imagine a nurse at work. The parish nurse, however, focuses specifically on other, independent functions identified in the state's Nurse Practice Act: assessing health needs, teaching, referring to services in the community, coordinating health care, counseling regarding health-related concerns, and advocating for those who need a voice.

What Is the Difference between Parish Nursing and Health Ministry?

Health ministry in a congregation is often, though not exclusively, led by a parish nurse, so health ministry and parish nursing go hand in hand. But they are not the same thing.

Some congregations have parish nurse programs. Such a program focuses somewhat more on the nurse's responsibilities and duties than on the ministry of members of the congregations and outcomes experienced by the parish. Health ministry is broader in scope. Congregations have music ministry, not church organist programs, and they have Christian formation programs, not Sunday school teacher programs. In the same way, congregations have health ministry. Sometimes the plural is used—health *ministries*—to emphasize the multiplicity of players.

Health ministry addresses health along the continuum of health, from excellent health to extremely poor health. It uses a public health model rather than the medical model, and balances the themes of wellness (health promotion, disease prevention) and healing (treating disease, recovery, chronic illness, and death). Health ministry is a ministry of the entire congregation and involves laity, clergy, and health professionals who are parishioners.

Why Should a Congregation Consider Health Ministry?

The health care system in the United States doesn't focus on health, too often doesn't seem to care, and isn't a cohesive, holistic system. Instead, it's primarily disease-oriented, fragmented, and enormously expensive.

The Reverend Dr. Granger Westberg, a pioneer in hospital chaplaincy and the initiator of the parish nursing movement, speaks of the mismatch between the resources allocated by the health care system and the people needing care. Westberg divides people into three categories, which he, tongue in cheek, describes as "The Well," "The Little Bit Sick," and "The Really Sick." In those groups, about 70 percent are "well," 29 percent are in the second category (visiting a doctor, asking help from the local pharmacist, getting routine care in a community hospital), and only 1 percent are in the third group, the "really sick people" who are in tertiary-care hospitals. Health professionals, on the other hand, are distributed in the opposite manner, with 1 percent of all health professionals working with "the well" to keep them well, 29 percent caring for those who are "a little bit sick," and 70 percent working with the 1 percent of the people who are "really sick." Westberg argues, therefore, that the institutional church can play a huge role in addressing health issues, particularly in keeping people well.

The disarray of the health care system is not the only reason congregations should become involved in health. The more compelling reason comes from the mouth of Jesus. The mission Christ gives to his followers is to preach, teach, and heal. The church's teaching and preaching have far exceeded its healing in this day. The church needs to be true to its calling. The health care system and the church offer plenty of space for health professionals and laity to work together to keep people well, to empower, to educate, to advocate, to teach, to care, and to offer the fullness of life that our Lord wants for us.

How Does Health Ministry Differ from Pastoral Care?

The spheres of pastoral care and health ministry overlap but are not synonymous. The following example demonstrates how health ministry stretched pastoral care, and included advocacy and empowerment:

> A parishioner spoke with her priest about her 91-year-old aunt, who was in a nursing home and was not eating. The quality of life for the elderly woman was quite good except for the eating. The doctor had asked the parishioner to grant permission to have a gastric feeding tube inserted in her aunt's stomach. Knowing that her aunt did not want dramatic measures, the parishioner nonetheless felt pressured to give permission for this procedure. The priest listened well, and after ethical reflection and discussion, he told the parishioner that he did not see that it was incumbent upon the parishioner to have the procedure done. It was caring and loving not to make the elderly aunt undergo any surgery, which the aunt greatly feared.
>
> The parishioner spoke with the parish nurse the next day, saying she had already spoken with the priest but wanted to gather all the information she could when making this decision about her aunt's care. The parishioner wondered if it were more humane to let someone die in surgery (the aunt was on intermittent oxygen and had cardiac problems as well as malnutrition) or to let someone starve to death. As the conversation unfolded, the nurse was able to suggest that other avenues were open.
>
> The nurse encouraged the parishioner to request a case

conference at the nursing home, and the nurse agreed to accompany her. The case conference included the dietician and the nursing staff. It became apparent that the gastric tube was the easiest answer for the nursing home, though it might not be the best answer for the patient or family. Together in the conference, they explored including the involvement of family and friends in food preparation and feeding.

The elderly aunt began eating again when the food was prepared in a familiar way and when time and attention were given to her and her dining experience.

Just What Does Health Ministry Look Like in a Congregation?

Health ministry is unique in each congregation. Its shape is drawn by the vision, the resources, and the needs of the particular congregation. Smaller congregations will have programs that differ from large parishes, and urban parishes will have programs different from rural ones. Each program has its own unique thumbprint.

The health ministries committee might work with the health department to offer health risk appraisals to parishioners. Someone might be recruited to teach classes on safe babysitting to the youth. People might commit to taking blood pressures after the Sunday worship service. A librarian might volunteer to maintain a resource bank with information on health and illness. A lecture series might be organized with topics like "The Healing Power of Humor" and "Psyche and Spirit: Mental and Spiritual Health." A letter-writing group might be organized to communicate with legislators regarding health care issues. The local YMCA might offer exercise programs in the church building. The possibilities are endless.

Health ministry contains a strong element of community health, with the parish itself as the community. Besides working with individuals and families, the parish nurse also works with the parish as a unit, paying attention to community concerns. Health ministry deals with the parish community, looking at its demographics, physical plant, and healthy or unhealthy practices.

What about Liability?

Licensed professionals need to carry personal liability insurance to cover their professional practice, whatever license it is that they carry.

Congregations also need to carry liability insurance on their staff and volunteers doing church-related work. The congregation needs to review its liability insurance policy and speak with the carrier about the kind of health ministry programming envisioned for the congregation. Companies often will add coverage for the parish nurse/health minister at no charge if it is clear that the work is noninvasive and doesn't require a doctor's order. It needs to be made clear to the insurance company that the nurse is not performing dependent duties (those only done under the direction of a physician), but independent functions as identified in the state's Nurse Practice Act.

If the congregation enters into partnership with another institution, say to hold a medical clinic in the church, the partnering health care organization needs to assure the congregation of adequate insurance coverage.

In What Kind of Situations Does a Parish Nurse Really Make a Difference?

The answer to this question comes from the people whose lives have been touched by this work.

- A mother stops in the health ministries office and says to the parish nurse, "I don't know what I should do, if anything. Our babysitter molested my little boy last night." She is hurt, confused, and angry. She doesn't know where to turn, so she turns to a health professional in her church, who listens, prays with her, refers her to community services that can help her, and stays in touch with her and the little boy.

- A young man stops the parish nurse after a Sunday worship service and says, "Do you see this lump on my neck? Do you think I should see a doctor? I don't have health insurance, so I've been putting it off." The nurse helps him understand that he needs immediate attention, and works with him to find a physician and get an emergency visit for the next morning.

- Another man comes for anointing and for prayers for healing after Eucharist. He says, "I think I might be alcoholic, and I know I can't handle it alone." The parish nurse and the priest pray with him. Afterward, he asks whether he can talk about his problem with the parish nurse, and over a cup of coffee, they discuss what it might be like to join the local AA group.

- A business executive in her thirties comes to talk with the parish nurse on her way back from getting a second opinion about her back pain. It isn't lupus after all—it's metastatic bone cancer. She comes in shock and disbelief. She meets with the parish nurse many times after that, seeking answers to practical questions, wanting to share her hopes and her fear of more pain, needing to talk about her life, her mistakes, and heaven, and making plans for advance medical directives. And she wants to talk through her burial service. When her condition stabilizes, the parish nurse suggests to this woman that she has something precious to give to her community—the ability to share her experience with others who have life-threatening illnesses. Together they form a support group, and in the midst of community, the woman continues to come to terms with her impending death.

Does Health Ministry Exclusively Serve the Parish, or Does It Serve the Neighborhood, Too?

There is an important element of outreach in health ministry. Again, depending on the vision and the resources of the congregation, health ministry might also minister to individuals in the community around the parish, all the while remembering that health ministry means helping people to integrate mind, body, and spirit, not delivering traditional medical care. A clinic to serve the needs of medically indigent people may be part of the vision of the congregation, but it is best accompanied by action to change a health care system that needs to be overhauled to become inclusive. It is too easy for churches to be charitable and merciful without owning responsibility for seeking justice.

The congregation itself is the locus of the health ministry. Everyone who is part of the parish is encouraged to both partake of services and to offer themselves and their gifts to others. This models to the wider community that the church is not the "dispenser of health" but a community of broken people who minister to each other to bring health and healing. Health ministry is a powerful tool for evangelism in the best sense of that word, sharing the good news of God's ready salvation for people. But it is not a tool for proselytizing.

How Do You Know Whether a Church Is Ready for a Health Ministry Program?

Most churches already have some aspect of health ministry in place, be it a corps of parishioners who deliver Meals on Wheels, an intercessory prayer group, a crisis care committee, or a Stephen Ministry. Many churches may not name these programs "health ministry," but they are part of health and caring. Most congregations have something on which to build. Current ministries tell where the interest of the parish can be found and provide a familiar place to start expanding health ministry.

Looking at the parish in terms of its resources and its energy is important. Resources don't have to be financial. They can be interest, skill, vision, or commitment. If these exist, it might be the right time to harness them into a fuller, more organized program.

Recognizing the specific health-related needs in a particular parish is also important. Does the parish have a large aging population, or is the parish full of young couples with little children? Are there obvious unmet needs? Necessity may be the mother behind beginning an organized, conscious health ministry program.

Where Does a Congregation Begin?

- Pray. Ask God for clarity, connections, direction, and insight. Pray seriously and with an open heart. Listen carefully. And continue praying throughout the process. Health ministry is not a human endeavor done with human talents.

- Become educated about health ministry. Read all you can, starting with the resources named in the appendix at the end of this book, and scan the Internet for "health ministry" and "parish nursing." Contact other congregations in your area to find out their experiences. Contact your local health care institutions and see if they have experience in partnering with congregations in this ministry.

- Contact your denominational headquarters to connect with like-minded congregations. When you find others of kindred spirit, spend time with them regularly. Toss around ideas, questions, and hopes. Listen for suggestions.

- Contact the Health Ministries Association (1-800-280-9919) and the International Parish Nurse Resource Center (1-800-556-5368) for information. You'll get encouragement, support, and linkage with others.

- Talk with the clergy of the congregation. Share your enthusiasm, and offer reading material. Allow time for reflection on your proposal, but be sure to get back in touch within a reasonable amount of time.

- Discuss and dream with the clergy who support this concept, and then plant seeds in the parish. Pass out articles to people who might be interested. Let parishioners know of your interest through the parish newsletter, and invite them to gather with you to learn more.

- Hold an informal meeting of interested parties. Show a videotape such as *Body & Soul* (available through National Episcopal Health Ministries) to offer a clear picture of the concept in action.

- See to it that someone from your congregation becomes educated in leading a health ministry by attending a basic course offered through a local university or national organization. These course offerings are coordinated through the International Parish Nurse Resource Center. Most courses are restricted to registered nurses, but some enroll other health professionals as well. The Health Ministries Association's annual meeting offers learning opportunities for many health professionals.

- Make a plan and act on it. Progress might not be swift, and it just might be that not everyone in the congregation will buy in to the idea. Some people need to experience health ministry for themselves before they comprehend it.

- Celebrate, both liturgically and otherwise, the growth and change that comes.

DIALOGUE WITH YOUR BODY ABOUT ILLNESS AND HEALTH
–Thomas A. Droege

Thomas A. Droege, Ph.D., has been a longtime friend of health ministry. He has been on the faculty at Valparaiso University in Valparaiso, Indiana, and has worked with the Interfaith Health Program at the Carter Center of Emory University's School of Public Health in Atlanta. He is a sage visionary, a true leader, and a practical pastor.

The very idea of having a dialogue with your body may seem strange to you. A dialogue between two people is not that difficult to imagine, but most of us tend to think of our body as an object rather than as a subject, an *it* rather than a *thou*. We often treat our bodies as possessions. We expect them to follow orders no matter how demanding or abusing we are. But we all know from experience that if we push our bodies too hard, they will rebel by refusing to do what we ask and by forcing accommodations on us. Suddenly our bodies are in control and we are the slaves.

Dialogue calls for a different relationship between self and body, a relationship Martin Buber would classify as I-Thou rather than I-It. Giving our bodies the status of persons rather than things requires a different attitude on our part. Rather than being property that we can put to any use we desire, a body-self calls for respect, love, reverence, and even awe. Then it is possible to carry on a dialogue in one's mind between two parties who are ready to listen and willing to change.

A dialogical relationship with one's body is particularly important in periods of illness, because then a feeling of estrangement from one's body is most likely to occur. You take your body for granted in times of relatively good health, but it has a way of getting your attention when you are sick. Like the whining of a tired and irritable child, your body's cries of distress are something you cannot ignore. This doesn't mean that you are ready to listen, really listen, to your ailing body, any more than you are ready to listen to a whining child. But remarkable things can happen if you can get beyond the irritating demand for attention and reach out to the wounded child underneath, who so desperately needs your understanding and unconditional love.

The following exercise is designed at least to initiate what can become a continuing dialogue with one's body. The exercise appears in two forms: one for use in a group, the other for the spiritual care of a person who is sick. Though both have the same goal, to improve the relationship between self and body, there are some clear differences. It is assumed that those using the exercise in a group setting are relatively healthy, while the spiritual care exercise assumes that the person is sick. Those doing the group experience are encouraged to express themselves in writing, but the sick person will probably prefer to respond orally. The spiritual care setting will be more personal and intimate, allowing the use of touch, and it will call for greater flexibility on the part of the guide.

Some form of preparation for a dialogue with one's body is called for no matter what setting is used. The following paragraph suggests how the exercise might be introduced:

> All too often we treat our bodies as our possessions, to use and misuse as we wish. Scripture speaks of the body as having a dignity equal to that of the self, both being expressions of yourself as a person. As a gift from God, your body is sacred and to be treated with the respect that belongs to the "temple of the Holy Spirit" (1 Cor 6:19). The voice of our body can be a vehicle for the voice of God. To give your body such a voice is the purpose of the dialogue that follows.

Exercise 1–Within a Group Setting

GUIDED IMAGERY

Let your body relax and sink into the chair on which you are sitting . . . letting your eyes close or keeping them focused on one particular spot in order not to be distracted by me or anything going on outside you . . . letting the sound of my voice guide you gently into the center of your inner being . . . attuning yourself to the world within rather than the world outside . . . becoming aware of your breathing as the natural rhythm of your body . . . breathing in . . . and breathing out . . . moving ever deeper to the center of your inner being . . . listening to the voice of your body . . . letting all the voices that have been demanding your attention fade into the background until they are no more than distant echoes. *(Pause for 20 seconds.)*

As you move more and more deeply into the region of your inner self, become aware of seeing your body from within rather than looking at your body as if it were some external object, like when you look in the mirror. Become aware of your body from within, your breathing in and out in a natural, regular rhythm. Scan different parts of your body for any tension that might be there, and then release that tension so that your body can feel relaxed and at ease. Pay attention to what your body is telling you about its needs: perhaps the need for nourishment . . . or for rest . . . or for exercise . . . or for touch. (Pause for 30 seconds.) Are you surprised at either the number or the intensity of the needs? Do those needs seem legitimate to you? What has kept you from meeting those needs? *(Pause for 1 minute.)*

The body that is you had its beginning long before you were aware of becoming a person. Return with the aid of your imagination to the beginning of your body. Since you can do anything that you want with your imagination, imagine that your beginning was like Adam's, God forming your body out of the dust of the ground to be absolutely unique, unlike anybody else who has ever lived.

Imagine that as God breathes into you the breath of life, your whole body suddenly becomes alive and fully functioning. Imagine your breath to be God's breath within you, your breathing in tune with the rhythm of the universe. *(Pause for 30 seconds.)*

Your body, for all the wonder of its created goodness, has been formed from the earth and will return to the earth, as subject to pain, suffering, and loss as every other earth creature. Let your body tell you the story of its woundedness from the beginning until now. Let your mind drift back over the years, and as you recall events of trauma to your body, record them on the paper in front of you with a word or phrase. The wound may have been a broken arm or leg, or it may have been a long or a short illness. The trauma may have been widespread throughout your body or localized in one place. It may have been on the surface for all to see or hidden deep inside. The trauma may have come and gone, or it may have left a wound that will never heal or a space that will never be filled. Take a moment to scan your body-memory and then list on the left-hand side of the paper the injuries and illnesses that you recall in whatever order they come to you. *(Pause for 2 minutes.)*

After you have completed the list, redo the sequence of items in the order of their importance: important for the lesson it taught you or for its lasting impact or because the wound is fresh and frightening. Let your judgments be spontaneous, flowing out of the story of your body. *(Pause for 1 minute.)*

With a deeper awareness of your body and its woundedness, you are ready for a dialogue with your body about illness and injury. Sitting in quietness with your eyes closed . . . focusing your attention inward . . . become aware of the presence of your body as a person, a person with a story to tell, a person with needs and fears and hopes. As you feel the presence of your body as a person grow stronger within you, you may be aware of an image of your body taking shape within your imagination: perhaps in the form of a person who bears the marks of many wounds on his or her body or in the form of a wise old man or woman. If such an image appears to your mind's eye, you may want to give the person a name in order that the dialogue may flow more smoothly. If not, simply be aware of your body as a presence within you. *(Pause for 30 seconds.)*

Remaining in quietness with your eyes closed, let the presence of your body as a person grow stronger. As you feel ready, greet the person who is your body and listen closely to what your body has to say about the wounds your body has suffered over the years, the threats of illness and injury in the past. Go back to each of the traumas you listed to refresh your body-memory about those wounds, asking about their meaning and what they have taught you. Listen to what your body needs from you in the future, especially in facing the trauma that will be the end of the story of your body. Let the dialogue between you and your body flow freely, recording both what you say and what your body-self says, your pen simply recording what is there without censoring or interpreting. Let the inner dialogue proceed in silence. *(Allow 10–15 minutes for writing.)*

Exercise 2–For the Spiritual Care of the Sick

The most frequent use of this exercise will likely be by individuals for spiritual self-care. It is well suited for that purpose, especially if your attention span is limited and you are looking for a relatively short exercise.

If you are using this exercise as a spiritual care guide, I suggest that you remain as flexible as possible in directing the guided imagery process. Much will depend on the personality, experience, capacity for imagery, and type and stage of illness of the person doing the exercise. The guide should have a map of the journey in mind, as well as a destination, but be ready to follow a number of different routes to get there, depending on the variables just mentioned. The exercise as written is one such map, which has as its goal the linking of the experience of the body as ill with the experience of the body as the temple of the Holy Spirit.

GUIDED IMAGERY

Let your body relax and feel at ease to the extent that this is possible in your present state of illness . . . letting your eyes close as your body relaxes . . . letting the sound of my voice guide you gently inside your body awareness . . . attuning yourself to the world inside rather than the world outside . . . becoming aware of your breathing as the natural rhythm of your body . . . moving deeper into the center of your inner being in order to listen to the voice of your body . . . paying attention only to the sound of my voice and the voice of your own body.

As you move more and more deeply into the region of your inner self, become aware of seeing your body from within rather than looking at your body as if it were some external object, like when you look in a mirror. As you become aware of your body from within, pay attention to your breathing, breathing in and out in a natural, regular rhythm. Your breathing is you. Feel a unity with your breathing. Feel a unity with your body.

Your body is a special creation of God. In order for you to have a deeper sense of that, go all the way back to the origins of your body-self, long before you had the capacity even to be aware of your body. Imagine that your beginning was like Adam's, God forming your body out of the dust of the ground to be absolutely unique, unlike anybody else who has ever lived. Imagine God breathing into you the breath of life so that your breath is God's breath, your breathing in tune with the rhythm of the universe, your being in the image of God.

St. Paul calls the human body a temple of the Holy Spirit, a sacred place. Other images can convey the same sense of holiness: a body filled with light that radiates outward, a body so filled with the Spirit of God that there is a tongue of fire on the head, a body with a face that glows with an inner light, a body with a halo surrounding it. Choose an image that fits with your felt sense of being filled with the Holy Spirit. *(Pause for 30 seconds.)* Tell me when you've found an image that seems right. Describe the image for me. If the image seems external to you, then step into that image right now so that you and your body are one and filled with the Holy Spirit. *(Pause for 15 seconds.)*

With the aid of your imagination, go to the place within your body where it feels the worst right now, the place within your body that is bearing the burden of the illness. Simply be aware of the pain or whatever it is that feels wrong. *(Pause for 30 seconds.)* Perhaps an image will form that will express how this feels, or maybe you will be aware of something that your body is trying to say that you haven't been hearing because other things have been demanding your attention. Don't try to force anything. Simply be aware of what is there. *(Pause for 1 minute.)* What have you been experiencing? Is there anything that surprises you? *(Pause for 30 seconds.)*

Return to the image you had before of your body as sacred, as filled with the Holy Spirit. Bring that image to the place within your body that is bearing the burden of your illness. If it's hard to unite your body as sacred with your body as sick, then imagine them side by side in two different chairs. What would they say to each other? Let your sick body speak first, and then let your sacred body answer. *(Pause for 1 minute.)*

(Bring the exercise to a close with a prayer that flows out of the imagery experience, and encourage the person to record the dialogue in writing if he or she feels strong enough.)

A DAY IN THE LIFE OF A PARISH NURSE
–*Jean Denton*

Jean Denton, RN, MA, is the founding director of National Episcopal Health Ministries. She has fifteen years' experience in parish nursing, and is a contributor to the standardized parish nursing curriculum of the International Parish Nurse Resource Center. Jean also served on the committee to develop the American Nurses Association's *Scope and Standards of Practice for Parish Nursing*. She is ordained to the Vocational Diaconate in the Episcopal Church.

A "typical day" in the life of a parish nurse does not exist. Many variables enter in—the size and needs of the congregation, the preparation and skills of the nurse, to name a few. The day I describe here is no day at all, though it might have been. It is a composite of experiences as seen through the lens of a staff member in a large congregation where I have been a member for a decade. Come and walk with me through my "day."

The door to my workplace at the church door bears the sign HEALTH MINISTRIES OFFICE, and I enter it early in the morning, knowing that having had a day off yesterday there will be mail and e-mail and voice mail waiting. I enjoy my office, which is just big enough for a small corner desk and a low file cabinet, a bookcase and a rocking chair for a visitor to enjoy. The cinderblock walls are painted a pale and gentle blue, and on one wall is pasted a mural of an open window with curtains blowing and a view of the sea and shore. The window serves to open the otherwise windowless room, and I want it to be an open place, a place where the Spirit can enter and move.

My calendar informs me that I have a meeting at the local chapter of the American Cancer Society today to continue planning for a workshop. The workshop is for clergy, and clergy are always ministering to parishioners who cope with cancer. I also have a home visit planned with Bill; he is awaiting the results of his MRI. His dizziness suggests a brain tumor, and he is frightened. Then there's lunch with a parishioner whose husband has just left the marriage, and she is anxious both for herself and the teenage children. There's also a report to finish for the vestry. Maybe then I can take the rest of the afternoon off, because I'm coming back this evening to teach the last of a five-week series on pastoral visiting for parishioners who want to be part of the church's Called to Care ministry.

At 8:30, the staff meets for morning prayer. Not everyone attends, but I find it important for me to be there. It's a time to remember why I am doing this work, and a time to be reminded that this is not my personal work. It is the work of the whole church, the body of Christ. In intercessory prayer, I am reminded that God's in charge of this endeavor. I am only a channel for God's grace—should I be so open!

On my way back to my office, a parishioner who is attending the Shepherd's Center program for seniors stops me. He tells me that his son-in-law, Charles, was admitted to Community North Hospital yesterday. It's probably cancer. He smokes a lot. Charles's wife is very distressed. Would I be able to stop by to see him? "Sure," I say. In my mind, I am reviewing what I know of the structure and dynamics of this family. I had given the homily at the burial service for this man's wife just two years ago. As I walk up the stairs, I consider the breadth of knowledge a parish nurse needs to do this ministry: counseling skills, the ability to work with groups, information on health as well as sickness, and the ability to navigate the health care system, all the while remaining conscious that it is God moving in each encounter and each situation.

Back in my office, I read over the agenda for the meeting at the Cancer Society. I find the article I want to share with the committee and put it aside to make copies. I lay out the material for the pastoral visiting class. I sit with a map to plan my day's itinerary: The Cancer Society is south, the lunch is in midtown, and the hospital visit is northeast. Bill lives west. Hmmm . . .

I move to the copy machine to reproduce the article, and the staff bookkeeper stops me. She asks, "Can I talk with you for a minute about a prescription?" "Sure," I say. "Why don't we meet in my office after I make this copy?" (I am assuming the copier won't jam and has adequate ink. And I am assuming it's a quick question about a dosage or side effect.) Back in my snug office, it's quiet and private. I close the door, and give her my full attention. After the first interrupting phone call—about a change of who is going to take blood pressures after the 8:00 a.m. service next Sunday—I ask the receptionist to please hold my calls. I'm in a conference.

The bookkeeper tells me that she has finally gone to see her doctor about the lack of energy and sleeplessness she has been having, and the unexplained tearfulness. The doctor did a physical workup and then sent her to a counselor. The counselor recommended a medication to help her with depression. The counselor faxed the request to the doctor; the doctor called it in to the pharmacy three days later. But it was called in to a pharmacy that didn't take her insurance. "What should I do?" she asks. She is too depressed to wend her way alone through the maze of the system, and we make a plan together.

I drive to the meeting, and enjoy being there. I relish the chance to connect with like-minded people from the community. I feel less alone. We work hard together, naming the issues clergy face in caring for parishioners with cancer. We write the objectives for the seminar, develop a time frame and a budget, make assignments, and identify possible speakers. Several health professionals are suggested. I propose hearing from a patient.

By now it's 11:45, and I go to the restaurant where I'll meet Sarah. After some small talk, I ask how she is—really. And she talks nonstop about her anger at her husband, her incredulity at finding herself in this predicament, her hope for reconciliation, her lack of money, and, when pressed, her feelings of shame and helplessness. I ask her, "Where is God in this?" She chews her thoughts as she chews her sandwich, then responds, "I'm glad you asked." And we go from there. Then I ask about her self-care, and she commits to take a fifteen-minute walk every day until we meet again next week.

As I walk to the car, I reflect on what supports there are for Sarah and the children—and her husband. I make a note to ask the priest to contact the husband, and also a note to speak with the leader of the Youth Group about the children. I wonder about a support group for Sarah—one that acknowledges that this is not just a social and psychological crisis, but a spiritual one as well, one that involves promises and vows said before God. I pray for Sarah's family as I am driving away. She and I hadn't said a formal prayer in the restaurant, but our hearts were raised to God.

It's 1:30 p.m. when I arrive at Bill's home. His wife welcomes me. He talks about the MRI, the weakness he feels, and the hope he holds that if it is a tumor it will be easily treated. I ask what it is that he fears most about this. Then I ask what he hopes for most strongly. We incorporate those into the closing prayer of the visit. I go to the car and use my cell phone to call the coordinator of Called to Care to see if someone could bring supper to them (there are frozen casseroles at church kept for just such occasions), and bring a few flowers from Sunday's altar flowers, and maybe listen a while.

It's time to go to the hospital. On the way, my cell phone rings. The parish secretary tells me that there is another parishioner at the same hospital. Could I please visit? (There goes my afternoon!) The secretary also lets me know that Mary called saying she needed to talk with the parish nurse—something about her teenage son. Returning that call will have to wait.

It's 3:30 when I get to the hospital. I look in on the newly admitted parishioner. A laboratory technician is drawing blood. I walk in and silently stand next to Gary, and offer my hand. He grabs it and holds tight. The doctor thinks Gary has a bleeding ulcer, and he is hooked up to an intravenous line, has a nasogastric tube threaded through his nose, and he wears a clip on his finger to monitor his oxygen level. He seems pale and frightened, and doesn't know why things are being done to him. I quietly talk through the hospital procedures, using English instead of medical jargon to explain what's happening. The technician leaves, and I help Gary get oriented to his room (even to the point of putting the needed urinal nearby but out of general view!). I ask an aide for mouth swabs; he can have nothing by mouth, and his lips are dry. He seems exhausted. I offer a prayer and a backrub, which he accepts gratefully. I write and leave a personal note for his wife when she comes to visit. I go to the nurses' station to let them know that Gary is a member of our congregation, and I give them my card and ask that it be put in his chart. I watch as they read the card. "You're a nurse? And you work in a church? Is that parish nursing? I've heard about that. . . . "

I walk down two flights of stairs to visit with Charles. I make the visit brief, partly because of my tiredness and partly because people from his office are in the room visiting. I tell him I will be back. His energy is high; he seems excited—almost too pumped up. Denial is a wonderful defense mechanism as long as it doesn't get overused.

I go home for supper, and call Mary. Last month she told me that the school called her because they found "grass" in Ben's locker at school. She had been beside herself—questioning her mothering skills, fearing Ben will become an addict, embarrassed to have her "A" student caught in something like this. I had referred her to Fairbanks Hospital and their excellent drug program for youth. She and he went there; since his urine test was positive, he stayed for observation and evaluation.

Mary now wants to get together with other parents who have similar experiences and see if there isn't something they can do to help themselves and their kids. She wants to know if this is something Health Ministries would want to sponsor. Did I know anyone who could facilitate such a group? I suggest the drug counselor at the local high school, to start. And I refer her to the chair of the Health Ministries Committee, reminding her that the members are committed to confidentiality. I applaud her healthy response to a very difficult situation.

At 7:00 p.m. I am back at the church, in the parlor, meeting with five parishioners who feel called to the ministry of active listening. They have been coming for several weeks, and they have been polishing their skills during the week. Each comes with a verbatim—a written snippet of pastoral conversation he or she has had this past week, accompanied by some reflections about the interaction. After some centering silence and opening prayer, we check in with each other, sharing our week's experiences. One of the parishioners volunteers to role-play his verbatim, seeking feedback from the group on his active listening skills. They learn much from each other and from the Spirit working in their midst.

I return home, feeling the wind at my back and gratitude in my heart for the ministry I am blessed to live out. I say my prayers, open the window for a night breeze, and settle in my bed, weary and satisfied.

CONGREGATIONAL PRACTICES HEAL US FROM DIS-EASE
–Brita L. Gill-Austern

Brita L. Gill-Austern, Ph.D., is the Austin Philip Guiles Professor of Psychology and Pastoral Theology at Andover-Newton Theological Seminary in Newton, Massachusetts, where she serves as the faculty director of the Faith, Health and Spirituality Program. She specializes in the integration of the healing arts and spiritual practices and in the role of congregations as healing communities. Ordained in the United Church of Christ, she has served parishes in California and Pennsylvania.

Health is a big-time business, consuming about 12 percent of our national product. Yet all is not well with our cultural pursuit of health and healing. Intractable diseases are among us, chronic diseases are on the rise, and many of us have become practically paranoid about what we eat. While the exercise industry is booming, still millions are spent each year on diets while millions go to bed each night hungry.

Something Is Missing

In the midst of these difficulties, people's faith in allopathic medicine and in doctors has decreased. More people make visits to alternative health care providers than to licensed medical doctors. Doctors and nurses are less and less satisfied with their professions, feeling the personal art of healing has become a business to be managed. A recent survey showed 36 percent of physicians, if they had to choose over again, would not choose medicine. Clearly something is missing not just for the recipients of health care, but also in the satisfaction of physicians in their profession.

Many see spirituality today as one more thing that they can add to other "cures du jour" to insure them a healthy and long life. But spirituality is not another technique; it belongs to an ecology of care which seeks to reweave the broken connections to our deepest selves, God, neighbor, and the natural world.

Although conferences on health and spirituality are proliferating, certain issues are not being addressed in the public square, such as how a focus on individual health can become an idol. Health is a good, but not the greatest of all goods. Our bodies are gifts from God for which we must care, but we must also avoid making personal health an idol that eclipses our faith in God and our commitment to a larger purpose.

To address the causes of disease requires awareness of environmental factors that contribute to disease. We must also address the single greatest vulnerability for disease: poverty. Without attention to violence, racism, poverty, and toxic wastes, our personal strategies of wholeness and wellness are woefully incomplete.

Separating Body and Soul

The growing interest in spirituality and healing is directly related to the increasing awareness among both the medical community and faith communities that the human being can only be understood as a "psychosomatic unity." We cannot separate body and soul, and when we do, our physical, spiritual and emotional health is threatened—not just our personal health, but the health of our common life. We need to see more clearly the connection between individual and communal well-being.

One of the early founders of holistic medicine, Richard Cabot, a physician at Massachusetts General Hospital, told a medical audience he believed the cause of almost every illness was "the wear and tear of the soul on the body." The fact that we are a psychosomatic unity is not an invention of our age, but this insight has been neglected too long.

Biblical Understanding of the Unity of the Person

An authentic spirituality for the twenty-first century will require recovering a Hebraic biblical perspective which sees no dualism between body and soul and which sees the person as a psychosomatic unity made in God's image. "Then the Lord God formed the human (*ha-adam*) of dust from the ground (*min ha adama*) and breathed into his nostrils the breath of life and the human (*ha-adam*) became a living soul" (Gen 2:7).

Soul comes into being as matter (dust) and God's spirit (breath) are joined together. Let human beings not pull apart what God has joined together. Recovering a notion of soul that is not simply a disembodied, ethereal, abstract concept helps us see the intimate connection between healing and the care of the soul. Donald Capps has asserted that we must recover the ancient tradition of locating the soul in the body.

Soul Loss

The root of the Hebrew word "soul" (*nephesh*) means appetite. The Hebrew

Scriptures are filled with passages that give voice to the appetitive nature of the soul. *Nephesh* craves, gets hungry, thirsty, and longs for something. The search for spirituality in our own time is related to the fact that our *nephesh* has become disconnected from the sources that feed the soul's appetite.

If the soul is not fed, it dies, shrinks, or grows faint, and because there is no soul/body dualism, the body breaks down or languishes. Beneath the intense interest in health and spirituality is an acknowledgment that in our culture, our churches, and our lives, there has been a loss of soul.

One of the most frequent words for healing in the Greek New Testament is *therapeuo*, which means to cultivate a garden or to render service to the gods. John Sanford writes: "The soul itself is like a garden: neglected she goes to seed and brings forth weeds, becoming weak and drying up for lack of attention."[1]

The words of Louise Gluck come to mind:

> When I made you, I loved you.
> Now I pity you.
> I gave you what you needed,
> Bed of earth, blanket of blue air.
>
> As I get farther away from you
> I see you more clearly.
> Your souls should have been immense by now,
> Not what they are,
> Small talking things.
> I gave you every gift
>
> Blue of spring morning,
> Time you didn't know how to use
> You wanted more. . . . [2]

Gluck captures what many speak about today as soul loss. The image is of anorectic souls that somehow have not grown to their own right size, souls that should have been immense by now are emaciated from lack of proper nutrients.

Lifestyle Diseases

Many of the major diseases of our time are called "diseases of civilization." Heart disease, cancer, lung ailments, accidental injuries, and alcoholism, to name just a few, are related in part to our loss of soul and to our collective way of life. Our lifestyle is killing us. Hurry sickness enslaves us in the pressures of time, with little capacity to enjoy the fullness of the moment. "Hurry is not of the devil," said Jung. "Hurry is the devil." Busyness keeps us so occupied that we dry up the well of compassion within us and the ties that bind us one to another become more frayed. The Chinese character for busyness is made up of two signs meaning kill/heart.

The conspicuous consumption that characterizes much of our culture diminishes overall pleasure and creates apathy to the needs of others. When success is defined as climbing the ladder, meaning ascendancy over someone else, we become more disconnected from one another.

Disconnection Contributes to Disease

Soul loss and soul sickness become visible in profound, pervasive, and persistent patterns of disconnection from God, others, our bodies, and our earth. These patterns of disconnection are at the root of some of our most intractable social problems: violence, poverty, racism, sexism, and heterosexism. These same patterns of disconnection lead to a sense of isolation and meaninglessness, two primary precursors of disease. The solution to these disconnections cannot, therefore, lie in our private individual efforts, in our self-help techniques, or in individual programs for wellness. When we are alienated and isolated, we become self-absorbed. The way of health and wholeness is always out of self-absorption to self-transcendence through self-giving. Sandra Schneider defines spirituality as "the experience of consciously striving to integrate one's life in terms, not of isolation and self-absorption, but of self-transcendence toward the ultimate value one perceives."[3]

Health understood within a relational theological framework is the opposite of disorder, fragmentation, and lack of harmony and integration. In Hebrew Scriptures the most complete word for health is *shalom*, which refers to the unity and harmony of all things in the commonwealth of God's love, where personal, social, and cosmic well-being all come together. To be healthy for the Hebrews meant that one's life was centered in the peace and wholeness of God. Within a Jewish and a Christian perspective, full health is only possible within a loving relationship with God, neighbor, self, and all being. As Gary Gunderson aptly puts it, "Health is not something that can be consumed one person at a time."[4]

Healing Happens in Connection

If we look at a pattern in Jesus' healing, we will also see that one of the central themes is the restoring of communion with God and neighbor—his passion is to restore us to our sense of oneness with one another. Among the most poignant words Jesus ever spoke are the last words on the cross. When he can no longer do anything for those whom he has loved so deeply, he turns to his beloved disciple and his mother and he says: "Woman, behold your son. Disciple, behold your mother." He heals grief and brokenness by giving the community to each other.

The healing stories of Jesus, like the story of Bartimaeus or of the hemor-rhaging woman, are stories where he draws persons into relation, out of isolation into community. Healing happens through connection, reconnection, meeting, and encounter. Health within a Christian and a Jewish perspective sees that personal bodily well-being is intimately connected to how we are related to the larger social body to which we belong.

Recovery of Practices

Spiritual practices are a way we rehearse how we want our life to be. Margaret Miles, in her book *Practicing Christianity*, argues that well-formed traditional devotional practices were used as a means to "deconstruct the socialization and conditioning inscribed on the body, mind and heart by the world and produce a new organizing center of the self."[5]

The spiritual practices we need for our time are soulful individual and communal practices that move us out of our solo quests. Solo quests, as Dorothy Bass writes, only mimic the patterns of disconnection that gave them birth.[6] We don't need any more self-help books, but rather we need to find practices that reconnect us to a larger whole and to community.

As we engage in soulful individual and communal practices, we discover, as Martin Luther King put it, that "our lives are tangled up with everyone else's in ways beyond our knowing, caught in an inescapable network of mutuality, tied to a single garment of destiny."

Health and ultimately salvation call us out of self-absorption. Therefore the recovery of soulful practices of healing must include not only private prayer and meditation (the staple of many stress-reduction programs), but also other practices that bring us into a deeper and more inclusive community with others. For example, the practice of communal fasting and intercessory prayer are key in deepening our identification and solidarity with those in need.

Particularly important in our culture and time are the return of the collective observance of a genuine Sabbath which includes communal worship, but is also about a day where we remember we are the receivers of God's creation and not its makers. Such an observance would return to some of the practices and understandings of Sabbath from Judaism and our Christian ancestors.

Hospitality to the Stranger

We cannot heal the deep divisions within our culture, world, and within our own souls without radically embracing a practice of hospitality to the stranger, or what I call hospitality to "otherness." No more important spiritual practice of our time exists; it cannot be sustained by solitary individuals, but requires the support and commitment of community.

The stranger and others invite us to come out of ourselves, to receive another, which means to open ourselves to their gifts as well as to care for them. In so doing, we sense that we are acting in accordance with what is deepest within us and thus opening ourselves to reality, to life as it is, and as it is meant to be.

Hospitality to the stranger is one means of grace by which we overturn and conquer the social, political, economic, racial, and gender stratifications we have invented as a means of control over others. In the words of the prophet Isaiah,

> *Is not this the fast that I choose:*
>   *to loose the bonds of injustice,*
>   *to undo the thongs of the yoke,*
> *to let the oppressed go free,*
>   *and to break every yoke?*
>
> *Is it not to share your bread with*
>   *the hungry,*
> *and to bring the homeless poor*
>   *into your house;*
> *when you see the naked, to*
>   *cover them,*
> *and not to hide yourself from*
>   *your own kin?*
> *Then your light shall break forth*
>   *like the dawn,*
> *and your healing shall spring*
>   *up quickly. . . . (Isa 58:6–9 NRSV)*

When we seek to enlarge the limits of our hearts, our homes, our churches, and our schedules and spread wide the curtains of our tent to include hospitality to otherness, to the stranger, the connections between us will begin to deepen, the illusion of our separateness will start to vanish, and we will grow healthy like a wound newly healed.

Every congregation has a treasure of spiritual practices that can contribute to the healing of individuals and community. Yet do we know their power for healing and are we making them a center of our life together? Health ministry is committed to helping people recover those practices of the Christian life which bring us in closer communion with God, one another, the earth, and our deepest selves and in so doing, contribute to the healing of individuals and the world.

Notes

1. John Sanford, *Healing Body and Soul: The Meaning of Illness in the New Testament and in Psychotherapy* (Louisville: Westminster, 1992), 34.

2. Lousie Gluck, *The Wild Iris* (Hopewell, NJ: Ecco Press, 1992), 15.

3. Sandra Schneider, "Spirituality in the Academy," *Theological Studies* 50, no. 4 (December 1989): 684.

4. Gary Gunderson, *Deeply Woven Roots: Improving the Quality of Life in Your*

Community (Minneapolis: Augsburg Fortress, 1997), 5.
    5. Margaret Miles, *Practicing Christianity* (New York: Crossroad, 1990), 96.
    6. Dorothy Bass, *Practicing Our Faith* (San Francisco: Jossey-Bass, 1997), 4.

FOR PERSONAL REFLECTION

1. From your personal experience with your congregation, what are the unmet needs of parishioners? Are there ways people in the congregation could address those needs?

2. What might your role be in a congregation's health ministry? How would you discern what God is calling you to be and to do?

3. In order to be part of health ministry, you would need support. Where would you go for support? Who could you count on for encouragement?

FOR GROUP DISCUSSION

1. Granger Westberg offers a very simple framework for categorizing peoples' health: "The Well," "The Little Bit Sick," and "The Really Sick." There are ways in which your congregation is already involved in health for those who are well, those who are a little bit sick, and those who are really sick and maybe dying. Identify these. In what ways might what is already established grow into a comprehensive health ministry in your congregation?

2. There are essential aspects to health ministry. Among them are:

   • Integration of faith and health

   • Health counseling

   • Health education

   • Advocacy

   • Referral

   • Empowering ministry

   Find examples of the components of health ministry in "A Day in the Life of a Parish Nurse." Name these components in your congregation today. What would it take to help these mature into bolder health ministry?

3. How would a health ministry change the life of your local faith community? What would be added to the congregation's life? What would be rearranged? What would cease?

Appendix

With a topic as broad as Christian spirituality and health, it is difficult to develop a human-size resource list. The following books are selected from numerous possibilities. They are chosen because of their focus on issues raised in this volume. The Web sites listed are those the editor has found most helpful.

BOOKS

Ackerman, Diane. *A Natural History of the Senses*. New York: Vintage Books, 1991.

Bakken, Kenneth L., and Kathleen H. Hofeller. *Journey Toward Wholeness: A Christ-Centered Approach to Health and Healing*. New York: Crossroad, 1992.

Beckman, Richard J. *Praying for Wholeness and Healing*. Minneapolis: Augsburg Fortress, 1995.

Brooke, Avery. *Healing in the Landscape of Prayer*. Harrisburg, PA: Morehouse Publishing, 2004.

Clinebell, Howard. *Anchoring Your Well Being, Christian Wholeness in a Fractured World*. Nashville: Upper Room Books, 1998.

Denton, Jean M. *Steps to a Health Ministry in Your Episcopal Congregation*. Indianapolis: National Episcopal Health Ministries, 2001.

Droege, Thomas A. *The Healing Presence: Spiritual Exercises for Healing, Wellness, and Recovery*. Minneapolis: Youth and Family Institute of Augsburg College, 1996.

Earle, Mary C. *Broken Body, Healing Spirit: Lectio Divina and Living with Illness*. Harrisburg, PA: Morehouse Publishing, 2003.

Epperly, Bruce G. *Spirituality & Health, Health & Spirituality: A New Journey of Spirit, Mind, and Body*. Mystic, CT: Twenty-Third Publications, 1997.

Evans, Abigail Rian. *Redeeming Marketplace Medicine: A Theology of Health Care*. Cleveland: Pilgrim Press, 1999.

———. *The Healing Church: Practical Programs for Health Ministries*. Cleveland,: United Church Press, 2000.

Fox, Matthew. *Sins of the Spirit, Blessings of the Flesh*. New York: Three Rivers Press, 1999.

Gary Gunderson. *Deeply Woven Roots: Improving the Quality of Life in Your Community*. Minneapolis: Augsburg Fortress, 1997.

Granberg-Michaelson, Karin. *Healing Community*. Geneva: WCC Publications, 1991.

Hale, W. Daniel, and Harold George Koenig. *Healing Bodies and Souls: A Practical Guide for Congregations*. Minneapolis: Fortress, 2003.

Kelsey, Morton. *Healing and Christianity: A Classic Study*. Minneapolis: Augsburg, 1995.

Kirk-Duggan, Cheryl A. *The Undivided Soul: Helping Congregations Connect Body and Spirit*. Nashville: Abington, 2001.

Kleinman, Arthur. *The Illness Narratives: Suffering, Healing, and the Human Condition*. New York: Basic Books/HarperCollins, 1988.

May, William F. *The Physician's Covenant: Images of the Healer in Medical Ethics*. Philadelphia: Westminster, 1983.

Moltmann-Wendel, Elisabeth. *I Am My Body: A Theology of Embodiment*. New York: Continuum, 1995.

Morhmann, Margaret E. *Medicine as Ministry: Reflections on Suffering, Ethics, and Hope*. Cleveland: Pilgrim Press, 1995.

Nelson, James B. *Body Theology*. Louisville, KY: Westminster/John Knox, 1992.

Newell, J. Phillip. *Echo of the Soul: The Sacredness of the Human Body*. Harrisburg, PA: Morehouse Publishing, 2001.

O'Brien, Mary Elizabeth. *Parish Nursing: Healthcare Ministry within the Church*. Sudbury, MA: Jones & Bartlett, 2003.

Patterson, Deborah. *The Essential Parish Nurse: ABC's for Congregational Health Ministry*. Cleveland: Pilgrim Press, 2003.

Paulsell, Stephanie. *Honoring the Body: Meditations on a Christian Practice*. San Francisco: Jossey-Bass, 2002.

Smith, David H. *Health and Medicine in the Anglican Tradition*. New York: Crossroad, 1986.

Smith, Linda L. *Called into Healing: Reclaiming our Judeo-Christian Legacy of Healing Touch*. Arveda, CO: HTSM, 2000.

Solari-Twadell, Phyllis Ann, and Mary Ann McDermott, eds. *Parish Nursing: Promoting Whole Person Health within Faith Communities*. Thousand Oaks, CA: Sage Publications, 1999.

Sulmasy, Daniel P. *The Healer's Calling: A Spirituality for Physicians and other Health Care Professionals*. Mahwah, NJ: Paulist Press, 1997.

Trembley, David, and Lo-Ann Trembley. *Pray with All Your Senses*. Chicago: Assisting Christians to Act, 1997.

Ulrich, Stephanie, and Allen Brown. *Health Ministry in the Local Congregation: An Introduction and Opportunity*. Indianapolis: National Episcopal Health Ministries, 1997.

Vaux, Kenneth L. *Being Well*. Nashville: Abington, 1997.

Westberg, Granger E., and Jill Westberg McNamara. *The Parish Nurse: Providing a Minister of Health for Your Congregation*. Minneapolis: Augsburg Fortress, 1990.

Wuellner, Flora Slosson. *Prayer and Our Bodies*. Nashville: The Upper Room, 1987.

WEBSITES

The following websites are dependable resources for further exploration of Christianity and health ministry. They are current as of this writing.

Health Ministries Association

http://www.hmassoc.org/

Health Ministries Association's mission is to encourage, support and develop whole-person ministries leading to the integration of faith and health. HMA is an interfaith membership organization, serving the people who serve the Faith Health Ministry movement. HMA supports members as they work toward an integration of faith and health, promotes and supports the expansion of the Faith Health Ministry movement, and brings together people of faith who work to improve the health of people and the communities in which they live.

International Parish Nurse Resource Center

http://ipnrc.parishnurses.org/

The mission of the International Parish Nurse Resource Center is to promote the development of quality parish nurse programs through research, education, and consultation. The International Parish Nurse Resource Center is organized:

- As a reference center for people desiring information about the philosophy and activities of nurses in congregations across the country.

- As a convener of annual educational programs where nurses can meet to learn about current developments in parish nursing.

- To provide consultation to institutions, agencies, and churches which organize parish nurse programs.

- To promote an understanding of the role of parish nurse professionals in promoting health and wellness within the church community.

Interfaith Health Program

http://www.ihpnet.org/

The Interfaith Health Program (IHP) at Emory University, Rollins School of Public Health, builds and nurtures broad, rich, and deep networks for learning within and across health and faith systems—local, national, and global. They state, "As participants within these rich streams of knowledge and wisdom, we discover models, technologies, tools, and visions that strengthen the abilities of health and faith communities to make Shalom. We synthesize and share these discoveries. . . ."

National Episcopal Health Ministries

http://www.EpiscopalHealthMinistries.org

National Episcopal Health Ministries (NEHM) seeks to promote health ministry in Episcopal congregations, assisting them to reclaim the Gospel imperative of health and wholeness. National Episcopal Health Ministries serves by:

- Offering education for Episcopal health ministry and parish nursing

- Providing resources to local congregations and dioceses

- Collaborating with other faith communities, institutions and health organizations, and

- Supporting those engaged in health ministry in Episcopal congregations

Health and Welfare Ministries of the United Methodist Church

http://gbgm-umc.org/health/congmin/congregational_health.stm

This site offers a "Congregational Health Ministries Resources Packet" which includes information about:

- Congregational Health Ministries

- Health Ministers

- Guidelines for the Lay Counselor

- Healing Congregations

- Participatory Health

- Holistic Health Scriptural References

- Health Ministries Activities

- Guidelines for the Health Committee

- Resources

Presbyterian Church (U.S.A.)

http://www.pcusa.org/health/usa/

The Office of Health Ministries of the Presbyterian Church USA provides ministry models, program resources, health awareness information, training and preparation to encourage, enable and support individual Presbyterians, congregations and governing bodies in mission-focused health ministry.

The Evangelical Lutheran Church in America

http://www.elca.org/dcs/wholehealth.html

This site offers "The Whole Church Catalog for Congregational Health Ministries."

http://www.elca.org/socialstatements/health/

The complete text of "Caring for Health: Our Shared Endeavor" is found on this Web page.

http://www.elca.org/dcs/healthmin.html

Included on this page are synod contacts and resource material.

Wheat Ridge Ministries

http://www.wheatridge.org/

"Wheat Ridge Ministries (originally called the Wheat Ridge Foundation) is an independent Lutheran charitable organization that provides support for new church-related health and hope ministries. Our mission statement says it well: 'Lutherans seeding new ministries of health and hope in the name of the healing Christ.'

"This mission statement continues to be a source of excitement as we encourage healing ministries being carried out by congregations, agencies, and church bodies. Reflecting Christ's concern for the whole person (John 10:10), our staff and board remain committed to seeding new and innovative ministries that focus on health of body, mind and spirit."

Lutheran Church Missouri Synod

http://www.lcms.org/pages/internal.asp?NavID=1889

The LCMS Health Ministries has two principal missions: (1) to support and promote Christ-centered health and wellness of body, mind, and spirit through congregational health ministries, and (2) to promote and encourage Christ-centered health and wellness among Lutheran Church-Missouri Synod Church workers.

Universal Health Care Action Network

http://www.uhcan.org/faith/

The Universal Health Care Action Network (UHCAN) is a national resource and strategic center supporting organizations and advocates working for comprehensive, affordable and publicly accountable health care for all in the United States. This site provides advocacy and organizing resources, as well as a specific focus on churches, "The Faith Project."

National Coalition for Health Care

http://www.nchc.org/

The National Coalition on Health Care's diverse membership is united in support of the following principles as a framework for improving our nation's health care:

- Health Insurance for All
- Improved Quality of Care
- Cost Containment
- Equitable Financing
- Simplified Administration

This site supplies articles, studies and reports about health care issues.

Cover the Uninsured

http://www.covertheuninsured.org

This site is a project of the Robert Wood Johnson Foundation, and is geared to consciousness-raising about the need to cover those without health care insurance by targeting one week a year as "Cover the Uninsured Week." Included are: a weekly news digest of related articles, specific guidelines about what individuals can do, resources for those now uninsured, and fact sheets about the issue.

Permissions

"Suffering, Spirituality and Health Care" from *The Healer's Calling* by Daniel P. Sulmasey, copyright © 1997 by Daniel P. Sulmasey. Used with permission of Paulist Press Inc., New York/Mahwah, NJ.

"Health Care in Crisis" pages 7–20 from *Redeeming Marketplace Medicine: A Theology of Health Ministry* (Cleveland: The Pilgrim Press, 1999) by Abigail Rian Evans, copyright © 1999 by Abigail Rian Evans. Used with permission.

"Dialogue with Your Body about Illness and Health" from *The Healing Presence: Spiritual Exercises for Healing, Wellness, and Recovery* by Thomas A. Droege, copyright © 1996 by Thomas A. Droege. Used by permission of The Youth & Family Institute, 1401 E. 100th Street, Bloomington, MN 55425, *www.youthandfamilyinstitute.org*.

"Congregational Practices Heal Us from Dis-ease" pages 3–7 from Today's Ministry: A Report from Andover Newton, Volume XIX, Issue Two, Summer 2002 by Brita L. Gill-Austern, copyright © 2002 by Brita L. Gill-Austern. Used by permission of Andover Newton Theological School and Brita L. Gill-Austern.

Poem from *A Winter's Love* by Madeleine L'Engle, copyright © 1984 by Madeleine L'Engle. Published by Ballantine Books. Permission sought.

"We Awaken in Christ's Body" [Symeon the New Theologian] from *The Enlightened Heart: An Anthology of Sacred Poetry*, edited by Stephen Mitchell. Copyright © 1989 by Stephen Mitchell. Reprinted by permission of HarperCollins Publishers Inc.

"Feet Addressing Head" from *At the Mercy Seat* by Susan McCaslin, copyright © 2003 by Susan McCaslin. Used by permission of Ronsdale Press, Vancouver, British Columbia.

"Pax" by D. H. Lawrence, from *The Complete Poems of D. H. Lawrence* by D. H. Lawrence, edited by V. de Sola Pinto and F. W. Roberts, copyright © 1964, 1971 by Angelo Ravagli and C. M. Weekley, Executors of the Estate of Frieda Lawrence Ravagli. Used by permission of Viking Penguin, a division of Penguin Group (USA) Inc.; and reproduced by permission of Pollinger Limited and the proprietor.

Excerpt from "A Lamentation" by Patricia Benner, copyright © by Patricia Benner. Unpublished. Used by Permission.

"Fact or Fiction: What Do You *Really* Know about U.S. Healthcare?" from *Seeking Justice in Health Care: A Guide for Advocates in Faith Communities*, published by the Universal Health Care Action Network (UHCAN) in Cleveland, Ohio. It was developed to support the efforts of members of faith communities working for health care for all. UHCAN can be contacted by telephone at (216) 241-8422 x15, e-mail at faithproject@uhcan.org, or through their website at www.uhcan.org. Used by permission.

Excerpt from "Caring for Health: Our Shared Endeavor," a social statement on health, healing, and health care, is used by permission of the Evangelical Lutheran Church in America, www.elca.org.

Excerpt from "A Framework for Comprehensive Health Care Reform: Protecting Human Life, Promoting Human Dignity, Pursuing the Common Good," a resolution of the United State Conference of Catholic Bishops dated June 18, 1993, used by permission of the United States Conference of Catholic Bishops.